HISTORICAL FIGURES

GEORGE WASHINGTON OR LIFE IN AMERICA ONE HUNDRED YEARS AGO

HISTORICAL FIGURES

Additional books and e-books in this series can be found on Nova's website under the Series tab.

HISTORICAL FIGURES

GEORGE WASHINGTON OR LIFE IN AMERICA ONE HUNDRED YEARS AGO

JOHN S. C. ABBOTT

Copyright © 2019 by Nova Science Publishers, Inc.

All rights reserved. No part of this book may be reproduced, stored in a retrieval system or transmitted in any form or by any means: electronic, electrostatic, magnetic, tape, mechanical photocopying, recording or otherwise without the written permission of the Publisher.

We have partnered with Copyright Clearance Center to make it easy for you to obtain permissions to reuse content from this publication. Simply navigate to this publication's page on Nova's website and locate the "Get Permission" button below the title description. This button is linked directly to the title's permission page on copyright.com. Alternatively, you can visit copyright.com and search by title, ISBN, or ISSN.

For further questions about using the service on copyright.com, please contact:
Copyright Clearance Center
Phone: +1-(978) 750-8400   Fax: +1-(978) 750-4470   E-mail: info@copyright.com.

NOTICE TO THE READER

The Publisher has taken reasonable care in the preparation of this book, but makes no expressed or implied warranty of any kind and assumes no responsibility for any errors or omissions. No liability is assumed for incidental or consequential damages in connection with or arising out of information contained in this book. The Publisher shall not be liable for any special, consequential, or exemplary damages resulting, in whole or in part, from the readers' use of, or reliance upon, this material. Any parts of this book based on government reports are so indicated and copyright is claimed for those parts to the extent applicable to compilations of such works.

Independent verification should be sought for any data, advice or recommendations contained in this book. In addition, no responsibility is assumed by the Publisher for any injury and/or damage to persons or property arising from any methods, products, instructions, ideas or otherwise contained in this publication.

This publication is designed to provide accurate and authoritative information with regard to the subject matter covered herein. It is sold with the clear understanding that the Publisher is not engaged in rendering legal or any other professional services. If legal or any other expert assistance is required, the services of a competent person should be sought. FROM A DECLARATION OF PARTICIPANTS JOINTLY ADOPTED BY A COMMITTEE OF THE AMERICAN BAR ASSOCIATION AND A COMMITTEE OF PUBLISHERS.

Additional color graphics may be available in the e-book version of this book.

Library of Congress Cataloging-in-Publication Data

ISBN: 978-1-53616-032-1

Published by Nova Science Publishers, Inc. † New York

CONTENTS

Preface		ix
Chapter 1	The Youth of George Washington	1
Chapter 2	The First Military Expedition	23
Chapter 3	The French War	43
Chapter 4	The Warrior, the Statesman, and the Planter	61
Chapter 5	The Gathering Storm of War	81
Chapter 6	The Conflict Commenced	101
Chapter 7	Progress of the War	121
Chapter 8	The Siege of Boston	139
Chapter 9	The War in New York	161
Chapter 10	The Vicissitudes of War	181
Chapter 11	The Loss of Philadelphia, and the Capture of Burgoyne	201
Chapter 12	Concluding Scenes	211

Index 223

Related Nova Publications 227

Figure 1. The House Where the First American Flag Was Made.

PREFACE[*]

As Columbus and La Salle were the most prominent of the Pioneers of America, so was Washington the most illustrious of its Patriots. In the career of Columbus we have a vivid sketch of life in the tropical portions of the New World four hundred years ago.

The adventures of La Salle, in exploring this continent two hundred years ago, from the Northern Lakes to the Mexican Gulf, are almost without parallel, even in the pages of romance. His narrative gives information, such as can nowhere else be found, of the native inhabitants, their number, character, and modes of life when the white man first reached these shores.

The history of George Washington is as replete with marvels as that of either of his predecessors. The world during the last century has made more progress than during the preceding five. The life of Washington reveals to us, in a remarkable degree, the state of society in our land, the manners and customs of the people, their joys and griefs, one hundred years ago.

We search history in vain to find a parallel to Washington. As a statesman, as a general, as a thoroughly good man, he stands pre-eminent.

---

[*] This is an edited, augmented and reformatted version of "George Washington or Life in America One Hundred Years Ago" By John S. C. Abbott, originally published by Dodd & Mead Publishers, dated 1875. The views, opinions, and nomenclature expressed in this book are those of the authors and do not reflect the views of Nova Science Publishers, Inc.

He was so emphatically the Father of his country that it may almost be said that he created the Republic. And now, that we are about to celebrate the Centennial of these United States—the most favored nation upon which the sun shines—it is fitting that we should recall, with grateful hearts, the memory of our illustrious benefactor George Washington.

Chapter 1

THE YOUTH OF GEORGE WASHINGTON

About two centuries ago there were two young men, in England, by the name of Lawrence and John Washington. They were gentlemen of refinement and education, the sons of an opulent and distinguished family. Lawrence was a graduate of Oxford University, and was, by profession, a lawyer. John entered into commercial and mercantile affairs, and was an accomplished man of business. The renown of Virginia, named after Elizabeth, England's virgin queen, was then luring many, even of the most illustrious in wealth and rank, to the shores of the New World. Lawrence and John embarked together, to seek their fortunes on the banks of the Potomac.[1]

It was a lovely morning in summer when the ship entered Chesapeake Bay, and sailing up that majestic inland sea, entered the silent, solitary, forest-fringed Potomac. Eagerly they gazed upon the Indian wigwams which were clustered upon the banks of many a sheltered and picturesque cove; and upon the birch canoes, which were propelled by the painted and plumed natives over the placid waters. The two brothers purchased an

---

[1] "There is no doubt that the politics of the family determined the two brothers, John and Lawrence, to emigrate to Virginia; that colony being the favorite resort of the Cavaliers, during the government of Cromwell, as New England was the retreat of the Puritans, in the period which preceded the Commonwealth."—*Life of Washington*, by Edward Everett, p. 24.

extensive tract of land, on the western bank of the Potomac, about fifty miles above its entrance into the bay. Here, with an estate of thousands of acres spreading around them, and upon a spot commanding a magnificent view of the broad river and the sublime forests, they reared their modest but comfortable mansion.

John married Miss Pope. We have none of the details of their lives, full of incidents of intensest interest to them, but of little importance to the community at large. Life is ever a tragedy. From the times of the patriarchs until now, it has been, to most of the families of earth, a stormy day with a few gleams of sunshine breaking through the clouds. Children were born and children died. There were the joys of the bridal and the tears of the funeral.

Upon the death of John Washington, his second son, Augustine, remained at home in charge of the paternal acres. He seems to have been, like his father, a very worthy man, commanding the respect of the community, which was rapidly increasing around him. He married Jane Butler, a young lady who is described as remarkably beautiful, intelligent—and lovely in character. A very happy union was sadly terminated by the early death of Jane. A broken-hearted husband and three little children were left to weep over her grave.

The helpless orphans needed another mother. One was found in Mary Ball. She was all that husband or children could desire. Subsequent events drew the attention of the whole nation, and almost of the civilized world, to Mary Washington, for she became the mother of that George, whose name is enshrined in the hearts of countless millions. It is the uncontradicted testimony that the mother of George Washington was, by instinct and culture, a lady; she had a superior mind, well disciplined by study, and was a cheerful, devout Christian.

Augustine and Mary were married on the 6th of March, 1730. They received to their arms their first-born child, to whom the name of George was given, on the 22d of February, 1732. Little did the parents imagine that their babe would go out into the world, from the seclusion of his home amid the forests of the Potomac, to render the name of Washington one of the most illustrious in the annals of our race.

George Washington was peculiarly fortunate in both father and mother. All the influences of home tended to ennoble him. Happiness in childhood is one of the most essential elements in the formation of a good character. This child had ever before him the example of all domestic and Christian virtues. The parental home consisted of a spacious, one-story cottage, with a deep veranda in front. It was, architecturally, an attractive edifice, and it occupied one of the most lovely sites on the banks of the beautiful and majestic Potomac.

Soon after the birth of George, his father moved from the banks of the Potomac to the Rappahannock, nearly opposite the present site of Fredericksburg. Here he died, on the 12th of April, 1743, at the age of forty-nine.

The banks of the Rappahannock were covered with forests, spreading in grandeur over apparently an interminable expanse of hills and vales. In those days there were but few spots, in that vast region, which the axe of the settler had opened to the sun. But the smoke from the Indian camp-fires could often be seen curling up from the glooms of the forests, and the canoes of Indian hunters and warriors often arrested the eye, as they were gliding swiftly over the mirrored waters.

Trained by such parents, and in such a home, George, from infancy, developed a noble character. He was a handsome boy, gentlemanly in his manners, of finely developed figure, and of animated, intelligent features. His physical strength, frankness, moral courage, courtesy, and high sense of honor, made him a general favorite. Every child has heard the story of his trying the keen edge of his hatchet upon one of the favorite cherry trees of his father's, and of his refusal to attempt to conceal the fault by a lie.[2]

Augustine Lawrence, the father of George, died when his son was but twelve years of age. Mary, a grief-stricken widow, was left with six fatherless children. She proved herself amply competent to discharge the

---

[2] The pleasing story may easily be perverted. A little boy, having read it, deliberately took his hatchet, went into the garden, and utterly destroyed a valuable young pear tree. Then entering the house, he said, while his face was beaming with satisfaction, "Grandpapa, it was I who spoiled your pear tree." Inexpressible was the astonishment and chagrin of my dear little grandson, on receiving a severe reprimand, and a prohibition from again going into the garden for a week. He could not understand why he should be censured, for that for which George Washington was so abundantly praised.

weighty responsibilities thus devolving upon her. George ever honored his mother as one who had been to him a guardian angel. In her daily life she set before him a pattern of every virtue. She instilled into his susceptible mind those principles of probity and piety which ever ornamented his character, and to which he was indebted for success in the wonderful career upon which he soon entered.

In the final division of the parental property, Lawrence, the eldest child of Jane Butler, received the rich estate called Mount Vernon, which included twenty-five hundred acres of land. George received, as his share, the house and lands on the Rappahannock. The paternal mansion in Westmoreland passed to Augustine.

Lady Washington, as she was called, was deemed, before her marriage, one of the most beautiful girls in Virginia. Through all the severe discipline of life, she developed a character of the highest excellence. And thus she obtained an influence over the mind of her son, which she held, unimpaired, until the day of her death.

The wealthy families of Virginia took much pride in their equipage, and especially in the beauty of the horses which drew their massive carriages. Lady Washington had a span of iron-grays, of splendid figure and remarkable spirit, and of which she was very fond. One of these, though very docile by the side of his mate in the carriage harness, had never been broken to the saddle. It was said that the spirited animal would allow no one to mount him. George, though then a lad of but thirteen years of age, was tall, strong, and very athletic.

One morning, as the colts were feeding upon the lawn, George, who had some companions visiting him, approached the high-blooded steed, and after soothing him for some time with caresses, watched his opportunity and leaped upon his back. The colt, for a moment, seemed stupefied with surprise and indignation. Then, after a few desperate, but unavailing attempts, by rearing and plunging, to throw his rider, he dashed over the fields with the speed of the wind.

George, glorying in his achievement, and inconsiderate of the peril to which he was exposing the animal, gave the frantic steed the rein. When the horse began to show signs of exhaustion, he urged him on, hoping thus to subdue him to perfect docility. The result was that a blood-vessel was burst, and the horse dropped dead beneath his rider. George, greatly agitated by the calamity, hastened to his mother with the tidings. Her characteristic reply was:

> "My son, I forgive you, because you have had the courage to tell me the truth at once. Had you skulked away, I should have despised you."

In school studies George was a diligent scholar, though he did not manifest any special brilliance, either in his power of acquiring or communicating information. He was endowed with a good mind, of well-balanced powers. Such a mind is probably far more desirable, as promotive of both happiness and usefulness, than one conspicuous for the excrescences of what is called genius. He left school the autumn before he was sixteen.[3]

There is still in existence a manuscript book, which singularly illustrates his intelligence, his diligence, and his careful business habits. This lad of thirteen had, of his own accord, carefully copied, as a guide for himself in future life, promissory notes, bills of sale, land warrants, leases, wills, and many other such business papers. Thus he was prepared, at any time, to draw up such legal documents as any of the farmers around might need.

In another manuscript book he had collected, with great care, the most important rules of etiquette which govern in good society.[4] Had some good

---

[3] "During the last summer that he was at school, we find him surveying the fields around the school house, and in the adjoining plantations, of which the boundaries, angles, and measurements, the plots and calculations, are entered with formality and precision in his books. He used logarithms, and proved the accuracy of his work by different methods."—Sparks' *Life of Washington*, p. 6.

[4] There were fifty-four of these rules. All were important. We give a few as specimens.
Read no letters, books, or papers, in company. But when there is a necessity for doing it you must ask leave.
Show yourself not glad at the misfortune of another, though he were your enemy.
Strive not with your superiors, in argument, but always submit your judgment to others with modesty.
Use no reproachful language against any one.
Associate yourself with men of good quality, if you esteem your own reputation; for it is better to be alone than in bad company.

angel whispered in the ear of George, at that early age, that he was in manhood to enter upon as sublime a career as mortal ever trod, and soaring above the rank of nobles, was to take position with kings and emperors, he could hardly have made better preparations for these responsibilities than his own instincts led him to make.

It may be almost said of George Washington, as Lamartine said of Louis Philippe, that he had no youth; he was born a man. At sixteen years of age George finished his school education. And though a Virginia school, in that day, and in the midst of so sparse a population, could not have been one of high character, George, by his inherent energies, had made acquisitions of practical knowledge which enabled him, with honor, to fill the highest stations to which one, in this world, can be elevated.[5]

George was fond of mathematical and scientific studies, and excelled in all those branches. With these tastes he was led to enter upon the profession of a civil engineer. There was great demand for such services, in the new and almost unexplored realms of Virginia, where the population was rapidly increasing and spreading farther and farther back into the wilderness. Notwithstanding the extreme youth of George, he immediately found ample and remunerative employment; for his commanding stature, and dignity of character, caused him everywhere to be regarded as an accomplished man.

His handwriting was as plain as print. Every document which came from his pen was perfect in spelling, punctuation, capitals, and the proper division into paragraphs. This accuracy, thus early formed, he retained through life.

Upon leaving school at Westmoreland, George ascended the river to visit his elder brother Lawrence, at Mount Vernon. It was then, as now, a

---

Speak not of doleful things in time of mirth, nor at the table. Speak not of melancholy things, as death and wounds, and if others mention them, change, if you can, the discourse.
When another speaks, be attentive yourself, and disturb not the audience. If any hesitate in his words, help him not, nor prompt him without being desired. Interrupt him not, nor answer him till his speech be ended.
Labor to keep alive in your breast that little spark of celestial fire called conscience.

[5] "At the age of fifteen, Washington received the appointment of midshipman, in the British navy, but surrendered it, at the earnest desire of his mother."—*National Portrait Gallery*, vol. i. p. 3.

lovely spot on the western bank of the river, commanding an enchanting view of land and water. Mr. William Fairfax, an English gentleman of wealth and high rank, had purchased a large tract of land in that vicinity, and had reared his commodious mansion at a distance of about eight miles from Mount Vernon. The aristocratic planters of the region around were frequent guests at his hospitable home. Lawrence Washington married one of his daughters.

Lawrence Washington was suddenly attacked with a painful and alarming sickness. A change of climate was recommended. With fraternal love George accompanied his brother to the West Indies. The invalid continued to fail, through the tour, and soon after reaching home died. Lawrence was a man of great excellence of character. His amiability rendered his home one of peculiar happiness. At the early age of thirty-four he died, leaving an infant child, and a youthful widow stricken with grief. He left a large property. The valuable estate of Mount Vernon he bequeathed to his infant daughter. Should she die without heirs, it was to revert to his brother George, who was also appointed executor of the estate.

Lord Fairfax visited William, his younger brother, and was so pleased with the country, and surprised at the cheapness with which its fertile acres could be bought, that he purchased an immense territory, which extended over unexplored regions of the interior, including mountains, rivers, and valleys. Lord Fairfax met George Washington at his brother William's house. He was charmed with the manliness, intelligence, and gentlemanly bearing of the young man. George was then but one month over sixteen years of age. And yet Lord Fairfax engaged him to survey these pathless wilds, where scarcely an emigrant's cabin could be found, and which were ranged by ferocious beasts, and by savages often still more ferocious. It may be doubted whether a boy of his age was ever before intrusted with a task so arduous.

It was in the month of March, in the year 1748, when George Washington, with an Indian guide and a few white attendants, commenced the survey. The crests of the mountains were still whitened with ice and snow. Chilling blasts swept the plains. The streams were swollen into torrents by the spring rains. The Indians, however, whose hunting parties ranged these forests, were at that time friendly. Still there were vagrant bands, wandering here and there, ever ready to kill and plunder. The enterprise upon which Washington had entered was one full of romance, toil, and peril. It required the exercise of constant vigilance and sagacity.

Though these wilds may be called pathless, still there were here and there narrow trails, which the moccasined foot of the savage had trodden for uncounted centuries. They led in a narrow track, scarcely two feet in breadth, through dense thickets, over craggy hills, and along the banks of placid streams or foaming torrents. The heroic boy must have found, in these scenes of solitude, beauty, and grandeur, some hours of exquisite enjoyment. In a sunny spring morning he would glide down some placid river, in the birch canoe, through enchanting scenery, the banks fringed with bloom and verdure. There were towering mountains, from whose eminences, the eye embraced as magnificent a region of lake and forest, river and plain, as this globe can anywhere present.

It was generally necessary to camp out at night, wherever darkness might overtake them. With their axes a rude cabin was easily constructed, roofed with bark, which afforded a comfortable shelter from wind and rain. The forest presented an ample supply of game. Delicious brook trout were easily taken from the streams. Exercise and fresh air gave appetite. With a roaring fire crackling before the camp, illumining the forest far and wide, the adventurers cooked their supper, and ate it with a relish which the pampered guests in lordly banqueting halls have seldom experienced. Their sleep was probably more sweet than was ever found on beds of down. Occasionally the party would find shelter for the night in the wigwam of the friendly Indian.

Strange must have been the emotions which at times agitated the bosom of this pensive, reflective, heroic boy, as at midnight, far away from the haunts of civilization, in the wigwam of the savage, he listened to the wailings of the storm, interrupted only by the melancholy cry of the night bird, and the howl of wolves and other unknown beasts of prey. By the flickering light of the wigwam fire, he saw, sharing his couch, the dusky forms of the Indian hunter, his squaw, and his pappooses. Upon one or two occasions they found the lonely cabin of some bold frontiersmen, who had plunged into the wilderness, and who was living at but one remove above the condition of the savage. From the journal which he kept we make the following extract, under date of March 15, 1748. He is describing a night at an emigrant's cabin.

> "Worked hard till night, and then returned. After supper we were lighted into a room; and I, being not so good a woodman as the rest, stripped myself very orderly, and went into the bed, as they call it, when, to my surprise, I found it to be nothing but a little straw matted together, without sheet or anything else, but only one thread bare blanket, with double its weight of vermin. I was glad to get up and put on my clothes, and lie as my companions did. Had we not been very tired, I am sure we should not have slept much that night. I made a promise to sleep no more in a bed, choosing rather to sleep in the open air before a fire."

One night, after a very hard day's work, when soundly sleeping, his camp and bed, which were made of the most combustible materials, took fire, and he very narrowly escaped being consumed in the flames. After spending several months on the survey, he wrote to a friend in the following strain:

> "The receipt of your kind letter of the 2d instant afforded me unspeakable pleasure. It convinces me that I am still in the memory of so worthy a friend; a friendship I shall ever be proud of increasing. Yours gave me the more pleasure, as I received it among barbarians and an uncouth set of people. Since you received my letter of October last, I have not slept above three or four nights in a bed. But after walking a good deal all the day, I have lain down before the fire, on a little hay, straw, fodder, or bearskin, whichever was to be had, with man, wife, and children, like dogs and cats and happy is he who gets the berth nearest the fire. I have never had my clothes off, but have lain and slept in them, except the few nights I have been in Fredericksburg."

Such experiences not only develop, but rapidly create character. George returned, from the successful accomplishment of this arduous enterprise, with all his manly energies consolidated. Though but seventeen years of age, he was a mature, self-reliant man, prepared to assume any of the responsibilities of manhood.

The imperial State of Virginia needed a public surveyor. This lad of seventeen years had already risen so high in the estimation of the community, that he was appointed to that responsible office. For three years he performed, with singular ability, the duties which thus devolved upon him. Great must have been the enjoyment which he found, in the field of labor thus opened before him. The scenes to which he was introduced must have been, at times, quite enchanting. The wonderful scenery presented to the eye in beautiful Virginia, the delicious climate, the grandeur of the star-bespangled sky, as witnessed from the midnight encampment, the majestic forests abounding in game, the placid lake, whose mirrored waters were covered with water-fowl of every variety of gorgeous plumage, the silent river, along which the Indian's birch canoe glided almost as a meteor—all these infinitely diversified scenes must, at times, have entranced a young man in the vigor of youth and health, and buoyant with the spirit of high enterprise.

Lord Fairfax had become the firm friend of George Washington. The opulent English nobleman had reared for himself a large and architecturally beautiful mansion of stone, beyond the Blue Ridge, in one of the most sheltered, sunny, and lovely valleys of the Alleghanies. This beautiful world of ours can present no region more attractive than that in which Lord Fairfax constructed his transatlantic home.[6]

His opulence enabled him to live there in splendor quite baronial. Many illustrious families had emigrated to this State of wonderful beauty and inexhaustible capabilities. There was no colony, on this continent, which could present more cultivated and polished society than Virginia. Distinguished guests frequented the parlors of Lord Fairfax. Among them all, there were none more honored than George Washington. He was one of

---

[6] "Lord Fairfax was a man of cultivated mind, educated at Oxford, the associate of the wits in London, the author of one or two papers in the "Spectator," and a *habitué* of the polite circles of the metropolis. A disappointment in love is said to have cast a shadow over his after life, and to have led him to pass his time in voluntary exile on his Virginia estates."—Everett's *Life of Washington*, p. 41.

the handsomest and most dignified of men, and a gentleman by birth, by education, and by all his instincts.

The tide of emigration, pouring in a constant flood across the Atlantic, was now gradually forcing its way over the first range of the Alleghanies, into the fertile and delightful valleys beyond. Still farther west there were realms, much of which no white man's foot had ever trod, and whose boundaries no one knew.

The French, who were prosperously established in Canada, and who, by their wise policy, had effectually won the confidence and affection of the natives, were better acquainted with this vast region than were the English; and they much more fully appreciated its wonderful capabilities. And still the English colonies, in population, exceeded those of the French ten to one.

Almost from the beginning, the relations of the English with the natives were hostile. And it cannot be denied that the fault was with the English. The Indians were very desirous of friendly intercourse. It was an unspeakable advantage to them, and they highly prized it, to be able to exchange their furs for the kettles, hatchets, knives, guns, powder and shot of the English. With the bullet they could strike down the deer at three times the distance to which they could throw an arrow. The shrewd Indian, who had used flints only to cut with, could well appreciate the value of a hatchet and a knife.

Our Puritan fathers were very anxious to treat the Indians with brotherly kindness. And so were the governmental authorities generally in all the colonies. But there was no strength in the Christian principles of good men, or in the feeble powers which were established in the colonies, to pursue, arrest, and punish the desperadoes who, from the frontiers, penetrated the wilderness with sword and rifle, shot down the Indians, plundered the wigwams, and inflicted every outrage upon their wives and daughters. No candid man can read an account of these outrages without saying:

"Had I been an Indian I would have joined in any conspiracy, and would have strained every nerve, to exterminate such wretches from the land they were polluting."

The untaught natives could draw no fine distinctions. When the Indian hunter returned to his wigwam, and found it plundered and in ashes, his eldest son dead and weltering in blood, and heard from his wife and daughters the story of their wrongs, he could make no distinction between the miscreants who had perpetrated the demoniac deed, and the Christian white men who deplored such atrocities and who implored God to interpose and prevent them. The poor Indian could only say:

"The white man has thus wronged me. Oh, thou Great Spirit, whenever I meet the white man, wilt thou help me to take vengeance."

Increasing population increased these outrages. There was no law in the wilderness. These British desperadoes regarded no more the restraints of religion than did the bears and the wolves. They behaved like demons, and they roused the demoniac spirit in the savages. Crime was followed by crime, cruelty by cruelty, blood by blood. But for man's inhumanity to man beautiful Virginia, with her brilliant skies, her salubrious air, her fertile fields, her crystal streams, her majestic mountains, her sublime forests, her placid lakes, might have been almost like the Garden of Eden. If the heart of man had been imbued with the religion of Jesus, the whole realm might have been adorned with homes, in some degree, at least, like those found in the mansions of the blest. But the conduct of depraved men converted the whole region into a valley of Hinnom, abounding in smouldering ruins, gory corpses, and groans of despair.

Rapidly, on both sides, the spirit of vengeance spread. The savages, with their fiend-like natures roused, perpetrated deeds of cruelty which demons could not have surpassed. They made no discrimination. The English were to be exterminated. When the frontiersman was roused, at midnight, by the yell of the savages, and being left for dead upon the ground, with his scalp torn from his head, after some hours of stupor revived to see his cabin in ashes, the mangled corpses of his children strewn around, with their skulls cleft by the tomahawk, and not finding the remains of wife or daughter, was sure that they were carried into Indian captivity, perhaps to be tortured to death, for the amusement of howling savages—as thus bleeding, exhausted, and in agony he crept along to some garrison house, he was in no mood to listen to the dictates of humanity. Thus the terrible conflict which arose, assumed the aspect of a war between maddened fiends.

George Washington had attained the age of nineteen years. Youthful as he was, he was regarded as one of the prominent men of the State of Virginia. Every day brought reports of tragedies enacted in the solitudes of the wilderness, whose horrors will only be fully known in that dread day of judgment when all secrets will be revealed. It became necessary to call the whole military force of Virginia into requisition, to protect the frontiers from the invasion of savage bands, who emerged from all points like wolves from the forest.

The State was divided into districts. Over each a military commander was appointed, with the title of Major. George Washington was one of these majors. The responsibilities of these officers were very great, for they were necessarily invested with almost dictatorial powers. The savages would come rushing at midnight from the wilderness, upon some lonely cabin or feeble settlement. An awful scene of shrieks and flame and death would ensue, and the band would disappear beyond the reach of any avenging arm. In such a war the tactics of European armies could be of but little avail.

The State of Virginia was then, as now, bounded on the west by the Ohio river, which the French called La Belle Rivière. England claimed nearly the whole North American coast, as hers by the right of discovery, her ships having first cruised along its shores. The breadth of the continent was unknown. Consequently the English assumed that the continent was theirs, from the Atlantic to the Pacific, whatever its breadth might be.[7]

---

[7] Sebastian Cabot, in the year 1498, sailed from Bristol, England, with two ships, in the month of May. He first made land on the coast of Labrador. He was seeking a passage to India. Cruising along the shores of Nova Scotia, and the whole length of the coast of Maine, he

But the ships of France were the first which entered the river St. Lawrence; and her voyagers, ascending the magnificent stream, discovered that series of majestic lakes, whose fertile shores presented inviting homes for countless millions. Her enterprising explorers, in the birch canoe, traversed the solitary windings of the Ohio and the Mississippi. Hence France claimed the whole of that immense valley, almost a world in itself, whose unknown grandeur no mind then had begun to appreciate.

It was then a law of nations, recognized by all the European powers, that the discovery of a coast entitled the nation by whom the discovery was made, to the possession of that territory, to the exclusion of the right of any other European power. It was also an acknowledged principle of national law, that the discovery and exploration of a river entitled the nation by whom this exploration was made, to the whole valley, of whatever magnitude, which that river and its tributaries might drain.[8]

These conflicting claims led to the march of armies, the devastations of fleets, terrific battles—blood, misery, and death. France, that she might retain a firm hold of the territory which she claimed, began to rear a cordon of forts, at commanding points, from the great lakes, down the Ohio and the Mississippi, until she reached the Spanish claims in the south. Though France had discovered the Mississippi, in its upper waters, the Spanish chevalier, De Soto, had previously launched his boats near its entrance into the Gulf, and his tragic life was closed by burial beneath its waves.

---

rounded Cape Cod, and continued his voyage to the latitude of Cape Hatteras. Thence he entered upon his homeward voyage.—Galvano's *Discoveries of the World*, p. 88. London, 1601.

[8] "The French insisted on the right of discovery and occupancy. Father Marquette, La Salle, and others, they said, had descended the Mississippi, and settlements had been made south of Lake Michigan and on the Illinois River, years before any Englishman had set his foot westward of the great mountains; and European treaties had repeatedly recognized the title of France to all her actual possessions in America. So far the ground was tenable."—Sparks' *Life of Washington*, p. 20.

But he immediately adds, in apparent contradiction to these statements: "It is clear that neither of the contending parties had any just claims to the land about which they were beginning to kindle the flames of war. They were both intruders upon the soil of the native occupants."

This is hardly fair to either party. Neither France nor England claimed the territory, to the exclusion of the rights of the original inhabitants. Their only claim extended to the right of purchasing the territory from the Indians, of trading with them, and of establishing colonies. And this right all the maritime nations of Europe recognized.

An awful struggle, which caused as great woes perhaps as this sorrowful world has ever endured, was now approaching, for the possession of this continent. France and England were the two most powerful kingdoms, if perhaps we except Spain, then upon the globe. The intelligent reader will be interested in a more minute account of the nature of those claims, which English historians, generally, have somewhat ignored, but upon which results of such momentous importance to humanity were suspended.

In the year 1497, John Cabot, with a fleet of four, some say five ships, sailed from Bristol, England, and discovered the coast of Labrador. But little is known respecting this voyage, for the journal was lost. He returned to England, greatly elated, supposing that he had discovered the empire of China.

The next year his son, Sebastian, who had accompanied his father on the former voyage, sailed from Bristol, with two ships, in the month of May, and touched the coast of Labrador, far away in the north. Finding it excessively cold, even in July, he directed his course south, and cruised along, keeping the coast constantly in sight, until, passing Nova Scotia, he entered the broad gulf of Maine. He continued his voyage, it is supposed, until, rounding the long curvature of Cape Cod, he found an open sea extending far to the west. He passed on until he reached the latitude of Cape Hatteras, when, finding his provisions failing him, he returned home. It was this voyage upon which England founded her claim to the whole of that portion of the continent whose coast had been thus explored. The breadth of the continent was entirely unknown.[9]

Upon this claim the grants to the Virginia, as also to the Connecticut colony, were across the whole breadth of the continent. King Charles I., in the fifth year of his reign, in the year 1630, granted to one of his favorites, Sir Robert Heath, all that part of America which lies between thirty-one and thirty-six degrees of north latitude, from the Atlantic to the Pacific.

---

[9] Galvano's "Discoveries of the World," p. 88, London; Biddle's "Memoir of Sebastian Cabot," p. 221, London.

This truly imperial gift included nearly the whole sea-coast of North and South Carolina, extending from sea to sea.[10]

The Spanish adventurer, De Soto, whose wonderful exploits are recorded in one of the volumes of this series, discovered the Mississippi, near its mouth, in the year 1541. Some years before this, in 1508, a French exploring expedition entered the Gulf of St. Lawrence, and framed a map of its shores. In 1525, France took formal possession of the country. Ten years after, in 1535, M. Cartier ascended the St. Lawrence, which he so named, as he entered the river on that saint's day. This wonderful stream, whose bed expands into a series of the most majestic lakes on this globe, presents a continuous water-course of over two thousand miles, and is supposed to contain more than one-half of all the fresh water on this planet.[11]

Several trading expeditions visited the region. In 1608 the city of Quebec was founded. French voyagers, in the birch canoe, extensively explored rivers and lakes, for the purchase of furs. They established a mission on the banks of Lake Huron, in the year 1641, and pushing their explorations to Lake Superior, established one there in 1660. Another mission was founded in 1671, at the Falls of St. Mary, which acquired much renown. In that same year France took formal possession of the vast regions of the north-west.

Two years after this, in 1673, Marquette and his companions discovered the Mississippi. In 1680, Father Hennepin explored that stream to its sources far away in the north. In 1682, La Salle performed his wonderful voyage down the whole length of the river, to the Gulf. A minute account of the romantic adventures he encountered, will be found in the History of La Salle, one of the volumes of this series. In 1699, Lemoine D'Iberville entered the Mississippi with two good ships, explored its mouths, and ascended the river about seventy-five miles, carefully sounding his way. One morning, greatly to his surprise, he saw a British corvette, with twelve cannon, under full sail, breasting the current. He ordered the British immediately to leave the river, stating that he had

---

[10] "A Description of the English Province of Carolina," by Daniel Coxe, Esq., p. 113.
[11] M'Culloch's Geographical Dictionary.

ample force to compel them to do so. The British officer felt constrained to obey, though not without remonstrance. He said:

> "England discovered this country fifty years ago; and has a better right to it than the French have. We will soon come back and teach you that the country is ours."

This was the first meeting of the two rival nations in the Mississippi valley. The bend in the river, where this occurrence took place, has since been called the "English Bend."[12]

Such was the nature of the conflicting claims advanced by France and England. France was proud; England haughty. Neither would consent to an amicable compromise, or to submit the question to the arbitration of referees. As the year rolled on, English emigrants, crowding the Atlantic coasts, were looking wistfully across the Alleghanies. The French, descending from Canada, had established several trading posts, which were also fortifications, in the beautiful valley of the Ohio.

There is much discrepancy in the details of these movements, which have descended to us through very unreliable sources. The writer has space here only to give the facts which are generally admitted. It is universally admitted that the French won the love of the Indians to an extraordinary degree. An aged chief of the Six Nations, said, at Easton, in 1758:

> "The Indians left you because of your own fault. When we heard that the French were coming we asked you for help and arms. But we did not get them. The French came. They treated us kindly, and gained our love. The Governor of Virginia settled on our lands for his own benefit, and, when we wanted help, forsook us."[13]

Governor Dinwiddie, of Virginia, hearing of these encroachments, as he regarded them, decided to send a commissioner across the Alleghanies, to one of these posts, with a double object in view. One, and the avowed

---

[12] "New France," vol. iii. p. 380; "Annals of the West," p. 57.
[13] "Plain Facts," p. 55; Pownal's "Memoir on Service in North America."

object, was to remonstrate, in the name of Great Britain, against this trespass, as he pronounced it, upon British territory. The other, and the true object, was to ascertain the number, strength, and position of the French garrisons, and to survey a route by which an army might be sent for their capture.[14]

It was indeed a perilous enterprise; one from which the boldest spirit might recoil. The first garrison which could be reached was on the Ohio River, about one hundred and twenty miles below the point where Pittsburg now stands. Here the French were erecting a strong fortress, to which the Indians resorted for trade. There was an intervening wilderness, from the settlements in Virginia, to be traversed, of pathless forests, gloomy morasses, craggy mountains, and almost impenetrable thickets, of nearly six hundred miles. Bands of savages, on the war-path or engaged in the hunt, were ever ranging these wilds. Many were exasperated by wrongs which they themselves had received, or of which they had heard, inflicted by the white men. The Indians, in all these north-western regions, had welcomed the French as brothers; and truly fraternal relationship existed between them. And they had nearly all learned to hate the English, who have never succeeded in winning the love of any people.

In such a journey, one must depend entirely, for subsistence, upon the game which could be taken. There was danger of being crippled by a strain or a broken bone, and of thus perishing, beyond the reach of all aid. There was no little danger from the tomahawk of the savage. It was also probable that the French officers would not allow the commissioner, whom they would regard as a spy, to return to the English colonies with information so valuable to their foes. Principles of justice and mercy have never had much control in military affairs. It would be very easy for the French so to arrange matters, that a band of savages should massacre and plunder the party of the commissioner, in the depths of the forest, under such

---

[14] "He (Washington) was furthermore to inquire, diligently and by cautious means, into the number of the French troops that had crossed the lakes, the reinforcements expected from Canada, how many forts they had erected, and at what places, how they were garrisoned and appointed, and their distances from each other; and, in short, to procure all the intelligence possible respecting the condition and object of the intruders."—Sparks' *Life of Washington*, p. 22.

circumstances that it would necessarily be regarded as merely a savage outrage.

There was no one to be found willing to expose himself to such hardships, and his life to such risks. At length George Washington, who was then but twenty years and six months old, came forward and volunteered his services. It was universally regarded, by the community, as an act of great heroism. Governor Dinwiddie, a blunt and sturdy Scotchman, eagerly accepted his proffered services. As he grasped the hand of the youthful Washington, he exclaimed:

"Truly you are a brave lad. And if you play your cards well, you shall have no cause to repent of your bargain."

The sobriety and dignity of character of Washington were such, that no one thought of accusing him of boyish fool-hardiness. And he had such experience in the deprivations and perils of the wilderness, that it could not be questioned that he fully understood the nature of the enterprise in which he had engaged.

On the 14th of November, 1753, Washington set out, from Williamsburg, Virginia, on this perilous expedition. His party consisted of eight men, two of them being Indian guides. The storms of winter were rapidly approaching. Already the crests of the mountains were whitened with snow. The autumnal rains had swollen the brooks into torrents. Warmly clad in furs, the party did not fear the cold. With their axes they could speedily rear a camp, which would shelter them from the fiercest storm. Wood was abundant; and the most dreary of midnight scenes may be enlivened by the blaze of the camp fire.

In such a shelter, before such a fire, with choice cuts of venison, the fattest of nature's poultry, and delicious trout fresh drawn from the brook, these hardy adventurers, accustomed to the woodman's lodging and the woodman's fare, could enjoy the richest of repasts, and all the comforts of the warm and bright fireside.

Many days were passed, full of incidents, romantic adventures, and hair-breadth escapes, when the barriers of the Alleghanies were safely surmounted, and the explorers, winding their way through the defiles, descended into the fertile and grand valley beyond. The Indian guides conducted them by a route which led to the upper waters of the Monongahela River. This stream, flowing toward the north, meets the Alleghany, which takes its rise near the great lakes. This union forms the Ohio.

Upon this solitary stream the Indians constructed birch canoes, and the little party paddled down, through sublime solitudes, a distance of nearly three hundred miles, to the mouth of the river, where Pittsburg now stands. The voyage occupied eight days. Occasionally they passed a small cluster of Indian wigwams. Silently the impassible children of the forest gazed upon them as they passed, offering no molestation. There was something truly awe-inspiring in the silence of the wilderness. No voice was heard. No blow of axe or hammer sent its reverberations to the ear. There was no report of the musket to break the solemn stillness. The arrow of the hunter, in its flight through the air, gave forth no sound.

Having reached the mouth of the Monongahela, they heard that the French had an important military fort on French Creek, called also Rivière aux Bœufs, about fifteen miles south of Lake Erie.[15] The French were in possession of a strong station at Presque Isle, on the southern coast of Lake Erie. From this point they had constructed a good wagon road to the head of boat navigation on French Creek. Here they reared another fort, as is supposed, about the year 1752.[16] "Through rivers and creeks, snow, rain and cold," Washington and his little party, toiling through the dreary wilderness, reached French Creek on the 11th of November. Washington had for his companion, Mr. Christopher Gist (who was a frontiersman of great energy and experience), beside his Indian guides, with four other white men and two Indians.[17] Forty-one days were spent in this arduous journey. They found a small French outpost at Venango, where the French

---

[15] "French Creek, New York and Pennsylvania, rises in Chautauque county, New York, passes into Pennsylvania, flowing by Meadville, and enters Alleghany river, at Franklin, Venango county. It is about 100 miles long."—M'Culloch's *Geographical Dictionary*.

[16] Washington's Journal of 1753.

[17] Gist's Journal of the Expedition may be found in the Massachusetts Historical Collections, 3d series, vol. v. pages 101–108.

commandant, Captain Joncaire, received them cordially, and guided them to the head-quarters.

On this journey, Washington very carefully examined the Forks of the Ohio, as a suitable place for the erection of a fort. He descended the Ohio about twenty miles to an Indian village called Logstown. Here, in a council with the chief, he endeavored to draw the tribe away from the French and into a friendly alliance with the English;[18] and also to obtain an escort of warriors to conduct him across the country, through the wilderness, to the French post, which was distant one hundred and twenty miles. In this he was but partially successful. Four Indians only accompanied him. This made his party amount to twelve. There were six white men and six Indians. Tanachanson, the chief sachem, and representative of the Six Nations, accompanied Washington's party.

---

[18] "The truth was, these Indians were in a very awkward position. They could not resist the Europeans, and knew not which to side with; so that a non-committal policy was much the safest; and they were wise not to return, by Washington, as he desired they should do, the wampum they received from the French, as that would be equivalent to breaking with them."—*Annals of the West*, p. 83.

Chapter 2

THE FIRST MILITARY EXPEDITION

A French officer, by the name of St. Pierre, was in command at Fort Le Bœuf. Though fully aware of the object of the commissioner's expedition, he received Washington with the courtesy characteristic of the French nation. Respectfully he received the remonstrance which was presented to him, and gave Washington a written reply, couched in dignified terms, in which he stated that he was placed at that post by the command of his government, and that he could not abandon it until officially instructed so to do.[19]

Washington was as hospitably entertained at the fort as if he had been a friend. In that remote frontier station, buried in the glooms of the wilderness, and with no society but that of rude soldiers and uncouth savages, a French officer, who was almost of necessity a gentleman of rank and refinement, must have enjoyed most highly a visit from an American of cultivated mind and polished manners. There was no opportunity to conceal anything of the strength of the French works from the English party, even if it had been deemed desirable to do so. Washington drew up

---

[19] "M. de St. Pierre, the commandant, was an elderly person, a knight of the military order of St. Louis, and courteous in his manners. At the first interview, he promised immediate attention to the letter from Governor Dinwiddie; and everything was provided for the convenience and comfort of Major Washington and his party while they remained at the fort."—Sparks' *Life of Washington*, p. 26.

an accurate plan of the fort, either secretly or by permission, which he sent to the British Government.[20] The reply which St. Pierre returned was obviously the only one which, as a servant of the crown, he could make. This must have been known as distinctly before the reply was given as afterward. And it certainly did not require a journey of more than twelve hundred miles, going and returning, through the wilderness, to learn that, if the French were to relinquish their claims to the valley of the Ohio, they must either be driven from it by force, or be persuaded to it by diplomatic conference at the court of Versailles.

The main object of the mission was however accomplished. A feasible route for a military force, over the mountains, was discovered, and the strength of the French garrisons, in those quarters, was ascertained. Washington was surprised in seeing with how much unexpected strength the French were intrenching themselves, that they might hold possessions which they deemed so valuable.

After a very friendly visit of two days, M. de St. Pierre, who had treated his guest with much hospitality, furnished him with a strong canoe, in which he could rapidly descend the St. Francis to the Alleghany, and that stream to the Ohio. Mr. Sparks writes:[21]

> "He had been entertained with great politeness. Nor did the complaisance of M. de St. Pierre exhaust itself in mere forms of civility. The canoe, by his order, was plentifully stocked with provisions, liquors, and every other supply that could be wanted."

The voyage down the winding stream to an Indian village, where Venango now stands, a distance of one hundred and thirty miles, was full of peril and suffering. The stream, swollen by wintry rains, was in some places a roaring torrent. Again it broke over rocks, or was encumbered by rafts of drifting timber, around which the canoe and all its freight had to be

---

[20] "Major Washington took an opportunity to look around and examine the fort. His attendants were instructed to do the same. He was thus enabled to bring away an accurate description of its form, size, construction, cannon, and barracks. His men counted the canoes in the river, and such as were partly finished."—Sparks' *Life of Washington*, p. 27.

[21] Sparks' *Life of Washington*, p. 27.

carried. Several times all had to leap into the icy water, to rescue the buoyant and fragile boat from impending destruction. At one place they carried the canoe over a neck of land a quarter mile in extent.

Soon after leaving Venango they found their progress so slow that Major Washington and Mr. Gist clothed themselves in Indian walking dresses, and with heavy packs on their backs, and each with a gun in his hand, set out through the woods on foot. They directed their course, by the compass, so as to strike the Alleghany River just above its confluence with the Monongahela.

This was indeed a weary and perilous journey to take, with the rifle upon the shoulder, the pack upon the back, and the hatchet suspended at the waist. With the hatchet, each night a shelter was to be constructed, should fierce gales or drenching rain render a shelter needful. With the rifle, or the fish-hook, their daily food was to be obtained. In the pack they carried their few cooking utensils and their extra clothing.

Washington's suspicions that there might be attempts to waylay him were not unfounded. Some Indians followed his trail, either instigated to it by the French, or of their own accord for purposes of plunder. A solitary Indian met him, apparently by accident, in a very rough and intricate part of the way, and offered his service as a guide. Through the day they journeyed together very confidingly. The Indian's sinews seemed to be made of iron, which nothing could tire. He led Washington and his companion along a very fatiguing route, until nightfall. Then, apparently supposing that, in their exhaustion, if one were shot the other would be helpless and could be followed and shot down at his leisure, he took deliberate aim, it is said, at Washington and fired, at a distance of not more than fifteen paces. The ball barely missed its target. The Indian sprang into the woods. Indignation gave speed to the feet of his pursuers. He was soon caught. The companion of Washington urged that the savage should immediately be put to death. But Washington recoiled from the idea of shooting a man in cold blood. Having disarmed the assassin, he turned him adrift in the wilderness.[22]

---

[22] Such is the story as generally received, and as narrated, essentially, by Mr. Gist. But it would appear that Washington had some doubt whether the Indian were treacherously disposed.

It was a cold December night. As it was thought not impossible that the Indian might have some confederates near, they pressed forward, through all the hours of darkness until the morning dawned, taking special care to pursue such a route that even savage sagacity could not search out their trail. They pressed on until they reached the Alleghany River but a short distance from its mouth. The whole region was then a silent wilderness. There were no signs of civilized or even of savage life to be seen. Though the broader streams were not yet frozen over, the banks of the rivers were fringed with ice, and immense solid blocks were floating down the rapid currents. It was necessary to cross the stream before them. With "one poor hatchet," Washington writes, it took them a whole day to construct a suitable raft. The logs were bound together by flexible boughs and grape vines. It was necessary to be very careful; for should the logs, from the force of the waves or from collision with the ice, part in the middle of the stream, they would be plunged into the icy river, and death would be almost inevitable.

They mounted the raft early in the morning, having finished it the night before, and with long setting poles endeavored to push their way across the whirling, swollen torrent. A piercing December wind swept the black waters. When about half-way across, the raft encountered a pack of floating ice. Washington's pole became entangled in the mud at the bottom of the river, and the raft was violently whirled around. One of the withes, which bound the logs together, parted; the raft was broken into fragments, and the occupants were plunged into the stream. The water was ten feet deep. Both were, for a moment, entirely submerged. Rising to the surface they clung to the floating logs. Fortunately, just below there was a small island, to which they were speedily floated.

According to his narrative the savage made no attempt to escape, but commenced reloading his gun. He said that his wigwam was so near, that he fired the gun to let the family know that he was coming. He had previously begged them to go with him to his cabin, and to pass the night. A careful examination of probabilities will lead many to believe that Washington was correct in his supposition. Mr. Sparks writes, "Whether it was the intention to kill either of them can only be conjectured. If it were, he showed a degree of stupidity very different from the ordinary cunning of the savage. They could only converse by signs and might easily have entirely misunderstood each other."

Here, drenched and freezing, they took shelter. Their powder, carefully protected, had not been wet. Despairingly they had clung to their guns. As soon as possible, as the island was well wooded, they constructed a shelter from the gale, and built a roaring fire. Its genial warmth reanimated them, so that they could even enjoy the wintry blasts which swept fiercely by. But before they had reared their shelter and built their fire, Mr. Gist's hands and feet were frost-bitten.

It is surprising with what rapidity men experienced in wood-craft will rear a camp, enclosed on three sides and open on one, which, roofed and sheathed with overlapping bark, will afford an effectual shelter from both wind and rain. Such a cabin, carpeted with bear-skins or with the soft and fragrant boughs of the hemlock, with a grand fire crackling in front, and a duck, a wild turkey, or cuts of tender venison roasting deliciously before it, presents a scene of comfort which, to the hungry and weary pioneer, is often truly luxurious. He would not exchange it for the most gorgeously furnished chambers in palatial abodes.

Our adventurers, accustomed to such mishaps, regarded their cold bath rather in the light of a joke. They piled the fuel, in immense logs, upon the camp fire; for on the torrent-encircled island they had no fear of being attacked by the savages. They dried their clothing, cooked and ate their savory supper, and, wrapped in their blankets, laid down and slept as sweetly, probably, as if they had been occupants of the guest chamber at Mount Vernon.

The dawn of the next morning revealed to them the fact that the night had been one bitterly cold; for the whole stream was firmly frozen over. They crossed the remaining channel on the ice to the eastern shore. Hence they continued their journey home, over the wide range of the Alleghanies. Without any remarkable incident occurring, they safely reached Williamsburg, then the capital of Virginia, on the 16th of January, 1754, having been absent eleven weeks. Washington seemed to be the only man who was unconscious that he had performed a feat of remarkable skill and daring.

At the confluence of the Monongahela and Youghiogeny rivers, there was an Indian princess, called Queen Aliquippa. Washington paid her a complimentary visit, and quite won her confidence by his friendly words and valuable gifts. He also came across a small trading post, recently established by Mr. Frazier. Here he remained two or three days, and succeeded in obtaining some horses for the rest of the journey.

He made his modest report to the governor. It was published, and was read with surprise and admiration, not only all over the State, but it was eagerly perused by statesmen in England, who were watching with great jealousy the movements of the French west of the Alleghanies. The all-important facts which the report established were, that the French had taken full possession of the valley of La Belle Rivière; that they were entrenching themselves there very strongly; that the native tribes were in cordial sympathy with them, and would undoubtedly enter into any military alliance with the French which they might desire; that it was very much easier for the French to bring down any amount of reinforcements and supplies from Canada, by the way of the great lakes and the natural water-courses, than for the English to transport such supplies across the wide, rugged, precipitous, pathless ranges of the Alleghanies; and finally that it was clear that the French would resist, with all their military force, any attempts of the English to establish their settlements in the valley of the Ohio.[23]

The intelligent reader will inquire who, according to the law of nations, was legitimately entitled to this region. The candid reader, laying aside all national predilections, will say:

> "It is very difficult to decide this question. The English ships had sailed along the coast. How far back, into the interior, did this entitle them to the country? The French had discovered these magnificent rivers, and had explored them in their canoes. Did this so entitle them to these valleys, as to limit the western boundaries of the English by the

---

[23] "As soon as Washington returned with the letter of St. Pierre, Governor Dinwiddie wrote to the Board of Trade, stating that the French were building another fort at Venango, and that, in March, twelve or fifteen hundred men would be ready to descend the Alleghany river with their Indian allies, for which purpose three hundred canoes had been collected; and that Logstown was then to be made head-quarters, while forts were built in various other positions, and the whole country occupied."—*Annals of the West*, p. 84.

Alleghany mountains, upon whose western declivities these valleys commenced?"

Such was the question. Alas! for humanity, that it could only be settled by war, carnage, and misery.

The Legislature of Virginia happened to be in session at Williamsburg when Washington returned. Soon after presenting his report he went, one day, into the gallery, mingling with the crowd, to witness the proceedings of the House. The speaker chanced to catch sight of him. He immediately rose from his chair and, addressing the assembly, said:

> "I propose that the thanks of this House be given to Major George Washington, who now sits in the gallery, for the gallant manner in which he has executed the important trust lately reposed in him, by his excellency the Governor."

These words called forth a spontaneous burst of enthusiasm. Every member sprang to his feet. Every eye was directed to the modest, confused, blushing young man. A shout of applause arose, which almost shook the rafters of the hall. There was no resisting the flood of homage. Two gentlemen conducted Washington to the speaker's desk. There was instant and universal silence.

Washington was entirely taken by surprise. To such scenes he was altogether unaccustomed. Be it remembered that he was then but twenty-one years of age; just entering the period of manhood. Thus suddenly was he brought before that august tribunal; and all were silently awaiting words for which he was utterly unprepared. In his great confusion he was speechless. There was a moment of silence, and then the speaker, perceiving the cruel position in which he was placed, happily relieved him from embarrassment, by presenting a chair and saying:

> "Sit down, Major Washington; sit down. Your modesty is alone equal to your merit."

Governor Dinwiddie, a reckless, headlong Scotchman, was governed mainly by impulse, and was accustomed to speak and act first, and reflect afterward. He despised the French, and could say with Lord Nelson, "I drew in hatred for the French with my mother's milk." He paid no respect whatever to the considerations upon which the French founded their claim to the valley of the Ohio; but affirmed it to be the height of impudence for Frenchmen to pretend to any title to territory, which Englishmen claimed as theirs. Such insolence, he declared, was not to be tolerated for a moment; and he determined that he would immediately drive the intruders, neck and heels, out of the valley.[24]

Arrogance is pretty sure to bring its own punishment. But we are often bewildered by the thought that, in the incomprehensible government of God over this world, the punishment often falls upon the innocent, while those who merit it go free.

Energetically the irate governor marshalled an army of four hundred men. The idea that the cowardly French could present any effectual resistance to his lion-hearted Englishmen, seems never to have entered his mind. The orders issued to this army, so formidable in those days, were very emphatic and peremptory.

> "March rapidly across the mountains. Disperse, capture, or kill all persons—not subjects of the king of Great Britain—who are attempting to take possession of the territory of his majesty, on the banks of the Ohio river, or any of its tributaries."

George Washington was appointed colonel of this regiment. A wiser selection could not have been made. His administrative abilities were of the highest order; his exalted reputation invested him with authority; he was acquainted with the route, as no other man in the colony could be; his

---

[24] "The Assembly was convened; and many of the most judicious members expressed doubts whether the king of England had an unquestionable claim to the valley, which France had discovered and occupied. 'You may well conceive,' the governor wrote, 'how I fired at this; that an English legislature should presume to doubt the right of his majesty to the interior parts of this continent, the back of his dominions.'"—Sparks' *Life of Washington*, p. 35.

bravery was above all suspicion, and his experience as a surveyor would enable him to select the best strategic points to command the vast territory.

At the confluence of the Monongahela and the Alleghany, he had spent a day in constructing a raft. There he had been wrecked. The delay which these incidents had caused, enabled him very carefully, with his practiced eye, to study the features of the country.

This spot, he decided, with instinctive military skill, to be the most appropriate place for England to rear a fortress and establish a garrison, which would constitute the most effectual *point d'appui* (point of support), from which expeditions could emerge for the destruction of the French trading posts. This whole region was then an unbroken, howling wilderness. Buried in the glooms of the forest, far away from all observation, Washington hoped to rear a strong fortress before the French should have any suspicion of what was going on. Having completed these works, and rendered them impregnable to any force which France could bring against them, he would then build strong flat-bottomed boats, armed with cannon, and manned with troops, in which they could drift down the Ohio, and attack by surprise, and destroy, all the French military and trading posts found upon the banks.

Contemplating this plan in the light of humanity, it was a very sad one. "War is cruelty. You cannot refine it." At these posts there were many humble emigrants, fathers and mothers, little boys and girls. They were innocent of all crime. Struggling against the enormous taxation, of king and nobles, in France, they had left the thatched cottages of their lowly ancestors, hoping to find homes of more comfort in the wilderness of the New World. It is dreadful to think of the consternation, which must have spread through such a little settlement of pioneers, when suddenly, on some bright, sunny morning, the terrible gun-boats, crowded with armed soldiers, rounded a bend in the river, and opened their fire. "Bayonets," says a French proverb, "must not think." Soldiers must obey orders, regardless of the tears and pleadings of humanity. The orders were peremptory.

"Apply the torch and lay every building in ashes. The dying matron, helpless in her bed, and the new-born babe, must look out for themselves. Disperse, capture, or kill all the inhabitants. Leave nothing behind but smouldering ruins and mangled corpses."

Such was the plan, in its awfulness, when contemplated by the eye of ordinary humanity. In a military point of view the plan, thus devised, was worthy of all admiration. As a means for the attainment of the desired end, it could not have been better. The expedition, however, was not popular, and it was found necessary to resort to impressment to fill the ranks. By the Provincial law, the militia could not be ordered to march more than five miles beyond the bounds of the colony. And it was at least doubtful whether the French were in Virginia, though Governor Dinwiddie declared the Pacific Ocean to be the western boundary of the State. Unfortunately for the success of the expedition, the French engineers were by no means behind the English in military skill. In descending to the Ohio, from the lakes, they had been accustomed to take canoes, on the upper waters of the Alleghany; and often, in fleets propelled by the paddles of friendly Indians, they had encamped, for the night, upon the forest-crowned eminences at the confluence of the Alleghany and Monongahela rivers. They also had decided that this was, above all others, the spot upon which France should rear her central fortress, and where she should store her abounding supplies.

The menace which Governor Dinwiddie had sent by Washington, was not unheeded by the French authorities. Immediately they commenced rearing a fortress, which they had, for some time, been contemplating. A thousand men from Canada descended the Alleghany River in sixty French bateaux and three hundred Indian canoes, taking with them a strong armament and a large supply of military stores. They commenced their fortress where Pittsburg now stands, calling it Fort Duquesne.[25] The forest

---

[25] It is said that there was a small party, of about forty men, in the employ of the Ohio Company, who had commenced throwing up entrenchments at the Fork. "On the 17th of April, Ensign Ward, then in command, saw, upon the Alleghany, a sight that made his heart sink; sixty bateaux and three hundred canoes, filled with men and deeply laden with cannon and stores. The fort was called on to surrender. Ward tried to evade the act; but it would not do.

resounded with the blows of the axe men. A thousand French soldiers, many of them skilled as masons and carpenters, plied all their energies in rearing the walls. Several hundred Indians eagerly aided, heaving along massive blocks of stone, and dragging heavy timbers.

Rapidly the works arose, fashioned by the most accomplished military engineers. Eighteen pieces of cannon were soon in position. And by the time the little army of Governor Dinwiddie had blindly commenced its march, the frowning walls of Fort Duquesne could have bid defiance to ten times the force the infatuated governor had sent to drive the French, "neck and heels," out of the valley.

Scarcely any mistake, in a military officer, can be greater than that of despising his enemy. The French authorities, in Canada, had carefully read Washington's report. They had made themselves intimately acquainted with all the discussions in the legislature. They had watched every movement. They had read Governor Dinwiddie's order to "disperse, capture, or kill" them all. They were as well acquainted with the number of troops sent to attack them, and with the strength of their armament, as was the youthful Colonel Washington himself. They knew the day and the hour when the march was commenced; and, by the aid of Indian runners, kept themselves pretty accurately informed of the progress which the army made in its advance.

The march, through the barren and rugged ranges of the Alleghanies, for a distance of nearly one hundred miles, was exhausting in the extreme. There was often suffering for food. Though in the rich and well-watered plains beyond, game was abundant, it was very scarce amid the bleak crags of the mountains. Experienced hunters accompanied the little band, whose duty it was to range the country for one or two miles on each side of the line of march, and bring in such game as could be shot down.

Slowly and painfully the soldiers toiled along, until they had accomplished the passage of the mountains, and, emerging from the rugged defiles, had entered hunting grounds which were abundantly stocked with

---

Contrecœur, with a thousand men about him, said 'Evacuate,' and the ensign dared not refuse. That evening he supped with his captor, and the next day was bowed off by the Frenchman, and, with his men and tools, marched up the Monongahela."—*Annals of the West*, p. 87.

every variety of game. The troops had reached the valley of the Monongahela, and, buoyant with hope, were pressing forward, sanguine in the expectation of the entire success of their enterprise, when their march was arrested by the appalling tidings which we have recorded.

They were within three or four days' march of the fortress when a courier communicated the alarming intelligence which we have related. To add to their consternation, he stated, that a combined and outnumbering force of French and Indians were on the rapid march to attack them in front, while a numerous array of Indian warriors had already reached their rear to cut off their retreat. More awful tidings for a young and ambitious soldier, can scarcely be conceived. Retreat was impossible. Even without encountering any foe, his exhausted troops, destitute of food, and with the game driven from their path, would inevitably perish by the way. But to add to his consternation he was told that the veteran soldiers of France, fresh from their barracks, in greatly outnumbering force, were coming down, at the double quick, upon his front; while Indian warriors, the strength of whose bands he could not compute, were lining the path of his retreat with their ambushes.[26]

To surrender his whole force, without striking a blow, was worse than death. In utter desperation to undertake a battle, would be an act of madness. It could, by no possibility, result otherwise than in the destruction of his little army. Though pride might dictate the act, the conscience of Washington recoiled from thus dooming his men to inevitable and useless death. France and England were then at peace. Though, as ever, each was regarding the other with a watchful and a jealous eye, still ostensibly friendly relations existed between the two governments.

France had discovered the valley of the Ohio, had explored it, and for more than half a century had been engaged in a lucrative traffic with the Indians, establishing trading posts, which were strongly fortified.

---

[26] It would seem that Washington had daily public prayers in the camp, reading the service himself. Mr. Irving writes, "It certainly was not one of the least striking pictures presented in this wild campaign—the youthful commander presiding with calm seriousness over a motley assemblage of half-equipped soldiery, leathern-clad hunters and woodsmen, and painted savages with their wives and children, and assisting them all in solemn devotion by his own example and demeanor."—*Life of Washington*, in two volumes, vol. i. p. 42.

Missionary operations, for converting and teaching the Indians, were connected with nearly all these stations. The claim of the French to the territory was founded, as France thought, upon the universally recognized laws of nations.

The measure of the hot-headed Governor Dinwiddie was totally unwarranted. Without any declaration of war, he had fitted out a military expedition, to take possession of the country, and to disperse, kill, or capture all the Frenchmen found in it. This was dishonorable warfare. It was the act of an individual, who was unfortunately invested with power. Such acts are almost invariably followed by calamity. But in this case, as in so many others, the calamity mainly fell, inexplicably, not so much upon him who had issued the orders, as upon the agents, who, unfamiliar with diplomatic right and wrong, were employed and almost forced to execute them.

As usual, rumor had exaggerated the facts. The French officers on the Ohio, who were rearing their homes in one of the most fertile and genial of earthly climes, who were living on terms of even affectionate relationship with the Indians, were very anxious to avoid any collision with the English colonists, which would involve the two kingdoms in war. They were in possession of the country; they were carrying on a very profitable trade with the natives, and were continually lengthening their lines and strengthening their posts.

Peace was evidently the policy for them to pursue. By war they had nothing to gain, but much to risk. Though minutely informed of the movements of Washington, and fully conscious that he might be crushed by a single blow, that blow would be but the beginning, not the end. It would surely inaugurate a terrible war, which would call into requisition all the fleets and armies of Great Britain. It would prove the signal for a conflict which would encircle the globe.

The French commandant at Fort Duquesne, who had nothing whatever to fear from the exhausted and half-famished little band which was approaching him, decided to send a friendly party to meet Colonel Washington, and to advise his return, assuring him that he could not be permitted, without the consent of the French government, to rear a fortress upon territory which France had long considered as exclusively her own. A civilian, M. Jumonville, was sent on this peaceful mission. He took with him, as an escort through the wilderness, but thirty-four men. This renders it certain that he had no hostile designs, for he sent not one to ten of the soldiers composing the regiment of Washington.

But Washington, young, inexperienced, and in a position of great responsibility, was agitated by indescribable embarrassment. It was a dark and stormy night. Jumonville, with his feeble escort, dreaming of no danger, for France and England were at peace, and he was on a friendly mission, had reared their frail shelter camps, and were quietly sleeping around the fires. Some Indians who had been sent forward as scouts, hurried back to Washington with the information that the advance-guard of the French army was encamped at the distance of but a few miles before him. The sagacious Indian scouts very accurately described their number and their position.

They were in a sheltered glen, on the banks of the Monongahela, which was quite shut in by rocks. An invisible foe could easily creep up in the darkness and the storm, and, aided by the camp fires, could take deliberate aim, and, by one volley, kill or disable almost every one of the unsuspecting and sleeping foe. Washington, who had no doubt that this party was advancing to attack him by surprise, unfortunately, unjustly, but not with dishonorable intent, adopted a resolve which introduced a war and ushered in woes over which angels might weep. It is altogether probable that, without this untoward event, France and England would have drifted into a war for the possession of this continent. But the candid mind must admit that the responsibility of opening these dreadful vials of woe, rests with the English and not the French.[27] Washington, who had commenced intrenching himself at a place called Great Meadows, and which he described as a "charming field for an encounter," took a strong detachment of his troops, and, leading them in person was, in an hour, on the march. The darkness was as that of Egypt. The rain fell in torrents, and the tree tops of the gigantic forest swayed to and fro in the howling gale. Savage

---

[27] It is said, on the other hand, that the French commenced the war by driving off the party under Ensign Ward, who was throwing up intrenchments on the site of Fort Duquesne.

warriors, whose eyesight seemed as keen by night as by day, led the party. Quite a band of friendly Indians joined in the enterprise, so congenial to their modes of warfare.

A march of two or three hours brought them to the glimmering fires of the French. Many of the sleepers were protected by the camps, which they had hurriedly reared. The assailants, with the noiseless, stealthy step of the panther, crept behind the rocks and into the thickets, and took careful aim at their slumbering victims. The Indians united with the English in two parties, so as entirely to surround the French, and prevent the possibility of escape.

Just as the day was beginning to dawn through the lurid skies, the signal for attack was given. A deadly volley was discharged, and the forest resounded with the yells of the Indians, so loud and hideous, that it would seem that the cry must have burst from thousands of savage throats. That one simultaneous discharge killed M. Jumonville and ten of his men. Others were wounded. The survivors sprang to their arms. But, in the gloom of the morning, no foe was visible. The assailants, entirely concealed, could take fatal aim at their victims who were revealed to them by the light of their fires. The French fought bravely. They were, however, overpowered; and after many had fallen, the survivors, twenty-one in number, several with bleeding veins and shattered bones, were taken captive. The prisoners were sent under guard to Virginia.[28]

This deplorable event, one of the greatest mistakes which was ever made, created, as the tidings spread, intense excitement throughout America, France, and England. France regarded it as one of the grossest of outrages, which the national honor demanded should be signally avenged. Though nothing is more certain than that Washington would recoil from any dishonorable deed, still it is impossible to palliate the impolicy of this act. His little army, as he well knew, was entirely in the power of the French. This act of slaughter could by no possibility extricate them, and

---

[28] The British admitted that so small a party, conducting a peace commissioner with a summons, could not have intended a hostile attack; but they affirmed that the French were spies. It is undoubtedly true that they were to gain what information they could; as was the case with Washington and his party when they visited the forts on French Creek. This was the main object of Washington's excursion. The summons was a mere pretext.

would certainly so exasperate his foes as to provoke them to the most severe measures of retaliation.[29]

The moment the tidings reached the French commandant at Fort Duquesne, he despatched an allied force of fifteen hundred French and Indians, to avenge the wrong. Washington, as we have said, could not retreat. Neither could he fight with the slightest prospect of success. Capitulation was inevitable. But his proud spirit could not stoop to a surrender of his force until he had protected his reputation by a desperate resistance. And such is the deplorable code of honor, in war, that it is deemed chivalric for an officer to consign any numbers of sons, husbands, fathers, to a bloody death, simply that he may enjoy the renown of having fought to the bitter end.

All the energies of Washington's little band were brought into requisition in throwing up breastworks. Appropriately he called the ramparts Fort Necessity.[30] At eleven o'clock in the morning of the 3d of July, the French and Indians, who are variously estimated at from nine to fifteen hundred, commenced the attack. Nature seemed in sympathy with the woes of man. It was a tempestuous day. The shrieks of the storm resounded through the forest, and the rain fell in torrents. And yet, far away in the solitudes beyond the Alleghanies, Frenchmen and Englishmen were all the day long killing each other, to decide the question, who should be permitted, of the human family, to rear their homes in these boundless wilds. The history of our fallen world teaches us, that the folly of man is equal to his depravity. God made this for a happy world. Man, in rebellion against his Maker, has filled it with weeping eyes and bleeding hearts.

The fratricidal strife continued until eight o'clock in the evening. Captain Vanbraam, the only one in the fort who understood French, was

---

[29] No transaction in the life of Washington has elicited more passionate attack and defence than this. The French court published a very full account of the occurrence in a duodecimo which was sent to all the governments of Europe. It was entitled, "Mémoire contenant le Précis des Faits, avec leurs Pièces justificatives, pour servir de Réponse aux Observations envoyées, par les Ministres d'Angleterre, dans les cours de l'Europe." A Paris, de l'Imprimerie Royale, 1756.

[30] "The site of this fort is three or four hundred yards south of what is now called National Road, four miles from the foot of Laurel Hill, and fifty miles from Cumberland at Wills' Creek."—Sparks' *Life of Washington*, p. 51.

then sent, with a flag of truce, into the camp of the assailants to ask for terms upon which the English might capitulate. He soon returned, bringing articles "which by a flickering candle in the dripping quarters of his commander, he translated to Washington; and, as it proved, from intention or ignorance mistranslated." In these terms, which Washington accepted, and which it is said his courier did not correctly translate, the death of Jumonville is spoken of as an "assassination."[31]

Washington, as we have mentioned, was a young man of ingenuous character and winning manners. He was in all respects a gentleman of dignified deportment, of firm moral principles, and of the highest sense of honor. Fortunately he fell into the hands of M. De Villiers, a French officer, who was also a gentleman, capable of admiring the character of his captive, and of sympathizing with him in the terrible embarrassments into which he had been plunged.

He treated Washington with magnanimity worthy of all praise. The terms of surrender were generous. The troops were to leave the fort with the honors of war, and were to return to their homes unmolested. They were to retain their small-arms, ammunition, and personal effects, surrendering their artillery, which indeed they had no means of moving, as their horses were all shot. They gave their word of honor not to attempt any buildings in the valley of the Ohio, for the space of one year. And they promised that all the French taken in the attack upon Jumonville, and who had been sent to Virginia, should be immediately restored.

Washington had sent a letter to Governor Dinwiddie, commending the prisoners to "the respect and favor due to their character and personal merit." But the British Governor threw them into close confinement, and treated them with great cruelty. He also, infamously regardless of the terms of capitulation, refused to surrender them. One of the officers, La Force, attempted to escape. He was recaptured, secured with double irons, and chained to the floor of his dungeon. Washington felt deeply mortified by

---

[31] M. De Villiers, in his despatches to the French Government, wrote, "We made the English consent to sign, that they had assassinated my brother in his camp."

this obtuseness of the governor on a point of military punctilio and honorable faith; but his remonstrances were unavailing.[32]

The next morning, Washington and his dejected troops commenced their forlorn march back through the wilderness. Encumbered with the wounded, who were carried on litters, but three miles were made that day. The next day they resumed their melancholy march, and, by slow stages, returned to their homes.[33]

On the whole, the character of Washington did not suffer permanently from this occurrence. His extreme youth, and the untried nature of the perplexities in which he was involved, and the fact that he *supposed* that Jumonville was approaching to attack him by surprise, disarmed the virulence of censure with all candid men. Indeed, his countrymen, somewhat oblivious of the extraordinary magnanimity of M. De Villiers, were disposed to applaud him for the military genius he had displayed in rescuing his little army from such imminent peril, and in conducting the troops back so safely to Virginia. The numbers engaged in the action at Fort Necessity, and the number killed and wounded, on the two sides, can never be known. Of the Virginia regiment alone, twelve were killed and forty-three wounded.

The rank and file of every army almost necessarily includes many of the most wild and depraved of men. The adventurers who crowd to the frontiers of any country, and especially those whose tastes have led them to abandon the more cultivated regions of civilization, and to plunge into the solitudes of the wilderness, have generally been those who have wished to escape from the dominion of laws and from the restraints of religion. In the little band enlisted under the banner of Washington there were many unprincipled and profane men. His ear was constantly pained by that vulgar cursing and swearing, which was exceedingly repugnant to his refined tastes, and to his Christian principles. He could not forget that, amid the thunderings and lightnings of Sinai, the law had been proclaimed:

---

[32] Irving's *Life of Washington*, vol. i. p. 51.
[33] "A gentleman, who had heard that Colonel Washington had said that he knew of no music so pleasing as the whistling of bullets, being alone in conversation with him, at Cambridge, Massachusetts, asked him whether it was as he had related. The general answered, 'If I said so, it was when I was young.'"—*Gordon's History*, vol. ii. p. 203.

"Thou shalt not take the name of the Lord thy God in vain, for the Lord will not hold him guiltless that taketh his name in vain."

And he recognized the divine authority of the words of our Saviour, when, in confirmation of this command, he said, "Swear not at all." Under the influence of these teachings, which he had received from the lips of his pious mother, and which had thus far governed his life, this young officer issued the following admirable, yet extraordinary order of the day.

> "Colonel Washington has observed that the men of his regiment are very profane and reprobate. He takes this opportunity to inform them of his great displeasure at such practices; and assures them that, if they do not leave them off, they shall be severely punished. The officers are desired, if they hear any man swear or make use of an oath or execration, to order the offender twenty-five lashes immediately, without a court-martial. For a second offence he shall be more severely punished."

Such was the character of the youthful Washington. Even those who do not emulate his example, can appreciate the excellence of his principles. Twenty years after this, when the war of the Revolution was deluging our land in blood, and when the infant colonies, which numbered a population of less than three million white inhabitants, were struggling, in deadly battle, against the armies of the most powerful empire on the globe. Washington, still recognizing the authority of God, and avowing his faith in the religion of Jesus Christ, was greatly distressed in the view of the contemptuous way in which the name of God was used by the officers, as well as by the common soldiers.

The feeble army he led was defeated, overwhelmed with disaster, and threatened with irretrievable ruin. Agonizing were the prayers which he had been heard offering to God, pleading with him to interpose to rescue our country from the gigantic power which was trampling out its life. In those dark hours, when nearly all patriotic hearts were engulfed in despair, General Washington, Commander in Chief of the Armies of America, in August, 1776, issued, at New York, the following order to the troops:

"The General is sorry to be informed that the foolish and profane practice of cursing and swearing, a vice hitherto little known in an American army, is growing into fashion. He hopes that the officers will, by example as well as by influence, endeavor to check it; and that both they and the men will reflect that we can have little hope of the blessing of heaven on our arms, if we insult it by our impiety and folly. Add to this, it is a vice so mean and low, without any temptation, that every man of sense and character detests and despises it."

Profanity must be exceedingly displeasing to God, or it would not have been so solemnly prohibited in those commandments which God issued for the regulation of the conduct of men in all ages. And yet it is our national vice. How many are there "who have no God to pray to; only a god to swear by." While speaking upon this very important subject it may be proper to refer to an anecdote of Washington, which was related to the writer by an officer in the United States Army, who was present on the occasion.

Washington had invited the members of his staff to dine with him in the city of New York. As they were sitting at the table, all engaged in that quiet conversation which the presence of Washington invariably secured, one of the guests very distinctly uttered an oath. Washington dropped his knife and fork as though he had been struck by a bullet. The movement arrested the attention of every one. For an instant there was perfect silence. Washington then, in calm, deliberate tones, whose solemnity was blended with sadness, said: "I thought that I had invited gentlemen only to dine with me." It is needless to add that no more oaths were heard at that table.

Chapter 3

THE FRENCH WAR

War between France and England had now became inevitable. The British cabinet, being resolved to drive the French from the continent of North America, had not only no apology to offer for her untoward military movement, but immediately made new and more formidable preparations for the accomplishment of her determined purpose. The task seemed not difficult; for the rapidly growing English colonies, scattered along the Atlantic coast, contained a population greatly outnumbering those gathered around the settlements on the banks of the St. Lawrence, and the few military and trading posts which were established on the borders of the great lakes, and in the valley of the Ohio.[34]

On the other hand, the pride of the court of France required that it should not submit to indignity; neither could France yield to the arrogant demands of the English, and surrender, at their dictation, territory which she had long considered as beyond all legitimate question her own. Thus the warfare became essentially one of attack on the part of England, one of defence on the part of France. England was to organize armies and send

---

[34] "As late as 1754 all the French colonies, from the St. Lawrence to the Gulf of Mexico, did not contain more than a hundred thousand white inhabitants, while the inhabitants of the English colonies were then estimated at twelve hundred thousand white and two hundred and fifty thousand blacks."—*History of the United States of America*, by Harvey Prindle Peet, LL.D., p. 156.

them across the mountains, to drive the French from the valley of the Ohio. France was to strengthen her fortresses in the valley so as to repel and drive back the invaders. Both nations did everything in their power to enlist the Indians warriors beneath their banners.

In the spring of the year 1755, the British government sent two regiments of regular troops from England, to cross the wilderness of the Alleghanies, and wrest Fort Duquesne from the French. The highly disciplined troops were well instructed in the tactics of European battlefields, but were entirely unacquainted with Indian strategy, and were quite unprepared to cope with the difficulties of Indian warfare. General Braddock, a proud, self-conceited Englishman, who despised all other nationalities, and who had a thorough contempt for the military ability of the Americans, was placed in command.

"Pride goeth before destruction and a haughty look before a fall." He was too proud to learn from those who were abundantly able to teach him. He was too haughty to listen to any warnings of danger from those who were far wiser than himself, but whom he regarded as ignorant and cowardly. He, in command of well drilled British regulars, had nothing to fear and nothing to learn from colonists, Frenchmen, or Indians.

General Braddock, at the head of his two highly disciplined and well uniformed regiments, commenced his march across the wide, rugged mountain ranges. From the eastern declivities, where the water commenced running into the Atlantic, to the western slopes where the gushing springs flowed into the Ohio, was a distance of more than one hundred miles. The path was narrow. In many places torrents were to be bridged, obstructions removed, and the trail widened through the vast masses of rock, by the corps of engineers. Thus there would be presented to the keen eyes of the Indians, who were sent by the French, to watch and report the progress of the foe, a straggling, broken line of men and wagons four miles in length.

There was something exceedingly exasperating in the contemptuous manner in which the British court and cabinet treated the colonial officers. It seemed to be, with them, an established principle that an Englishman must, of necessity, be superior to an American. Governor Dinwiddie reduced Colonel Washington to the rank of a captain, and placed over him officers whom he had commanded. This degradation was, of course, not to be submitted to by a high-minded man. Washington at once resigned his commission, and retired from the army.

Governor Sharpe, the crown-appointed Governor of Maryland, received, from the king, the appointment of Commander-in-Chief of the forces employed against the French. He was well acquainted with Washington's exalted character, and valuable experience, and yet he had the presumption to write, urging him to accept the office of *captain* of a Virginia company, intimating to him that he might nominally hold his former commission as colonel. Washington replied:

> "This idea has filled me with surprise; for if you think me capable of holding a commission that has neither rank nor emolument annexed to it, you must entertain a very contemptible opinion of my weakness, and believe me to be more empty than the commission itself."

When General Braddock landed at Alexandria, in Virginia, with his two regiments, hearing of the fame of Washington, and of his previous excursions across the mountains, he invited him to take part in the campaign, as one of his staff, retaining his former rank. The chivalric spirit of Washington was roused; for the pageantry of war was quite conspicuous from his quiet retreat at Mount Vernon.

British ships of war, with their gay banners, and transports crowded with troops, were continually sailing by his door, to Alexandria, which was but a few miles above. The booming of cannon, and the music of well-trained bands, woke the echoes of those vast forests. Washington mounted his horse, and rode to Alexandria. The love of adventure, of heroic military achievements, inspired him. He eagerly accepted the offer of Braddock, to become a member of the general's military household, but without any emolument or any distinct command. The position recognized his full rank, and gave him the opportunity of acquiring new experience, and of becoming acquainted with the highest principles of martial tactics as then practised by the armies of Europe.

His widowed mother entreated him not again to expose himself to the perils of a campaign. But he found the temptation too strong to be resisted. On the 20th of April, 1755, the army commenced its march, from Alexandria. Washington was announced as one of the general's aides. Benjamin Franklin, then forty-nine years of age, visited the army when it had reached Fredericktown. Braddock was so confident of the success of the expedition, that he said to Franklin:

> "After taking Duquesne, I shall proceed to Niagara; and having taken that, to Frontenac, if the season will allow time. And I suppose it will, for Duquesne can hardly detain me above three or four days. Then I can see nothing which can obstruct my march to Niagara."[35]

Franklin, with his customary good sense and modesty, replied, "To be sure, sir, if you arrive well before Duquesne, with these fine troops, so well provided with artillery, the fort, though completely fortified, and assisted with a very strong garrison, can probably make but a very short resistance. The only danger I apprehend, of obstruction to your march, is from the ambuscades of the Indians, who, by constant practice, are dexterous in laying and executing them. And the slender line, nearly four miles long, which your army must make, may expose it to be attacked by surprise on its flanks, and to be cut, like thread, into several pieces, which, from their distance, cannot come up in time to support one another."

Franklin adds, "He smiled at my ignorance, and replied, 'These savages may indeed be a formidable enemy to raw American militia, but upon the king's regular and disciplined troops, sir, it is impossible they should make any impression.'

"I was conscious of an impropriety in my disputing with a military man on matters of his profession, and said no more."[36]

---

[35] "It is evident that the sense of the people was but little wakened to the necessity or importance of those enterprises against the French; and that they looked upon them rather as the results of political objects in Great Britain, than as immediately concerning themselves."—Sparks' *Life of Washington*, p. 51.

[36] *Autobiography of Franklin*, Sparks' edition, p. 90.

There were many delays; and it was not until the 20th of May, that the army reached Wills' Creek, where there was a frontier post called Fort Cumberland. Here again there were delays, which Washington deemed the result of want of judgment. On the 10th of June, the march was resumed, and the army commenced, what Washington called, "the tremendous undertaking," of dragging the artillery and the heavily-laded wagons up the steep and rugged mountain road, which the engineers had been sent forward to open.

Washington very strongly disapproved of the great number of horses and wagons required by the officers for the transportation of their baggage, with many needless luxuries. He was astonished and appalled at the recklessness with which the march was conducted; and he could not refrain from warning his superior officer of the peril to which the army was exposed in its thin line several miles in extent.

"The French officers," said he, "through their Indian runners, will keep themselves informed of every step of our progress. The eyes of these savage scouts, from the glooms of the forest and the distant crags, are continually fixed upon us. We are in danger, every hour, of falling into an ambush, when our men and horses will be shot down by volleys of bullets from an invisible foe. And that foe can instantly take flight, beyond all possibility of pursuit. The French officers can lead hundreds of the savage warriors to plunge, in a sudden onset, upon our straggling line, and striking fiercely on the right and left, plunder and burn many wagons, throw the whole line into confusion, and retire unharmed, before it will be possible to concentrate any force to repel them."

It would seem that such suggestions would be obvious to any man of ordinary intelligence. General Braddock, with a smile of incredulity and contempt, listened to these warnings of his youthful aide, and politely intimated that a Major-General in the regular army of his majesty the king of Great Britain was not to be taught the art of war by a young American provincial, who had never seen even the inside of a military school.

When the army commenced its march from Fort Cumberland, Washington was quite dazzled by the brilliance of the scene. He declares it to have been the most beautiful and inspiring spectacle he had ever beheld. The British troops were dressed in full and gaudy uniform. They were arranged in columns, and marched with precision of drill such as Washington had never seen before. The beams of the unclouded sun were reflected from silken banners and burnished arms, while well-trained musical bands caused the forests to resound with their martial strains. The officers were mounted on prancing steeds, in the highest condition. The river flowed tranquilly by, an emblem, not of horrid war, but of peaceful, opulent, and happy homes. All were inspirited with hope and confidence.

Such was the commencement of the campaign. How different the scene presented, when, at the close of a few weeks, the fragments of this army returned, bleeding, exhausted, starving—a struggling band of fugitives, one half of their number having been killed and scalped by the Indians.

Washington soon became convinced of the incapacity of General Braddock to conduct such an enterprise as that upon which he had entered. He writes:[37]

> "I found that, instead of pushing on with vigor, without regarding a little rough road, they were halting to level every mole-hill, and to erect bridges over every brook, by which means we were four days in getting twelve miles."[38]

On one occasion Washington said, "If our march is to be regulated by the slow movements of the train, it will be very tedious." Braddock smiled contemptuously at this indication of the ignorance of the young American officer in reference to the march of armies.

Without encountering any opposition, the army surmounted the rugged acclivities, and threaded the long defiles of the mountains, until, from the dreary expanse, they entered upon the luxuriant, blooming, magnificent valley of apparently boundless reach beyond. This successful passage of

---

[37] "Braddock's own secretary, William Shirley, wrote confidentially to Governor Morris, 'We have a general most judiciously chosen for being disqualified for the service he is employed in, in almost every respect.'"—*Colonial Records*, p. 405.

[38] Walpole wittily wrote, "The Duke of Brunswick is much dissatisfied at the slowness of General Braddock, *who does not march as if he was at all impatient to be scalped*." This was unjust. Want of courage was not one of the faults of General Braddock.

the mountains inspired Major-General Braddock with renewed self-confidence. His deportment said, every hour, to his youthful American aid, "You see that a British officer cannot be instructed in the art of war by a young Virginian."

The lips of Washington were sealed. Not another word could he utter. But he knew full well that an hour of awful disaster was approaching, and one which he could do nothing whatever to avert. On the 9th of July the sun rose over the Alleghanies, which were left far away in the east, in cloudless splendor. The army, in joyous march, was approaching the banks of the Monongahela.

It was one of those lovely days in which all nature seems happy. The flowers were in their richest bloom. The birds were swelling their throats with their sweetest songs. Balmy airs scarcely rippled the surface of the rivulet, along whose banks the troops were marching. All the sights and sounds of nature seemed to indicate that God intended this for a happy world; where he wished to see his children dwelling lovingly together, in the interchange of all deeds of fraternal kindness. It was such a day as Herbert has beautifully pictured in the words:

> "Sweet day, so still, so calm, so bright,
> The bridal of the earth and sky."

The troops were defiling through a ravine which presented a natural path for their march. On either side the eminences were covered with the majestic forest and dense and almost impenetrable thickets of underbrush. The narrow passage was very circuitous. It was just the spot which anyone familiar with Indian warfare would carefully explore, before allowing a long line of troops to become entangled in its labyrinthine trail. But there was no pause in the march; no scouts were sent along the eminences to search for an ambush; no precautions whatever were adopted to guard against surprise.

The troops were now within a few miles of Fort Duquesne. The march had been triumphantly accomplished. Braddock was sanguine in the assurance that before the sun should set his banners would float, in triumph, over the fortress, and his army would be sheltered within its walls. He was exulting. Washington was appalled in view of the danger which still menaced them. Proudly Braddock hurried along, with his straggling band. Jokes and laughter resounded, as the burnished muskets and polished cannon of the British regulars brilliantly reflected the sunbeams.

The hour of doom had come. Suddenly there was a thunder-burst of musketry, as from the cloudless skies. A storm of bullets, piercing the flesh, shattering the bones, swept the astounded ranks. It was like a supernatural attack from invisible spirits. Not a musket was revealed. Not an individual was to be seen. But from hundreds of stentorian throats the hideous war-whoop burst, leading those, who had never heard those shrill yells before, to apprehend that they were assailed, not by mortal foes, but by incarnate fiends.

The Indians were unerring marksmen. They were allies of the French, and their savage ferocity was guided by European science. Crash followed crash in rapid succession. The ground was instantly covered with the dead and the dying. The horses, goaded by bullets and terrified to frenzy, reared and plunged, and tore along the line, dragging fragments of wagons after them, and trampling the living and the dead into the mire. The ranks were thrown into utter consternation. There was no defence that could be made. And still the deadly storm of bullets fell upon them, while a feeble return fire was attempted, which merely threw its bullets against the rocks, or buried them in the gigantic trees. The Indians were derisively laughing at the convulsive and impotent struggles of their victims.

Washington, who had been appalled as he anticipated this terrific scene, now that the awful hour had come, was perfectly calm and self-possessed. He had previously made the arrangement with some of the provincial officers, precisely what to do in the emergence. The Virginia troops were somewhat scattered. Washington was on horseback. Almost instantly his horse was shot beneath him. He sprang upon another, from which the rider had fallen; but scarcely was he seated in the saddle, ere that horse dropped to the ground, pierced by the bullet. Four bullets passed through his clothing. All this occurred in almost less time than it has taken to describe it.

The scene was one to appall the stoutest nerves. The yells of the savages, the clamor of the panic-stricken soldiers, the frantic plungings of the wounded steeds, the utter and helpless confusion, the unceasing rattle of musketry, the storm of leaden hail, the incessant dropping of the dead, and the moans of the wounded, all united in presenting a spectacle which could scarcely be rivalled in the realms of despair. How different this awful scene of battle from the picture of loveliness, peace, and happiness, which the valley exhibited, reposing in its Maker's smiles, as that morning's sun flooded it with its beams.

Braddock was a Briton, and, almost of course a man of physical courage. Even pride was sufficiently strong to prevent any display of cowardice. With bull-dog daring, he stood his ground, and issued his orders, endeavoring in vain to marshal his troops in battle array. At length a bullet struck him, and he fell mortally wounded. An awful scene of confusion and horror was presented. There were six hundred invisible foes in ambush. They were armed with the best of French muskets, and were supported by a small band of highly disciplined French troops.

Washington rallied all the Americans within his reach, and each man, posting himself behind a tree, fired not a bullet without taking deliberate aim. The English huddled together, and senselessly, in their frenzy, firing at random, presented a fair target to the Indian marksmen, and fell as fast as the savages could load and fire. As the Indians rushed from their covert, with tomahawk and scalping-knife to seize their bloody trophy of scalps, from the dead and the wounded, who were struggling upon the ground, the Americans, with their rapid and deadly fire checked them, and drove them back. But for this the army would have been utterly destroyed. The English regulars were helpless. "They ran," wrote Washington, "like sheep before the hounds."

The rout was complete. Braddock, bleeding, exhausted, and experiencing the intensest mental anguish, begged to be left upon the field to die. Everything was abandoned. The wagoners and artillery-men, cutting the traces, mounted the horses and fled. Fortunately, the savages were too much engaged in plunder to pursue. The carnage had been awful. Out of eighty-six officers, twenty-six were killed and thirty-six wounded. Over seven hundred of the rank and file fell. The tomahawk of the savage soon numbered the wounded with the slain.

Braddock was hurried from the field in a litter, and his wounds dressed about a mile from the scene of carnage. He could not mount a horse, and had to be carried. A woe-stricken band of eighty soldiers formed his escort. For four days he lingered in great pain, and then died. Once he was heard to exclaim: "Who would have thought it." It is also said that he apologized to Washington for the manner in which he had rejected his advice. His remains were buried in the road, and all indications of his grave concealed, lest the Indians might discover the spot. In the gloom of night the melancholy funeral ceremonies were performed. Washington read the burial service. It is probable that not even a volley was fired over his grave. Seldom has there been recorded a more sad close of an ambitious life.

The army of Braddock was annihilated. The French, conscious that it could do no further harm, left the starving, staggering, bleeding remains to struggle back to Virginia. They returned to Fort Duquesne, to rejoice over the victory, and to strengthen their works, in preparation for another assault, should the attempt be renewed.

There was, at that time, an English officer, Colonel James Smith, a captive at the fort. He has given a minute and exceedingly interesting account of the scenes which had transpired, and which continued to be enacted there. His narrative throws much light upon the character of the conflict, and upon the woes with which man's inhumanity can crush his brother man.

He says that Indian scouts were every hour watching, from mountain crags and forest thickets, the advance of the army. Every day swift runners came to the fort with their report. The French commandant was kept as intimately acquainted with the condition of the army, and its position, as Braddock could have been himself. These warriors, intelligent men, with established military principles, loudly derided the folly of Braddock, declaring that he was nothing but a fool. As they described his straggling and defenceless line, its utter exposure, the course which they knew he must pursue, and the ambush they were preparing for his destruction, they would burst into boisterous laughter, saying, "We will shoot 'em all down, same as one pigeon."

It is a great mistake to imagine that men must be simpletons because they can neither read nor write. It is said that Charlemagne could not even write his own name. And many of the most illustrious warriors of ancient days had no acquaintance whatever with books. No one can read, with an impartial spirit, the history of the Indian wars, without admitting that there were in many cases, Indian chiefs who entirely outgeneralled their English antagonists. The scene of events at the fort is very vividly presented by Colonel Smith.

Early in the morning of the day in which the attack was to be made, there was great and joyous commotion in and around the fort. The Indians, some six or seven hundred in number, were greatly elated. They seemed to be as sure of victory then as they were after it had been attained.

There was hurrying to and fro, examining the muskets, filling the powder-horns from open kegs of powder, storing away bullets in their leathern pouches, and hurrying off in small bands, in single file, through the trails of the forest. About an equal number of French troops accompanied the Indians.

Soon all were gone, save the small garrison left in charge. Slowly and silently the hours of the long summer day passed, when late in the afternoon the triumphant shouts of fleet-footed runners were heard in the forest, announcing the tidings of the great victory—tidings which awoke the garrison to enthusiasm, but which filled the heart of Colonel Smith with *dismay*. They brought the intelligence that the English were huddled together and surrounded, in utter dismay and confusion, in a narrow ravine, from which escape was almost impossible. The Indians, from their concealments, were shooting them down as fast as they could load and fire. They said that before sundown all would be killed.

The whoops or yells of the savages had various significations. There was the war-whoop, with which their fierce natures were roused to the attack. There was the cry of retreat, at whose signal all seemed instantaneously to vanish. And there was the exultant, triumphant "scalphalloo," with which they made the forests resound, when they returned to the camp, dangling the gory trophies of victory.[39]

Soon a band of about a hundred savages appeared, yelling like so many demons in their frantic, boisterous joy. It was the greatest victory they had ever known or conceived of. Braddock's army was laden not only with all conveniences but with all luxuries. The Indians were astounded, bewildered, at the amount and richness of the plunder they had gained. It was more than they could carry away, and it presented to them a spectacle of wealth and splendor such as the fabled lamp of Aladdin never revealed. The savages returned stooping beneath the load of grenadiers' caps, canteens, muskets, swords, bayonets, and rich uniforms which they had stripped from the dead. All had dripping scalps, and several had money. Colonel Smith writes:

> "Those that were coming in and those that had arrived, kept a constant firing of small-arms, and also of the great guns in the fort, which was accompanied by the most hideous shouts and yells from all quarters; so that it appeared to me as if the infernal regions had broke loose. About sundown I beheld a small party coming in with about a dozen prisoners, stripped naked, with their hands tied behind their backs. Their faces, and parts of their bodies were blackened. These prisoners they burned to death on the banks of the Alleghany River, opposite to the fort. I stood on the fort walls until I beheld them begin to burn one of these men. They tied him to a stake and kept touching him with fire-brands, red-hot irons, etc., and he screaming in the most doleful manner. The Indians, in the meantime, were yelling like infernal spirits. As this scene was too shocking for me to behold, I returned to my lodgings, both sorry and sore.[40]

---

[39] Mr. Irving, writing of the assailants says, "They were not the main force of the French, but a mere detachment of 72 Regulars, 146 Canadians, and 637 Indians, 855 in all, led by Captain de Beaujeu. Such was the scanty force which the imagination of the panic-stricken army had magnified into a great host, and from which they had fled, in breathless terror, abandoning the whole frontier."—*Life of Washington*, vol. i. p. 206.

[40] There can be no possible excuse for the French officers, in permitting this barbarity. The Indians were their allies, instigated to the war by their influence, marching under their banners, led by their officers, and paid by their money. They were therefore responsible for the conduct of these their allies. To permit them, under the very walls of Fort Duquesne, to

"From the best information I could receive, there were only seven Indians and four French killed in this battle. Five hundred British lay dead in the field, besides what were killed in the river, after their retreat. The morning after the battle, I saw Braddock's artillery brought into fort. The same day also I saw several Indians in the dress of British officers, with the sashes, half moons, laced hats, etc., which the British wore."

On the 17th of July, Washington, at the head of his sad cavalcade, reached Fort Cumberland. Fugitives had already brought reports of the disaster. Washington, knowing the terrible anxiety of his family wrote as follows to his mother.

"The Virginia troops showed a good deal of bravery, and were nearly all killed. The dastardly behavior of those they called Regulars, exposed all others, that were ordered to do their duty, to almost certain death. At last, in despite of all the efforts of the officers to the contrary, they ran, as sheep pursued by dogs, and it was impossible to rally them."

The American troops, who, in silent exasperation, had allowed themselves to be led, by the folly of Braddock, into the valley of death, had, in some way, become acquainted with the warnings and remonstrances of Washington. This foresight, combined with the perfect courage he had displayed on the battle-field, gave them the highest opinion of his military abilities. They proclaimed his fame far and wide. Thus the ignominious defeat of the British Major-General rebounded to the honor of his American aide.

After the lapse of eighty years a gold seal of Washington, containing his initials, was found upon the battle-field. A bullet had struck it from his person. The precious relic is in possession of one of the family.

This total defeat of the English, established, for a time, the entire ascendency of the French in the valley of the Ohio and on the great lakes. Washington reached Mount Vernon on the 26th of July, in a very feeble condition of bodily health. He was probably well satisfied that there is but

---

put the captives to death by torture, was an atrocious crime meriting the execration of humanity.

little pleasant music to be found in the whistling of hostile bullets. To his brother Augustine he wrote, in reference to his frontier experience:

> "I was employed to go a journey in the winter, when I believe few or none would have undertaken it. What did I get by it? My expenses borne. I was then appointed, with trifling pay, to conduct a handful of men to the Ohio. What did I get for that? Why, after putting myself to a considerable expense in equipping and providing necessaries for the campaign, I went out, was soundly beaten and lost all! Came in, and had my commission taken from me; or, in other words, my command reduced, under pretence of an order from home [England]. I then went out a volunteer with General Braddock; and lost all my horses and many other things. But this, being a voluntary act, I ought not to have mentioned it; nor should I have done it, were it not to show that I have been on the losing order, ever since I entered the service, which is now nearly two years."

The French and the English now alike infamously engaged in enlisting the Indians to aid them in the conflict. These benighted savages seem to have had no more idea of mercy than had the wolves. They burned the lonely cabins, tomahawked and scalped women and children, carried mothers and maidens into the most awful captivity, and often put their helpless victims to the torture. And yet the nobility of France and the lords of England looked complacently on, while they goaded the savages to their infernal deeds.

The English settlers outnumbered the French more than ten to one. But the French, in actual possession of the lakes and the valley, could rally around their banners a vastly more powerful force of savages than the English could summon. Thus the English were much more exposed than the French. The savages having lapped blood, and generally hating the English, entered eagerly upon the work of conflagration, plunder, and slaughter.

There were American hamlets of log huts, and lonely American farmhouses, scattered through the wilderness for a distance of four hundred miles along the western frontier of Virginia. But the court and cabinet of Great Britain considered their weal or woe a matter of but little consequence compared with the national glory to be obtained in driving the French from this whole continent.[41]

Fifteen hundred plumed, painted, howling savages were soon the allies of France, perpetrating deeds which one shudders to record. At midnight these demons of the human race would burst from the forest, and rush howling upon some hut where the poor defenceless emigrant, with his wife and his children, was tremblingly sleeping. In an hour the dreadful tragedy was completed. The yells of the savages drowned the shrieks of the mother and her babe, as they fell beneath the tomahawk. The cabin was in ashes. The savages had disappeared. The rising sun revealed but the gory corpses in their shocking mutilation.

For the protection of the frontier, thus exposed to the greatest woes of which the imagination can conceive, Virginia raised a force of seven hundred men, which was placed under the experienced command of Colonel Washington. For three years he was engaged in these arduous but almost unavailing labors. No one could tell at what point the wary Indian would strike a blow. Having struck it, the demoniac band vanished into the glooms of the wilderness, where pursuit was impossible. There is some excuse to be found for the fiend-like deeds of the savages, in the ignorance, and in the principles of war which they and their ancestors had ever cherished. But there is no excuse whatever to be found for those French and English statesmen, who employed such agents for the accomplishment of their ambitious projects. The scenes of woe, which Washington often witnessed, were so dreadful that, in after life, he could seldom bear to recur to them. We will give one instance, which he has related, as illustrative of many others.

One day as, with a small detachment of troops, he was traversing a portion of the frontier, he came to a solitary log cabin, in a little clearing, which the axe of a settler had effected in the heart of the forest. As they

---

[41] The plan of the British campaign of 1755, in which Braddock met his disaster, was four-fold: first to capture Nova Scotia; second, to drive the French from their posts on Lake Champlain; third, to seize the important French fort at Niagara, between Lake Ontario and Lake George, and fourth, to expel all French settlers from the frontiers of Pennsylvania and Virginia, and take entire possession of the Ohio valley.—Irving's *Life of Washington*, vol. i. p. 152.

were approaching, through the woods, the report of a gun arrested their attention. Cautiously they crept through the underbrush, until they came in full sight of the cabin. Smoke was curling up through the roof, while a large party of savages, with piles of plunder by their side, were shouting and swinging their bleeding scalps, as they danced round their booty. As soon as they caught sight of the soldiers they fled into the forest with the swiftness of deer. In the following words Washington describes the scene which was then opened before them:

> "On entering we saw a sight that, though we were familiar with blood and massacre, struck us, at least myself, with feelings more mournful than I had ever experienced before. On the bed, in one corner of the room, lay the body of a young woman, swimming in blood, with a gash in her forehead, which almost separated the head into two parts. On her breast lay two little babes, apparently twins, less than a twelve-month old, with their heads also cut open. Their innocent blood which once flowed in the same veins, now mingled in one current again. I was inured to scenes of bloodshed and misery, but this cut me to the soul. Never in my after life, did I raise my hand against a savage, without calling to mind the mother with her little twins, their heads cleft asunder."

The soldiers eagerly pursued the fugitive savages. They had gone but a short distance from the house, when they found the father of the family and his little boy, both dead and scalped in the field. The father had been holding the plough, and his son driving the horse, when the savages came upon them. From ambush they had shot down the father, and the terrified little boy had run some distance toward the house, when he was overtaken and cut down by the tomahawk. Thus the whole family perished. Such were the perils of a home on the frontiers, in those sad days. In allusion to these awful scenes Washington wrote:

> "On leaving one spot, for the protection of another point of exposure, the scene was often such as I shall never forget. The women and children clung round our knees, beseeching us to stay and protect them, and crying out to us, for God's sake, not to leave them to be butchered by the

savages. A hundred times, I declare to heaven, I would have laid down my life with pleasure, could I have insured the safety of those suffering people by the sacrifice."

During the years 1756 and 1757, the English met a constant series of disasters. The French furnished their Indian allies with the best muskets, and amply supplied them with ammunition. A small band of French, under skillful officers, would take lead. They could call to their aid any number almost they wished of Indian warriors. These hardy men, cautious and sagacious, were highly disciplined in the kind of warfare in which they were engaged. They were by no means to be despised. In such enterprises they were far more valuable than European troops could have been. If there be fiendish work to be done, fiends are needed as the agents.

In February 1756, some matters of state called Washington to Boston. He travelled the distance, five hundred miles, on horseback, and in considerable state. He was accompanied by two aides. The three officers had each black servants dressed in livery. All were well mounted. In Philadelphia and New York Washington was received with distinguished honors.

Almost every man must have his first love. It is very confidently asserted that Washington, young, rich, handsome, and renowned, became an ardent and open admirer of a beautiful and highly accomplished lady, Miss Philipse.[42] It is even said that he sought her hand, and was refused. This is not probable. He remained in Boston but ten days; the press of business demanding a speedy return. The lady subsequently married Captain Morris.[43]

Napoleon once said that he could easily imagine himself surrounded from infancy by family influences, education and companionship, which

---

[42] Mr. Sparks gives the name, Miss Mary Phillips; Mr. Everett spells it Phillipse; and Mr. Irving gives it as Philipse.

[43] "He had before felt the influence of the tender passion. At the age of seventeen he was smitten by the graces of a fair one, whom he called a 'Lowland beauty,' and whose praises he recorded in glowing strains, while wandering with his surveyor's compass among the Alleghany Mountains. On that occasion he wrote desponding letters to a friend, and indited plaintive verses, but never ventured to reveal his emotions to the lady who was unconsciously the cause of his pains."—Sparks' *Life of Washington*, p. 73.

should have led him, instead of espousing the cause of the people, to have been an ardent defender of the ancient régime. Mr. Everett writes:

> "One cannot but bestow a passing thought on the question, What might have been the effect on the march of events, if Washington, at the age of twenty-five, and before the controversies between the mother country and the colonies had commenced, had formed a matrimonial alliance with a family of wealth and influence, in New York, which adhered to the royal cause and left America, as loyalists, when the war broke out? It is a somewhat curious fact, that Washington's headquarters, during a part of the campaign of 1776, were established in the stately mansion of the Morrises, on the Harlem River."[44]

---

[44] *Life of George Washington*, by Edward Everett, p. 87.

Chapter 4

THE WARRIOR, THE STATESMAN, AND THE PLANTER

The remonstrances of Washington against the folly of cutting a new road were unavailing. As we have mentioned, the people were not in sympathy with these war measures. They were unwilling to enlist, and still more unwilling to furnish supplies. Washington, at this period of his life, had very high notions of military authority. He was then by no means a democrat, and not even a republican. In his view, it was the duty of the people to obey the orders of the court, not to question them. He was compelled to impress both wagons and wagoners. They could be obtained in no other way. In his indignation he wrote:

> "No orders are obeyed but such as a party of soldiers or my own drawn sword enforces. Without this, not a single horse, for the most earnest occasion, can be had; to such a pitch has the insolence of this people arrived, by having every point hitherto submitted to them. However, I have given up none, where his majesty's service requires the contrary, and where my proceedings are justified by my instructions; nor will I, unless they execute what they threaten, and blow out our brains."[45]

---

[45] "One is tempted to smile at this tirade about the 'insolence of the people,' and this zeal for 'his majesty's service,' on the part of Washington; but he was yet a young man and a young

Figure 2. Washington's Head-Quarters at Newburgh.

Washington was at Winchester, gathering troops for the new expedition. The savages were ravaging the frontier, murdering travellers, burning farm-houses, butchering and scalping the inhabitants. They had even crossed the western ridge of the Alleghanies and penetrated the valley of the Shenandoah. Even the baronial home of Lord Fairfax was menaced by them. Greenway Court, as his stately mansion was called, was surrounded by the majestic forest, where the savages, in large numbers, could gather unseen. The scalp of his lordship would be considered by them an inestimable trophy. His friends urged that he should abandon the place and take refuge in some of the lower settlements. The British nobleman, with spirit characteristic of his race, replied to his nephew, Colonel Martin, who was urging this measure:

---

officer. What he thus terms insolence was the dawning spirit of independence, which he was afterward the foremost to cherish and promote."—Irving's *Life of Washington*, vol. i. p. 215.

"I am an old man, and it is of but little importance whether I fall by the tomahawk or die of disease and old age. But you are young, and, it is to be hoped, have many years before you; therefore decide for us both. My only fear is that, if we retire, the whole district will break up and take to flight; and the fine country, which I have been at such cost and trouble to improve, will again become a wilderness."

It was decided to remain, and convert Greenway Court into a sort of fortress, garrisoned by the slaves of Lord Fairfax, and his numerous other retainers. Aid could also be speedily summoned from Winchester. Washington, at Winchester, organized a band of Americans familiar with forest life, and explored the hiding places in the mountains and valleys in search of the prowling bands of savages.

The panic at Winchester was dreadful. Every hour brought its tale of horror. Only twenty miles from the town, in the Warm Spring Mountain, a scouting party of the English was attacked by the savages, all on horseback. The captain and several of the soldiers were shot down. The rest were put to flight by the victorious Indians. It was daily expected that the town would be attacked. All looked to Washington as their only protector. The consternation of the women was dreadful. They came to him, with their children in their arms, and implored him to save them from the savages. The heart of Washington was often wrung with anguish. He wrote to Governor Dinwiddie:

"I am too little acquainted with pathetic language to attempt a description of this people's distress. But what can I do? I see their situation. I know their danger and participate their sufferings, without having it in my power to give them further relief than uncertain promises.

"The supplicating tears of the women, and petitions of the men, melt me into such deadly sorrow that I solemnly declare, if I know my own mind, I could offer myself a willing sacrifice to the butchering enemy, provided that would contribute to the people's ease."

Washington himself was bitterly assailed. Every outrage inflicted by the Indians was charged to his neglect or incompetency. His sensitive nature was stung to the quick. His situation was indeed deplorable. He derived neither honor nor emolument from his command. He was shut up in a frontier town, surrounded by savage hordes, whose ravages his feeble band could by no means arrest. He declared that nothing but the imminent danger of the times prevented him from resigning his command. His friend Mr. Robinson, Speaker of the House of Burgesses, wrote to him:

> "Our hopes, dear George, are all fixed on you, for bringing our affairs to a happy issue. Consider what fatal consequences to your country your resigning the command, at this time, may be; especially as there is no doubt most of the officers will follow your example."

The House of Burgesses was in favor of the policy of erecting a chain of frontier forts to extend a distance of about four hundred miles, through the solitudes of the Alleghany Mountains, from the Potomac to the borders of North Carolina.

Washington considered this measure quite injudicious. To render it of any avail, it would be necessary that the forts should be within about fifteen miles of each other, so that the intervening country could be daily explored. Otherwise the Indians would rush between, and, having effected their ravages would escape back to the forest where pursuit would be fruitless. The forts would have to be very strongly garrisoned, for French artillery could be brought against them, and almost any number of savage warriors. The cost of rearing so many forts would be immense. They could not be suitably garrisoned by less than two thousand men. Washington, therefore, proposed that, instead of this series of forts, there should be a strong central fortress at Winchester, and three or four large fortresses, at convenient distances on the frontier, from which parties could easily explore the surrounding country. He also made many other suggestions of reform in the military service, which developed, thus early, the sagacity and forethought which so signally characterized him in future life. Many of the suggestions of Washington, Governor Dinwiddie rejected. But the central fortress at Winchester and the frontier posts were reared.

The repeated inroads of the savages had driven nearly all the inhabitants out of the beautiful valley of the Shenandoah. The woes which these poor fugitives endured cannot well be imagined. It was the object of the British government, not only to expel the French from the valley of the Ohio, but also from the valley of the St. Lawrence. The necessity of collecting troops from Pennsylvania and Virginia, to attack the French in Canada, greatly weakened the power of the Americans in the more southern States, to protect their homes.

Every man who attains celebrity pays a heavy price for the attainment. Washington, in one of his hours of anguish, when he was thwarted in his most important plans, and assailed by a constant torrent of abuse, wrote, in reference to a very unwelcome order he had received:

> "The late order reverses, confuses, and incommodes everything; to say nothing of the extraordinary expense of carriage, disappointments, losses, and alterations which must fall heavily upon the country. Whence it arises, or why, I am truly ignorant. But my strongest representations of matters relative to the peace of the frontiers are disregarded as idle and frivolous; my propositions and measures as partial and selfish; and all my sincerest endeavors, for the service of my country, are perverted to the worst purposes. My orders are dark, doubtful, uncertain; to-day approved, to-morrow condemned.
>
> "Left to act and proceed at hazard, accountable for the consequences, and blamed without the benefit of defence, if you can think my situation capable of exciting the smallest degree of envy, or affording the least satisfaction, the truth is yet hidden from you, and you entertain notions very different from the case."[46]

Care, exposure, and sorrow threw Washington into a burning fever. He retired to Mount Vernon, where he was reduced very low, and four months passed away before he was able to resume his command. This was on the 1st of March, 1758.

Much to the relief of Washington, Governor Dinwiddie, in January, had sailed for England. The Earl of Loudon succeeded him. But, busily

---

[46] Sparks' *Life of Washington*, p. 81.

engaged in organizing an expedition for the invasion of Canada, the earl did not immediately enter upon the duties of his office in Virginia. William Pitt was now prime minister of Great Britain.

As one of his first measures, in the year 1758 a strong expedition was organized, consisting of six thousand men, to march against Fort Duquesne. General Forbes was appointed to the command of the whole force. Virginia raised two thousand troops. These were divided into two regiments. Washington, who had been appointed by the Assembly, commander-in-chief of all the Virginia troops, was also colonel of the first regiment. Colonel Byrd led the second. Colonel Bouquet, in command of the British regulars, was in the advance, marshalling his forces in the centre of Pennsylvania.

Early in July, Washington, with his troops, marching from Winchester, reached Fort Cumberland. Two of his companies he dressed in Indian costume. To Colonel Bouquet he wrote:

> "My men are bare of regimental clothing, and I have no prospect of supply. So far from regretting this want, during the present campaign, if I were left to pursue my own inclinations, I would not only order the men to adopt the Indian dress, but cause the officers to do it also, and be the first to set the example myself. Nothing but the uncertainty of obtaining the general approbation causes me to hesitate a moment to leave my regimentals in this place, and proceed as light as any Indian in the woods. It is an unbecoming dress, I own; but convenience rather than show, I think, should be consulted."

Notwithstanding the earnest remonstrances of Washington, it was decided to cross the mountains by a new route. With immense labor, a road had been cut for the passage of wagons and artillery, along which Braddock's army had passed. Slight repairs would put this road in good condition. Washington presented an accurate estimate, showing that the whole army could be at Fort Duquesne in thirty-four days, with a supply of provisions remaining on hand for eighty-seven days. But Colonel Bouquet was firm in his resolution to open a new route, from Raystown, through

Pennsylvania. Washington, after an interview with Bouquet, wrote, on the 2d of August, to a friend, Major Halket:

> "I have just returned from a conference with Colonel Bouquet. I find him fixed—I think I may say unalterably fixed—to lead you a new way to the Ohio, through a road every inch of which is to be cut, at this advanced season, when we have scarce time to tread the beaten track, universally confessed to be the best passage through the mountains. If Colonel Bouquet succeeds in this point, all is lost—all is lost indeed. Our enterprise will be ruined, and we shall be stopped at the Laurel Hill this winter; the southern Indians will turn against us, and these colonies will be desolated by such an accession to the enemy's strength. These must be the consequences of a miscarriage; and a miscarriage is almost the necessary consequence of an attempt to march the army by this new route."

Quite a large band of Indians were engaged as allies of the English on this expedition. They were led by a very intelligent and distinguished chief, called Scarvoyadi. There were several tribes who recognized his chieftainship. They had kept aloof, for some time, from military alliance with either party. At length, with some hesitancy, they joined the English. Washington considered the aid of these bold warriors as of the utmost importance. He knew that they were proud, and would quickly discern and keenly feel any insult. He therefore urged that they should be treated with consideration, and that they should be consulted on important questions.

But the British officers had but very little respect for ignorant savages. Many of the warriors, disgusted with the long delay, deliberately shouldered their muskets and marched back through the wilderness to their homes. They were ready at once to respond to the invitations of the French, whoever treated them as equals. Scarvoyadi, who still personally adhered to the English, wrote to the Governor and Council of Pennsylvania, in reference to the defeat of Braddock, as follows:

> "As to the defeat at the Monongahela, it was owing to the pride and ignorance of that great general who came from England. He is now dead.

But he was a bad man when he was alive. He looked upon us as dogs. He would never hear anything we said to him. We often endeavored to advise him, and tell him of the danger he was in. But he never appeared pleased with us. That was the reason why a great many of our warriors left him."[47]

We have no space here to allude to the great and successful campaign in the north, against Canada, with which Washington had no connection. But operations went on very slowly on the frontiers of Virginia. General Forbes, who was commander-in-chief, was long detained in Philadelphia. Colonel Bouquet, who was to command the advance, assembled his corps of British regulars at Raystown, in the heart of Pennsylvania. There were about three thousand five hundred American troops, Provincials, as they were called, at other appointed places of rendezvous.

Washington summoned his two regiments of Virginia troops to meet at Winchester. They numbered about nineteen hundred men. There were also about seven hundred friendly Indians, who came into his camp, lured by the high reputation of Washington and the prospect of the plunder of Fort Duquesne.

But when the American young men, from their scattered farm-houses in the wilderness, some of them distant two hundred miles, arrived at the rendezvous, they found themselves destitute of everything needful for so momentous a campaign. They were in want of horses, arms, ammunition, tents, field equipage, and almost everything else essential to the enterprise.

It was necessary for Washington immediately to repair to Williamsburg, to present the state of the case to the Council. When he reached the Pamunkey River, where there was no bridge, he was carried across, with his horse, in a ferry-boat. In the crossing he chanced to meet a Virginia gentleman of the name of Chamberlain, who was wealthy and who occupied a mansion in the neighborhood, where he entertained his distinguished guests with almost baronial hospitality.

He urged Washington so importunately to accompany him to his dwelling, at least to dine, that Washington, though with great reluctance, as

---

[47] Hazard's "Register of Pennsylvania," vol. v. p. 252.

it might cause the delay of an hour, felt constrained to accept the invitation. Among the guests at the table was a very beautiful young widow, by the name of Martha Custis. She was wealthy, and both by birth and marriage was connected with the most distinguished families in Virginia.

She was high-bred, accustomed to the most polished society, intelligent, and very beautiful. Her husband, who had been dead about three years, had left her with two children and a large fortune. Washington seemed to be, at first sight, deeply impressed with her surpassing loveliness and her social and mental attractions. The dinner hour rapidly passed. The horses, according to appointment, were at the door. But Washington decided to remain until the next morning. The afternoon and evening passed rapidly away, and at an early hour the ensuing day Washington was again in the saddle, endeavoring to make up for lost time as he urged his steed toward Williamsburg.

The beautiful and opulent widow had many suitors. The somewhat stately mansion, reared upon her large estate, was known as the White House. It was situated in New Kent County, not far from Williamsburg. Washington, apprehensive that he might lose the prize, improved the brief time which remained to him, to the utmost. The result was that their mutual faith was soon plighted. The marriage was to take place as soon as the campaign against Fort Duquesne was at an end.

Washington was continually urging upon the British officers the necessity of an immediate and vigorous advance. But these men, though winning the admiration of all by their bravery in the field, being generally the sons of the nobles, and accustomed to luxurious indulgence, deemed it necessary to make provisions for their comfort on the campaign, which, to the hardy Americans, seemed quite preposterous. The troops became daily more restless and demoralized by the temptations of an idle camp. The Indians, quite disgusted, in a body retired.

At length Washington, to his great relief, received orders to repair to Fort Cumberland. He reached that frontier fort on the 2d of July, and immediately commenced cutting a road through the forest, a distance of thirty miles, to Raystown, where Colonel Bouquet was stationed. Scouting parties of Indians were ranging the woods, firing upon the workmen, and upon the expresses passing between the posts, and worrying the laborers in every possible way. Washington succeeded in engaging the services of a band of Cherokee warriors, whom he sent out in counter parties against the hostile Indians. Colonel Bouquet thought that no one but an American could be guilty of the folly of imagining that Cherokee warriors could, in any emergence, be equal to British regulars. He insisted that each party should be accompanied by an English officer and a number of English soldiers. Washington was annoyed by the encumbrance, but was obliged to yield. He said:

> "Small parties of Indians will more effectually harass the enemy, by keeping them under continual alarms, than any parties of white men can do. For small parties of the latter are not equal to the task, not being so dexterous at skulking as the Indians. And large parties will be discovered by their spies early enough to have a superior force opposed to them."[48]

While affairs were moving thus slowly, Washington was quite enthusiastically chosen, by the electors of Frederick County, as their representative to the House of Burgesses. On the 21st of July, tidings arrived of the capture of Louisbourg, and the island of Cape Breton, by the English. This increased the impatience of Washington to be on the move. The rumor reached him that Colonel Bouquet intended to send a body of eight hundred troops in advance toward the fort. He immediately wrote to the Colonel, entreating that his command might be included in the detachment.

"If any argument," said he, "is needed, to obtain this favor, I hope, without vanity, I may be allowed to say, that from long intimacy with these woods, and frequent scoutings in them, my men are at least as well acquainted with all the passes and difficulties as any troops that will be employed."

Notwithstanding the remonstrances of Washington, and the indignation of the Virginia Assembly, Colonel Bouquet persisted in his plan of cutting a new road over the mountains, to Fort Duquesne. Sixteen hundred men

---

[48] Irving's *Life of Washington*, vol. i. p. 230.

were sent forward, from Raystown, to engage in the work. Thus July and August passed away; Washington was still encamped at Fort Cumberland, in the extreme of impatience, with nothing to do. He learned, by his spies, that on the 13th of August there were but eight hundred men, Indians included, at Fort Duquesne. There can be no question, that had Washington's counsels been followed, the fort would, by that time, have been in the hands of the British.

In September, Washington received orders to repair, with his troops, to Raystown, where he was to join Colonel Forbes. It was the middle of the month. And yet, with incredible toil the new military road had been opened but about forty-five miles, where a fort of deposit was built, called Loyal Hannan, a short distance beyond Laurel Hill, a distance of fifty miles, through the wilderness, was still to be traversed.

Colonel Bouquet, who commanded two thousand men there, sent forward about eight hundred men, under Major Grant, to reconnoitre. The Major was a boastful, conceited bravado. A part of his force consisted of Highlanders, and another part of Americans, under Major Andrew Lewis. They were all brave men. Grant was not aware that Indian scouts were watching every step of his advance. The farther they could draw him from the main body, the more easy and signal would be their victory. Supposing that he had approached the fort unperceived, Major Grant decided to make a sudden attack, thinking to take it by surprise, and thus to win great glory. Major Lewis thought the attempt very imprudent. There was certainly danger of failure. The failure might prove exceedingly disastrous. Whereas, by obeying orders, and waiting for the main body of troops to come up, the fort could certainly be taken, and probably with but very little, if any, bloodshed. With characteristic contemptuousness Major Grant replied:

> "You and your Americans may remain behind, with the baggage. I will go forward, with the British regulars, and show you how a fort can be taken."

He then placed Major Lewis in the rear, with the American troops, to protect the baggage. With martial music and unfurled banners, as if in proud challenge of the garrison, he marched his troops to an eminence, near the fort, where he encamped for the night. There was no movement in the fort. Not a gun was fired. Not a voice was heard. Nearly two thousand Indians were encamped nearby, waiting to cooperate with a sally from the fort the next morning.

The morning came. With its early dawn there was opened one of those awful scenes of tumult, blood, and woe, which have so often disfigured this sad world. The sally from the garrison attacked in front. The Indians in ambush, with hideous yells, opened fire upon the flanks. The scenes of Braddock's defeat were renewed. The British officers, with coolness and courage which could not be surpassed, endeavored to rally their men according to European tactics, which was the most foolish thing they could possibly do. The soldiers were thus presented to the foe, in such a concentrated mass, that every bullet of the savages accomplished its mission.

The British regulars, for a little time, held their ground bravely, though almost deafened by the yells of two thousand savages, and assailed by perhaps as terrific a storm of leaden hail as soldiers ever encountered. But no mortal courage could long withstand this merciless slaughter. Panic ensued, and a tumultuous flight. Major Lewis, leaving Captain Bullit with fifty men to guard the baggage, hurried forward, with the remainder of the Virginia troops, to the scene of action. The ground was covered with the dead and wounded, and the English utterly routed, were in frantic flight. The yells of two thousand Indians, in hot pursuit, blended into one demoniac scream.

Lewis was surrounded and captured. A French officer came to his rescue, and saved him from the tomahawk. Major Grant was likewise captured, and his life was saved by a French officer. Captain Bullit endeavored to make a forlorn stand, by forming a barricade with the baggage wagons. It was the work of a moment. The fugitives rallied behind it. Every man could see that escape, by flight, pursued by two thousand fleet-footed savages, was impossible. Concealed behind this bulwark, as the savages drew near, a deadly fire, by a concerted signal, was simultaneously opened upon them. This held the savages in check for a little time, but it manifestly could not be for long. We regret to add that the brave Captain Bullit then resorted to a stratagem, which, had it been adopted by the Indians, would have been denounced as the vilest perfidy. We give the occurrence, in the mild, and certainly not condemnatory language, of Washington Irving.

> "They were checked for a time, but were again pressing forward in greater numbers, when Bullit and his men held out the signal of capitulation, and advanced, as if to surrender. When within eight yards of the enemy, they suddenly levelled their arms, poured a most effectual volley, and then charged with the bayonet. The Indians fled in dismay, and Bullit took advantage of this check to retreat, with all speed, collecting the wounded and scattered fugitives as he advanced."[49]

The routed detachment, in broken bands, after the endurance of terrible sufferings, reached the Fort, Loyal Hannan. Here we are informed, by Mr. Irving, that Bullit's behavior was "a matter of great admiration." He was soon after rewarded with a major's commission.[50]

In this disastrous campaign, fraught with woe to so many once happy homes, twenty-one officers and two hundred and seventy-three privates were either killed or taken captive. There was something in the dignity, thoughtfulness, and heroism of Washington's character which caused, notwithstanding the incessant attacks to which he was exposed, his reputation to be continually on the advance. The weary weeks still lingered slowly away, and but little was accomplished. The Indians were ravaging the frontiers, almost unopposed. Life had become a burden in hundreds of woe-stricken homes. In many a lonely log-cabin, the widowed mother gathered her orphan children around her, and in terror awaited the war-

---

[49] Irving's *Life of Washington*, vol. i. p. 94.
[50] Washington, commenting upon this movement of Major Grant, writes: "From all accounts I can collect, it appears very clear that this was a very ill-concerted, or a very ill-executed plan. Perhaps both. But it seems to be very generally acknowledged that Major Grant exceeded his orders."—Irving's *Life of Washington*, vol. i. p. 286.

whoop of the savage. Washington was given the command of a detachment of American troops to do what he could for the protection of these homes where anguish dwelt.

If there be pestilence, famine, earthquake, God is responsible for the consequences; for He sends the scourge. But for these woes, these terrific woes, caused simply by ambitious warfare between the courts of England and France, God is not responsible. They were the work of man. The responsibility rests upon human hearts. Who will be held, by God, accountable for them in the day of judgment? There are some persons who must have cause to tremble.

It was not until the 5th of November, that the whole army was assembled at Loyal Hannan. Dreary winter was at hand. Snow capped the summits, and ice filled the gorges of the mountains. Freezing blasts moaned through the forests and swept the plains. Fifty miles of rugged mountain ranges were to be traversed, through which no road had yet been opened. The march was commenced, without tents or baggage, and with but a light train of artillery, in consequence of the ruggedness of the way.

Washington was in the advance. His route led along the path by which the fugitives of Grant's army had retreated. It was a melancholy march. The road presented continued traces of the awful defeat. It was strewed with human bones, picked clean by the wolves. These were the remains of beloved sons, husbands, fathers. Some had been cut down and scalped by the Indians. Some had thrown themselves on the ground, to die alone of exhaustion and hunger. Their panic-stricken companions could not remain, in their desperate flight, to nurse the sick or to bury the dead.

As the troops drew near Fort Duquesne the more numerous these mementoes of the awful past appeared. Washington advanced with the greatest caution, until he arrived within sight of the fort. He had anticipated a vigorous defence. But the signal successes of the British armies in Canada had prevented any reinforcement or supplies from being sent to Fort Duquesne. The intelligent officers saw, consequently, that they were in no condition to repel the very formidable army which Great Britain was marching against them.

The commandant had but five hundred men, and his provisions were nearly exhausted. As soon as the English army was within one day's march of the fort, he at night embarked his troops, and nearly all the valuable material of the fortress, in several large flat-bottomed boats, blew up the magazine, reduced all the works to ashes, and, leaving but blackened ruins behind him, drifted down the rapid current of the Ohio.

In the chill and the gloom of the 25th of November, the English army reached the confluence of the Alleghany and the Monongahela rivers. There was neither fort, village, cabin, or wigwam there. Not an Indian or a Frenchman was to be seen. Not a gun, not a cartridge, not a particle of food was left behind. The grand eminences rose sublimely, as now. The two tranquil streams flowed rapidly along, as if eager to unite in forming La Belle Rivière. The primeval forest, in almost awful grandeur, covered hill and valley as far as the eye could extend. Silence and solitude reigned supreme. The French were driven out the valley, and the British flag was triumphantly unfurled.

Vigorous measures were adopted to erect another fort. It was called Fort Pitt, in honor of England's illustrious minister. The domination of the French, in the valley of the Ohio, was at an end. The Indians promptly gave in their adhesion to the conquering power, entered into alliances with the English, and, for a short time, allowed peace to exist in that beautiful valley, which God apparently intended as one of the fairest gardens of our world.

Washington, with somewhat accumulated fame, returned to Virginia. On the 6th of January his marriage union with Mrs. Custis took place, at the White House, the attractive residence of the wealthy bride. A numerous assemblage of the distinguished gentlemen and ladies of the land graced the festive scene.[51]

---

[51] An old negro servant of the household of Mrs. Custis gave the following account of the impression Washington produced upon the family:
"Never seed the like, sir—never the like of him, though I have seen many in my day—so tall, so straight! And then, sir, he sat on a horse and rode with such an air! Ah, sir, he was like no one else! Many of the grandest gentlemen, in the gold lace, were at the wedding; but none looked like the man himself."—*Soldier and Patriot*, p. 58.

Washington remained for three months, a happy man, with his bride at the White House. He then repaired to Williamsburg, to take his seat as representative in the House of Burgesses.[52] His prospects for a happy life were brilliant indeed. From his own family he had inherited a large fortune. His mental and personal attractions were extraordinary. His fame was enviable. Mr. Custis, the first husband of his wife, had left, in addition to a very large landed estate, money, well invested, amounting to two hundred and twenty-five thousand dollars. One-third of this fell to his widow in her own right. Two-thirds were inherited equally by her two children: a son of six years, and a daughter of four. Washington's bride was, in all respects, everything his heart could wish. The two children were intelligent, amiable, and lovely in a high degree.

At the close of the session of the Assembly, he conducted his happy family to his favorite abode of Mount Vernon. In those blessed days of peace and domestic joy he wrote to a friend.[53]

> "I am now, I believe, fixed in this seat, with an agreeable partner for life; and I hope to find more happiness in retirement than I ever experienced in the wide and bustling world."

Most of our readers are familiar with the home of Washington, as it has been presented to them in the many engravings which have found their way to almost every fireside. The mansion, very spacious on the ground floor, was architecturally quite pleasing. It stood upon a smooth, green, velvety lawn, spreading several hundred feet down to the river which washed its eastern base. The prospect it commanded was magnificent. The eminence, in the rear, was crowned with the stately forest. The spacious estate, of two thousand five hundred acres, was divided into many highly

---

[52] William Wirt, in his Life of Patrick Henry, has assigned to this date, the enthusiastic reception of Washington by the Assembly. Others, as we think more correctly, have given it the date to which we have assigned it in this volume.

[53] To a nephew, who was entering the Assembly for the first time, he wrote, "The only advice I will offer, if you have a mind to command the attention of the House, is to speak seldom, but on important subjects, except such as particularly relate to your constituents; and, in the former case make yourself perfectly master of the subject. Never exceed a decent warmth, and submit your sentiments with diffidence. A dictatorial style, though it may carry conviction, is always accompanied with disgust."—Sparks' *Life of Washington*, p. 101.

cultivated farms. Much of the region was still covered with the forest, which the axe of the settler had never disturbed. Game of every variety abounded on the hills, and in the meadows and streamlets. A nobler hunting ground could perhaps nowhere be found. Washington, when but a stripling, had often ranged its vast expanse, where deer, foxes, and rabbits had found their favorite haunts; and where water-fowl floated, often in countless numbers, upon the creeks and lakelets. In one of Washington's letters he writes enthusiastically, and yet truly:

> "No estate in United America is more pleasantly situated. In a high and healthy country; in a latitude between the extremes of heat and cold; on one of the finest rivers in the world—a river well stocked with various kinds of fish at all seasons of the year, and, in the spring with shad, herring, bass, carp, sturgeon, etc., in great abundance. The borders of the estate are washed by more than ten miles of tide water. Several valuable fisheries appertain to it. The whole shore, in fact, is one entire fishery."

Washington was, from his natural disposition, and also from the teachings of his mother, a devout man. The society in the midst of which he was born, and by which he was from childhood surrounded, was aristocratic in all its habits and tastes. Most of the wealthy planters were connected with the aristocratic families of England. They had brought over large sums of money, purchased extensive estates and were living in a style of splendor and of profuse hospitality unknown in any of the other colonies.

The governors, in particular, being appointed by the crown and who were generally men of wealth and high birth, endeavored to form their establishments on the pattern of miniature royalty. The Episcopal church, or church of England, was altogether predominant throughout the Dominion. Many of these haughty men maintained it merely as an essential part of the political organization of the British government. But

Washington was a religious man in heart and in life. He was vestryman[54] of two parishes: Fairfax and Truro.

The parochial church of Fairfax was at Alexandria, ten miles from Mount Vernon. The church of the Truro parish was at Pohick, about seven miles distant. Washington had presented the plan of the latter church, and had built it almost at his own expense. He attended one or the other of these churches when the weather and the state of the roads would permit. He and Mrs. Washington were both communicants.

Notwithstanding the rapid increase of wealth and splendor in our land, the style of living, which prevailed among these opulent families in Virginia, has long ago faded away. Massive side-boards were generally, seen covered with glittering plate. The burglar was not feared in these large households. Superb carriages, drawn often by four blooded horses, all imported from England, conveyed the richly dressed families, through the forest roads, from mansion to mansion in their stately calls.

Washington had his chariot and four.[55] His black postilions, chosen for their manly beauty, were richly clad in livery. When he accompanied Lady Washington in any one of her drives, he, a splendid horseman, almost invariably appeared mounted, and their equipage would often surpass that of the minor dukes and princes of Europe.

Mr. Irving writes: "A large Virginia estate, in those days, was a little empire. The mansion-house was a seat of government, with its numerous dependencies, such as kitchens, smoke-house, workshops and stables. In this mansion the master ruled supreme; his steward, or overseer, was prime minister and executive officer. He had his legion of house negroes for domestic service, and his host of field negroes for the culture of tobacco, Indian corn, and other crops, and for other out-door labor.

"Their quarters formed a kind of hamlet, composed of various huts, with little gardens and poultry yards, all well stocked; and swarms of little

---

[54] "Vestryman—Episcopal church; one belonging to a select number of persons, in each parish, who manage its temporal concerns."—*Webster.*

[55] "His stable was well filled, and admirably regulated. His stud was thorough-bred and in excellent order. His household books contained registers of the names, ages, and marks of his favorite horses; such as Ajax, Blueskin, Valiant, Magnolia (an Arab), etc. Also his dogs, chiefly fox-hounds, Vulcan, Singer, Ringwood, Sweet-lips, Forester, Music, Rockwood, and Truelove."—Irving's *Life of Washington*, vol. i. p. 314.

negroes gambolling in the sunshine. Then there were large wooden edifices for curing tobacco, the staple and most profitable production, and mills for grinding wheat and Indian corn, of which large fields were cultivated for the supply of the family, and the maintenance of the negroes.

"Among the slaves were artificers of all kinds: tailors, shoemakers, carpenters, smiths, wheelwrights, and so forth. So that a plantation produced everything within itself for ordinary use. As to articles of fashion and elegance, and expensive clothing, they were imported from London; for the planters on the main rivers, especially the Potomac, carried on an immediate trade with England. Their tobacco was put up by their own negroes, bore their own marks, was shipped on board of vessels which came up the rivers for the purpose, and consigned to some agent in Liverpool or Bristol with whom the planter kept an account."[56]

---

[56] Irving's *Life of Washington*, vol. i. p. 315.

Chapter 5

THE GATHERING STORM OF WAR

Many of the Virginia planters were devoted to pleasure alone. They lived high, gambled, hunted, and left the management of their estates very much to overseers. Washington was a model planter. He carried into the administration of his estate all the sagacity, integrity, punctuality, and industry, which had thus far characterized him in public affairs. He was his own book-keeper, and his accounts were kept with methodical exactness. His integrity was such, that it is said that any barrel of flour, which bore his brand, was exempted in the West India ports from the ordinary inspection.[57]

He was very simple in his domestic habits, rising often, in midwinter, at five o'clock. He kindled his own fire, and read or wrote, by candle-light, until seven o'clock when he breakfasted very frugally. His ordinary breakfast was two small cups of tea, and three or four cakes of Indian meal, called hoe-cakes. After breakfast he mounted one of his superb horses, and in simple attire, but which set off to great advantage his majestic frame, visited all those parts of the extended estate, where any work was in progress. Everything was subjected to his careful supervision. At times he dismounted, and even lent a helping hand in furtherance of the operations

---

[57] Speech at laying the corner stone of the Washington Monument, by Robert C. Winthrop.

which were going on. He dined at two o'clock, and retired to his chamber about nine in the evening.[58]

He was kind in word and deed to his negro slaves, and while careful that they should not be overtasked, was equally careful that they should not be permitted to loiter away their time in idleness. The servants were proud of their stately, dignified, wealthy master, and looked up to him with reverence amounting almost to religious homage. Washington was very fond of the chase. Often, when riding to a distant part of the estate, he would take some of the hounds with him, from the hope that he might start up a fox. There was not perhaps, in all Virginia, a better horseman, or a more bold rider. The habits and tastes of the old English nobility and gentry prevailed in Virginia to an extraordinary degree. The passion for following the hounds was thoroughly transplanted from the broad estates of the English land-holders to the vast realms which nature had reared and embellished on the banks of the Potomac, and amid the ridges of the Alleghanies.

Mount Vernon was always crowded with guests. Even the most profuse hospitality was no burden to the princely proprietor. Frequently, in the season, Washington would three times a week engage in these hunting excursions with his guests. He could mount them all superbly from his own stables. The Fairfaxes were constant companions on these festive occasions. These opulent and high-bred gentlemen would often breakfast at one mansion, and dine at another. It is said that Washington, notwithstanding his natural stateliness of character, greatly enjoyed these convivial repasts.

Washington was, however, by no means engrossed in these pleasures in which he sought frequent recreation. The care of his vast estates demanded much of his time. His superior abilities and his established integrity led him to be in demand for public services. He was appointed Judge of the County Court, and being a member of the House of Burgesses, was frequently called from home by public duties. Whatever

---

[58] "My manner of life," Washington wrote to a friend, "is plain; and I do not mean to be put out of it. A glass of wine and a bit of mutton are always ready, and such as will be content to partake of them, are always welcome. Those who expect more will be disappointed."—*Soldier and Patriot*, p. 62.

trust Washington assumed, was discharged with the utmost fidelity. The diary which he carefully kept was headed with the words, "Where and How my Time is Spent."[59]

The great Dismal Swamp, that vast, gloomy morass, thirty miles long and ten miles wide, had then been but very partially explored. Washington, with several other gentlemen of enterprise in his vicinity, formed a project to drain it. Imagination can hardly conceive of a more gloomy region. A dense, luxuriant forest, of cedar, cypress, hemlock, and other evergreen and deciduous trees, sprang up from the spongy soil. Many portions of this truly dismal realm were almost impenetrable, from the density of thickets and interlacing vines. Stagnant creeks and pools, some of which were almost lakes, were frequently interspersed. It was the favorite haunt of venomous reptiles, and birds and animals of ill omen.

Washington undertook to explore this revolting region. There were portions of the quaking bog over which he could ride on horseback. But often he had to dismount and carefully lead his horse from mound to mound. In the centre of the morass he found a large sheet of water, six miles long and three broad. It is appropriately called the Lake of the Dismal Swamp. Upon the banks of this lake there was some firm land. Here Washington encamped on the first night of his exploration. As the result of this survey a company was chartered, under the title of the Dismal Swamp Company. Through the efficiency of this company great improvements were made in this once desolate region.

In the spring of 1763, the peace of Fontainebleau was signed; and the two great kingdoms of England and France sheathed their swords. During the conflict, the British government, through the arrogance and haughty assumptions of its officers, had become increasingly unpopular. The British had driven the French from the continent. They had been accustomed to treat the Americans, officers and privates, as contemptuously as they had treated the Indians. A man born in America was deemed of an inferior grade to one born in England. This spirit, which

---

[59] "Washington was fond of hunting, and sport of all kinds. He kept a beautiful barge on the Potomac, rowed by six negroes in uniform dress."—*Soldier and Patriot*, p. 61.

met the Americans at every turn, was rapidly severing the ties of kindly feeling which had bound the emigrants to the mother country.

It was a constant endeavor of the British government to impose taxes upon the Americans, while refusing them the right of any representation in parliament. From the earliest period, when such a measure was attempted, the colonists had, with great determination, remonstrated against it. We cannot enter into the detail of the attempts made to impose taxes, and the nature of the resistance presented. At one time the colonists resolved not to purchase British fabrics, but to clothe themselves in home manufactures. This, in Boston alone, cut off the sale of British goods to the amount of more than fifty thousand dollars in a single year.

The question was discussed in parliament, in the year 1764, George Grenville being prime minister; and it was voted that England had a right to tax America. There were, however, many Englishmen who were opposed to the wrong, and who vehemently denounced it. In accordance with this vote the Stamp Act was passed. By this act, no legal instrument was binding, unless written upon paper stamped by the British government, and purchased of their agents.

It is a little remarkable that aristocratic Virginia was the first effectually to rise, in a burst of indignation, against this decree. Thus far it had been strong in its devotion to the British crown, church, and constitution. Washington was then a member of the Virginia House of Burgesses. Patrick Henry, one of the most renowned of the early patriots, presented the celebrated resolution, that "The General Assembly of Virginia has the exclusive right and power to lay taxes and impositions upon the inhabitants; and that whoever maintained the contrary should be deemed an enemy to the colony."[60]

It was in the speech of great eloquence which he made upon this occasion, that he uttered the sentence which became world renowned:

---

[60] Though the first burst of opposition to the Stamp Act came from Virginia, the New Englanders were the first to take the field against the whole project of Parliamentary taxation.—See Irving's *Washington*, Mount Vernon edition, vol i. p. 110.

"Cæsar had his Brutus; Charles his Cromwell; and George the Third"—"Treason; treason," shouted several emissaries of the crown. Patrick Henry, bowing to the chairman, added, with great emphasis, "may profit by their example. Sir; if this be treason, make the most of it."

The storm was gathering. Washington foresaw it. With gloomy forebodings he returned to Mount Vernon. He wrote to Francis Dandridge, his wife's uncle, then in London:

"The Stamp Act engrosses the conversation of the speculative part of the colonists, who look upon this unconstitutional method of taxation as a direful attack upon their liberties, and loudly exclaim against the violation."

The alarming posture of affairs led the General Court, or Assembly of Massachusetts, to invite a Congress to meet, of delegates from the several colonies. The meeting was held in New York, in October, 1765. There were delegates representing Massachusetts, Rhode Island, Connecticut, New York, New Jersey, Pennsylvania, Delaware, Maryland, and South Carolina.

With great unanimity they denounced the acts of parliament imposing taxes without their consent, and some other measures, as violations of their rights and liberties. An address, in accordance with these resolves, was sent to the king, and petitions to both houses of parliament. In Boston, the stamp distributor was hung in effigy, and the stamps were seized and burned. Similar demonstrations were made in several other places. In Virginia, Mr. George Mercer was appointed distributor. On his arrival at Williamsburg he declined the office. The bells were rung, the town illuminated, and Mercer was greeted with acclaim.

The 1st of November, 1765, was the appointed day for the Stamp Act to go into operation. In many of the colonies the day was ushered in with funereal solemnities. The shops were closed, bells were tolled, flags were at half-mast, and many of the promoters of the act were burned in effigy. In New York, a copy of the act was paraded through the streets, in large letters on a pole, surmounted by a death's head, with an inscription beneath:

"The Folly of England and the Ruin of America."

Innumerable were the scenes of popular reprobation and violence which the obnoxious measure brought forth. The merchants of the great commercial marts of Boston, New York, and Philadelphia, mutually pledged themselves not to purchase any goods of British manufacture, until the act was repealed.

Washington took no active part in these demonstrations. All his associations allied him with the aristocracy. The native dignity and reserve of his character rendered it difficult for him to throw himself into the turbid current of popular indignation. He was constitutionally cautious, being careful never to take a step which he might be compelled to retrace. He remained quietly at Mount Vernon, absorbed in the complicated cares of the large estates there subject to his control.

The commotion so increased that the British government became somewhat alarmed. Dr. Franklin was called before the House of Commons to be examined on the subject. He was asked:

"What was the temper of America toward Great Britain before the year 1763?"

The philosopher replied, in calm, well ordered phrase, characteristic of the extraordinary man:

"The best in the world. They submitted willingly to the government of the crown. Numerous as the people are, in the several old provinces, they cost you nothing in forts, citadels, garrisons, or armies to keep them in subjection. They were governed, by this country, at the expense only of a little pen, ink, and paper. They had not only respect, but affection for Great Britain, its laws, its customs and manners, and even a fondness for its fashions, that greatly increased the commerce. Natives of Great Britain were always treated with particular regard. To be an Old England man was, of itself, a character of some respect, and gave a kind of rank among us."

"And what is their temper now?" Franklin was asked.

He replied, "Oh! it is very much altered. If the Stamp Act is not repealed there will be a total loss of the respect and affection the people of America bear to England; and there will be the total loss of the commerce which depends on that respect and affection."

"Do you think," the question was asked, "that the people of America would consent to pay the tax if it were moderated?"

"No," Franklin replied; "never, unless compelled by force of arms."[61]

These representations probably exerted very considerable influence. The act was repealed on the 18th of March, 1766. Washington was in entire harmony with the philosophic Franklin in his views upon this subject. To a friend he wrote:

> "Had the Parliament of Great Britain resolved upon enforcing it, the consequences, I conceive, would have been more direful than is generally apprehended, both to the mother country and her colonies. All therefore, who were instrumental in securing the repeal, are entitled to the thanks of every British subject, and have mine cordially."[62]

The Americans were struggling for the establishment of a principle which they deemed vital to their liberties. The petty pecuniary sum involved in that one case was of but little moment. The repeal of the act was attended with the obnoxious and insulting declaration that the king and parliament "had the right to bind the people of America in all cases whatever."

In correspondence with this assumption, a tax was speedily imposed on tea, glass, and sundry other articles. Troops were also sent out to hold the Americans in subjection, and the colonies were ordered to pay for their support. Two regiments of British regulars were sent to Boston. This was

---

[61] "Parliamentary Register," 1776.
[62] "Writings of Washington," Jared Sparks, vol. ii. p. 345, note.

indeed shaking the rod over the heads of the people. A town meeting was called. It was resolved that the king had no right to quarter troops upon the citizens, without their consent. The selectmen refused to provide lodgings for them.

Most of the troops were encamped on the common, while the governor, as agent of the crown, converted the State House and Faneuil Hall into barracks for others. The indignation of the people was at the boiling point. To overawe them, cannon, charged with grape-shot, were planted, to sweep the approaches to the State House and Faneuil Hall, and sentinels, with loaded muskets and fixed bayonets, challenged all who passed.

These regiments paraded the quiet streets of puritanic Boston with their banners and glittering weapons, and the martial music of bugles, drum and fifes was heard, even on the Sabbath, and every note fell upon the ears of the people like an insult and defiance. Washington, in his beautiful retreat at Mount Vernon, was steadfastly and anxiously watching all these proceedings. His feelings, in reference to the conduct of the British government, were very frankly expressed in the following letter to a friend, George Mason.[63]

> "At a time when our lordly masters in Great Britain will be satisfied with nothing less than the deprivation of American freedom, it seems highly necessary that something should be done to avert the stroke, and maintain the liberty which we have derived from our ancestors. But the manner of doing it, to answer the purpose effectually, is the point in question. That no man should scruple or hesitate a moment, in defence of so valuable a blessing, is clearly my opinion. Yet arms should be the last resource. We have already, it is said, proved the inefficacy of addresses to the throne and remonstrances to Parliament. How far their attention to our rights and interests is to be awakened or alarmed, by starving their trade and manufactures, remains to be tried."

---

[63] "He had some few intimates in his neighborhood, who accorded with him in sentiment. One of the ablest and most efficient of these was Mr. George Mason, with whom he had occasional conversations on the state of affairs."—Irving's *Life of Washington*, vol. i. p. 341.

Washington clearly foresaw how terrible the sacrifice which he and his opulent associates must make, in entering into a conflict with the British government. He alluded to this in the following words:

> "I can see but one class of people, the merchants excepted, who will not, or ought not, to wish well to the scheme; namely those who live genteelly and hospitably on clear estates. Such as these, were they not to consider the valuable object in view, and the good of others, might think it hard to be curtailed in their living and enjoyments."

It required the highest patriotic heroism for these wealthy men to peril their earthly all in such a conflict. An appeal to arms, followed by defeat, would inevitably lead to the confiscation of their estates, and to their execution upon the scaffold, as guilty of high treason. Mr. Mason nobly replied, in harmony with the spirit of Washington:

> "Our all is at stake; and the little conveniences and comforts of life, when set in competition with our liberty, ought to be rejected, not with reluctance but with pleasure. We may retrench all manner of superfluities, finery of all descriptions, and confine ourselves to linens, woollens, etc. It is amazing how much this practice, if adopted by all the colonies, would lessen the American imports, and distress the various trades and manufactures of Great Britain."

The result of this correspondence was the draft, by Mr. Mason, of the plan of an association, each member of which was to pledge himself not to use any article of British merchandise upon which a duty was imposed. Washington was to submit this plan to the House of Burgesses, on its approaching session. A somewhat similar resolve had already been adopted by the people of Boston.

The king had appointed Lord Botetourt[64] Governor of Virginia. It was the plan of the British court to crush the Puritans of Massachusetts by the

---

[64] Junius, in his celebrated letters, describes Botetourt as "a cringing, bowing, fawning, sword-bearing courtier." The witty Horace Walpole wrote of him, "If his graces do not captivate

gleam of bayonets and the rumbling of artillery. But the Cavaliers of Virginia were to be dazzled and seduced by such a display of regal splendor as had never before been witnessed on this continent. It was supposed that the *title* of the noble lord would quite overawe the wealthy, splendor-loving plebeians of the Potomac. The king presented Lord Botetourt with a very magnificent coach of state, and also with a gorgeous dining service of solid silver.[65] When the governor reached Williamsburg, he surrounded his petty court with all the etiquette of royalty. He opened the session of the Assembly with the pomp of the monarch opening Parliament. His massive coach of state, polished like a mirror, and with the panels emblazoned with his lordship's family coat-of-arms, was drawn from his mansion to the capitol by six milk-white horses in the richest caparisons.

The poor negroes gazed upon the pageant, with mouths wide open with wonder, awe, and admiration. The bedizened lord, seated upon luxurious cushions, with his outriders, his brilliantly liveried coachman and footman, appeared to them but little less than an archangel from some higher sphere. But the pompous display was not in the least calculated to overawe George Washington, George Mason, and their gentlemanly associates, who well knew the value of human rights, and the worthlessness of tawdry splendor.

The souls of these men were moved by stern responsibilities pressing upon them. Several members presented spirited resolves denouncing the late acts of Parliament in imposing taxes. It was declared, emphatically, that the power to impose taxes was vested in the House of Burgesses alone. Washington was prepared to submit the plan of agreement which Mr. Mason had drawn up. The plan was publicly canvassed, and everywhere met with approval. An address was voted to the king, in which it was urged that all trials for treason, alleged to be committed in one of the colonies, should be tried before the courts of that colony. It was very clear that if anyone, who had incurred the displeasure of the crown, should be dragged to London for trial, he would stand a very poor chance of acquittal.

---

them (the Virginians), he will enrage them to fury; for I take all his *douceur* to be enamelled on iron."—*Grenville Papers*, vol. iv. p. 330, note.

[65] The wits of London quite amused themselves in lampoons upon this extraordinary splendor of outfit, of "a minister plenipotentiary to the savage Cherokees."

The Gathering Storm of War 91

Lord Botetourt was astonished by these bold declarations and demands. He promptly repaired to the capitol, authoritatively summoned the speaker and his council to his audience chamber, and said to them imperiously:

> "Mr. Speaker and Gentlemen of the House of Burgesses, I have heard of your resolves, and augur ill of their effects. You have made it my duty to dissolve you; and you are dissolved accordingly."

The Burgesses, as the members of the colonial Assembly were called, unintimidated by this exercise of the royal prerogative, repaired, in a body, to a private house. They were no longer the House of Burgesses, but merely a collection of citizens. They chose for moderator their late speaker, Peyton Randolph.[66] Washington then presented his draft of an association to discountenance the use of all British merchandise, taxed by Parliament to raise a revenue in America. It was signed by every member. Then, being printed, it was sent throughout the country, and to other colonies, and soon became almost universally adopted.

The king and parliament were not alarmed; they were only astonished to see that the helpless worm should have presumption thus to squirm beneath their gigantic tread. Lord Botetourt soon began to feel the influence of the society which surrounded him. He found that the opulent, highly cultivated gentlemen of Virginia, were quite his equals; that they were men who could not be dazzled from their paths, by any display of ribbons and gilding and courtly pomp.

Nay, more than this; he soon began to feel the power of their superior intelligence. As he listened to their courteous and logical representations, he became convinced that their cause was a just one; that their grievances were many, and that he had entered upon his office, with entirely erroneous impressions respecting the true posture of affairs. His pompous equipage was laid aside. He reduced his establishment to the simplicity of that of a

---

[66] Peyton Randolph was one of the most distinguished of the Virginia patriots. He was attorney-general of the Province, and was subsequently elected President of the Second Colonial Congress.

well-bred gentleman. He even did not hesitate to declare that the taxes ought to be repealed, and that sundry other reforms were called for.

In Boston, a committee called upon the royal governor to state that the General Court could not deliberate, with self-respect, when the State House was surrounded by soldiers, and cannon were pointed at its doors, and men-of-war were in the harbor, with their guns directed menacingly against the town. They requested therefore that the governor, as the representative of his majesty the king, would have such forces removed from Boston during the session of the court.

The governor curtly replied, "I have no authority to order the removal of either ships or troops."

The General Court responded firmly but respectfully, "The General Court cannot then undertake to transact any business, while thus menaced by cannon and muskets."

The governor was embarrassed. There was business of pressing importance to come before the court. He endeavored to extricate himself by ordering the court to meet in Cambridge, beyond the reach of the guns of the fleet, and where there were no troops. The court met, and the governor immediately sent in a requisition for money to pay to British soldiers, and for quarters to be assigned for their board and lodging.

The blood of the Puritan was as red and pure as that of his equally patriotic brother the Cavalier. After a solemn discussion, for it was a solemn moment, involving issues of fearful magnitude, these noble men returned an answer, in brief as follows:

> "The establishment of a standing army in this colony, in a time of peace, is an invasion of our natural rights."

There was no offer to provide for these British regulars, and no refusal to do so, save what might be implied in the resolve. The governor again sent to know whether the Assembly would or would not make provision for the British troops. The decisive reply was returned that it was "incompatible with their own honor and interest, and their duty to their constituents," to pay the expenses of British soldiers thus unconstitutionally billeted upon the American people.

The governor, much annoyed, prorogued the Assembly, and ordered it to meet again in Boston, on the 1st of January, 1770.

The "Non-Importation Associations," as they were called, produced the effect, on British commerce, which the advocates of those measures had anticipated. The British merchants were in great trouble. They flooded Parliament with petitions that the taxes might be repealed, so that commerce might be restored.

Lord North became prime minister. He was one of the most haughty of England's nobles, with limited capacity, but an obstinate will. He revoked all duties excepting that on tea. Thus he adhered to the *principle* that England had a right to impose taxes upon America, without allowing the Americans any representation in Parliament. He distinctly announced that this single tax was continued, "to maintain the parliamentary right of taxation." It was foolishly thought that, because the tax was only three-pence on the pound, the Americans would therefore consent to be betrayed into the establishment of the principle.

There were many Englishmen in Parliament whose sympathies were entirely with the Americans. In strains of eloquence equal to any which have ever proceeded from human lips, they argued the cause of colonial rights. George III was one of the most obstinate of men. Lord North was bound to obey his behests. He but gave utterance to the sentiments of his royal master in saying:

> "The properest time to exert our right of taxation is when the right is refused. To temporize is to yield. The authority of the mother country, if it is now unsupported, will be relinquished forever. A total repeal cannot be thought of, till America is prostrate at our feet."[67]

The British soldiers, established in Boston, were exceedingly obnoxious to the citizens, and bitter hostility soon sprung up between them.

---

[67] Holmes' *American Annals*, vol. ii. p. 173.

These veterans, inured to the cruelties of war, as, in their gay uniform they paraded the streets, with gleaming bayonets and loaded muskets, looked very contemptuously upon the towns-people, and often treated them with great insolence.

One day there was some collision between a party of young Bostonians and a small band of soldiers. The unarmed young men were put to flight, and the soldiers pursued them. The alarm bells were rung. Excited crowds swept through the streets. The mob, armed with clubs and stones, assailed the troops fiercely. They defended themselves with bullets. Four of the populace were killed. Several others were wounded. The exasperation had now risen to such a pitch that the governor deemed it expedient to remove the troops from the town. Tidings of the "Boston Massacre" swept through all the colonies, and added additional fuel to the flame already so fiercely burning.

Lord Botetourt found no friendly response to his representations at the British Court. He had been sent to Virginia to overawe the inhabitants, and to bring them into servile obedience to the British crown. He had thought that the same views of truth, which had influenced his mind, would exert a conciliatory influence upon the king and his cabinet. But he was bitterly disappointed. Opprobrium was his only reward. Desponding and enfeebled, he was attacked by a bilious fever and died. He had become endeared to the people by his noble espousal of their cause. Washington testified that he was disposed "to render every just and reasonable service to the people whom he governed." The House of Burgesses erected a statue to his memory, in the area of the capitol.

The path of this world, as of all its nations and individuals, has ever been through darkness, clouds, and storms. While the tempest of national war, which was to doom our land to the most awful woes, was thus deepening its folds, Washington undertook another expedition, across the mountains, to the Ohio. He was influenced by public as well as private considerations. The State of Virginia had offered a bounty of two hundred thousand acres of land, to be divided among the officers and soldiers, who had served during the French war, according to their rank. Washington was one of the Virginia Board of Commissioners. There had been great neglect in settling these claims. The zeal of Washington was aroused that they should be promptly and fully paid.

The treaties made with the Indians in those days, will seldom bear minute investigation. The purchasers were not careful to ascertain the validity, of the title of the chiefs, to the lands which they sold. And many of the chiefs were ready, for a suitable compensation, to sell all their right and title to lands to which they had no claim whatever.

There was a powerful confederacy of tribes living in the vicinity of the great northern lakes, called the Six Nations.[68] By a treaty, in 1768, these chiefs sold to the British crown all the land possessed by them south of the river Ohio. Speculators were rushing in. It was the object of Washington to visit these fertile acres, and affix his seal to such tracts as he might deem suitable to pay off the soldiers' claim.

It was an enterprise fraught with considerable danger. There was no law in these vast wilds, which were ranged by Indians, and by white men still more savage in character. Several of the tribes in that region remonstrated against the sale. Among these were the powerful Delawares, Mingoes, and Shawnees. They said that the chiefs of the Six Nations had withheld from them their share of the consideration which was paid; and that they were as legitimate owners of those vast hunting grounds as were any chiefs of the Six Nations. They therefore openly avowed their intention of exacting the deficiency, which they deemed due to them, from the white men who should attempt to settle on their hunting-grounds. Thus there had been several robberies and murders, perpetrated by no one knew who. White vagabonds, dressed in Indian costume, could scarcely be distinguished from the Indians themselves. And lawless bands of savages, roving here and there, were the burglars and highway robbers of the wilderness, for whose outrages no tribe could be held responsible.

Washington selected, for his companion, on this expedition, his very congenial friend and neighbor, Dr. Craik.[69] Washington took two of his

---

[68] These nations, or tribes, consisted of the Mohawks, the Oneidas, the Onondagas, the Senecas, the Cayugas, and the Tuscaroras.—See Drake's *Book of the Indians*, B. v. p. 2.

[69] Dr. James Craik was a Scotchman by birth, and a very noble man. He accompanied Washington in the unfortunate expedition rendered memorable by the disaster of Jumonville. Washington cherished, for him, a life-long friendship.

negro servants to accompany him, and the doctor took one. Thus the party consisted of five persons. All were well mounted. A single led horse carried the baggage of the party. A journey of twelve days conducted them, through this unpeopled wilderness, to Fort Pitt, which, it will be remembered, had been reared on the ruins of Fort Duquesne.

It was the 17th of October, 1770, when they reached the fort. It was garrisoned by two companies of Irishmen. Around the fort a little hamlet had sprung up, of about twenty log houses. It was called the town. These rude dwellings, in comfort but little above the wigwam of the savage, were occupied by a rough, coarse set of men, who had been lured into the wilderness to trade with the Indians. Such was the origin, scarcely one hundred years ago, of the present beautiful city of Pittsburg, with its opulent, refined, and highly cultivated population.

One of these cabins they called a tavern. Nominally, Washington and his companion took up their quarters there. But they were entertained within the fort with all the hospitality that frontier post could afford. Washington met, at the fort, Colonel George Crogan, a man of great renown in frontier adventures. He had reared his hut on the banks of the Alleghany River, about four miles above the fort. Washington visited the colonel, at his spacious and well-guarded cabin. There he met several chiefs of the Six Nations. The fame of Washington had reached their ears. They greeted him fraternally, and assured him of their earnest desire to live in peace with the white men.

Washington and his party, returning to Fort Pitt, left their horses there, and embarked in a large canoe to sail down the beautiful and placid Ohio, as far as the Great Kanawha. Colonel Crogan engaged two Indians attendants and an interpreter to accompany the party, as they floated down the sublime solitudes of this majestic stream. He also, with several other officers, descended the river with them in a canoe, about thirty miles, as far as the Indian village called Logstown. It will be remembered that Washington had held an interview with the Indian chiefs here on a former excursion.[70]

---

[70] "At that time (1770) there were no inhabitants on the Ohio, below Pittsburg, except the natives of the forest. A few traders had wandered into those regions, and land speculators had sent

It was the lovely month of October. Nothing can be imagined more beautiful than the luxuriant banks of the Ohio, with their swelling mounds, crowned in their autumnal vesture. It was the favorite hunting season of the Indians. The river valley abounded with game. The roving Indians were alike at home everywhere. They had a taste for lovely scenery. In every cove their picturesque wigwams could be seen. They feasted abundantly upon the choicest viands the forest and river could afford. Often, at night, the picturesque scenery would be illumined, far and wide, by their camp fires, while the echoes of hill and valley were awakened by their boisterous revelry.

Blessed peace reigned; and our voyagers were cordially welcomed and hospitably entertained at all these encampments. As they drifted down the tranquil current, they found themselves in the paradise of sportsmen. Herds of deer were browsing in the rich meadows, and unintimidated by the passage of the boats, were coming down to the waters edge to drink. At times the whole surface of the stream seemed to be covered with water-fowl, of every variety of gay plumage. Flocks of ducks and geese, in their streaming flight were soaring through the air. These skilful sportsmen, without landing, could fill their canoes with game. When night came, selecting some sheltered and attractive spot, they would land, erect their hut, imperious to wind and rain, spread their couch of rushes or fragrant hemlock boughs, build their fires, and, with appetites whetted by the adventures of the day, enjoy as rich a repast as earth can give.

The banks of the Ohio are now fringed with magnificent hotels, and the stream is ploughed with steamers palatial grandeur. But probably no voyagers on that river now can find the enjoyment, which Washington experienced in his canoe, one hundred years ago.

Washington had a spirit of romance in his nature which led him intensely to enjoy such scenes. And yet he was at the farthest remove from a mere pleasure-seeker. His journal shows that his mind was much engrossed with the great object of the expedition. He carefully examined

---

out emissaries to explore the country; but no permanent settlements had been formed."—Sparks' *Life of Washington*, p. 111.

the soil, the growth of timber, and the tracts of land most suitable for immediate settlement.

At Logstown, Colonel Crogan, and the officersof the fort returned up the river, and left the adventurers to pursue their voyage into the solitary realms beyond. About seventy-five miles below Fort Pitt they came to quite an important Indian village, called Mingotown. Here again, amid all these scenes of peace and beauty, where man might enjoy almost the bliss of Eden, they came to the sad evidences of our fallen race. The whole population was in turmoil. Sixty warriors, hideously painted and armed to the teeth, were just setting out on the warpath.

Their savage natures were roused to the highest pitch of hatred against the Cherokees, for some real or imagined wrong. With demoniac rage they were going to rush upon some Cherokee village, at midnight; to apply the torch, to dash out the brains of women and children, to tomahawk the men; and, having made such captives as they could, to bring them back to their villages, and there, burning them at the stake, to inflict upon them the most fiend-like torture.

It was also said that, about forty miles farther down the river, two white men had been recently killed. Who their murderers were was not known, or whether their object was plunder or revenge. This troubled state of affairs led Washington to hesitate whether to continue his voyage. He, however, decided to proceed, though with great circumspection. Having arrived at the spot, at the mouth of Captema creek, where the murder were said to have taken place, he found a small Indian village, two women only being there, as the men were all absent hunting. Here he learned that rumor had, as usual, been exaggerating the facts. Two traders had attempted to cross the Ohio, on the backs of their horses, swimming them; and one of them had been drowned. This was all.

The voyage of two additional days, through unbroken solitudes, brought the party to an Indian hunting camp, at the mouth of the Muskingum River. An illustrious chieftain resided here, by the name of

Kiashuta. He was a sachem of the Senecas, and was considered head chief of the river tribes.[71]

Kiashuta was a renowned warrior. He had been one of the most energetic of the Indian chieftains in Pontiac's conspiracy for the extermination of the English. The chief instantly recognized Washington. Seventeen years before, in 1753, he had formed one of the escort of the youthful Washington, across the wilderness country, to the French posts near Lake Erie.

The chief received Washington with every demonstration of friendship, presented him with a quarter of a fine buffalo, just killed, aided him in establishing his camp, and, at the camp fire, engaged in earnest conversation until near the dawn of the morning. He was a very intelligent man, of decided views as to Indian policy, and was well informed respecting the plans and measures of the English. As was the case with nearly all the chiefs, he was very anxious for peace with the white men. He expressed the earnest desire, to Washington, that friendly relations might continue to exist between them and the English, and that trade might be carried on between them upon equitable terms. Impartial history must declare that the Indians seldom if ever commenced hostilities, unless goaded to do so by intolerable wrongs.

Early the next morning the delightful voyage was resumed, beneath unclouded skies, through charming scenery, over a placid river, and in the enjoyment of as genial a clime as this earth can anywhere afford. They reached the mouth of the Great Kanawha. Here, upon a spot on the southern, or Kentucky shore, appropriately called Point Pleasant, they encamped for several days to explore the solitudes of the grand realms spreading around them.[72]

---

[71] The Muskingum is one of the largest rivers that runs wholly in the State of Ohio. It flows down, from its sources far away in the north, with a gentle current, over a pebbly bottom, and is navigable for large boats, for a distance of about one hundred miles. The beautiful city of Marietta now stands at its mouth, where the wigwam of the Indian only was seen at the time of Washington's visit.—M'Culloch's *Geographical Dictionary*.

[72] The Great Kanawha, after flowing through a garden-like region four hundred miles in extent, enters the Ohio about two hundred and fifty miles below Pittsburg.—M'Culloch's *Geographical Dictionary*.

Washington describes the country as charming in the extreme. There were, in the vicinity, many beautiful lakelets of crystal water fringed with the grand forest in its autumnal vesture. Over these still waters, ducks, geese, and swans floated in numbers which could not be counted. Their gambols and their joyous notes excited the mind with the most pleasurable emotions. Flocks of fat turkeys would scarcely step aside from the path of the hunter, while buffalo, deer, and other similar game, met the eye in great abundance. The larder of our voyagers was profusely stored, and among those back woodsmen there were cooks who knew well how to find the tender cuts, and how to prepare them for their repasts with the most appetizing effect.

Chapter 6

THE CONFLICT COMMENCED

"Sorrow is for the sons of men
And weeping for earth's daughters."

Washington, on his return to Mount Vernon, found his beloved stepdaughter, Martha Custis, in the very last stages of pulmonary consumption. She was a beautiful girl of but seventeen summers, whom Washington loved as his own child. While in anguish he was praying at her bedside, her spirit took its flight. She died on the 19th of June, 1773.

John Park Custis, a petted boy of about sixteen, and the heir of a large fortune, remained the idol of his indulgent mother. It is pretty evident that he had his own way in all things, and that the sound judgment of the father often reluctantly yielded to the injudicious fondness of the mother. His education had been irregular and imperfect. The impetuous youth fell in love with a young daughter of a wealthy neighbor, Benedict Calvert, Esq. There was no objection to the marriage, excepting the youth of the children. It is pretty evident that Washington had considerable difficulty in inducing the impulsive lad to consent to the postponement of the marriage for a year or two, that he might prosecute his studies; for his education was exceedingly defective.

He accordingly took John to New York, and placed him under the care of Rev. Dr. Cooper, who was president of King's College, now called Columbia. The lad went reluctantly, and the fond mother was so pliant to his wishes, that but a few months passed away when she consented to his return, and to his premature marriage. The disapproval of Washington is expressed in the following letter to President Cooper:

> "It has been against my wishes that he should quit college in order that he may soon enter into a new scene of life, which I think he would be much fitter for some years hence than now. But having his own inclination, the desires of his mother, and the acquiescence of almost all his relatives to encounter, I did not care, as he is the last of the family, to push my opposition too far. I have therefore submitted to a kind of necessity."

The bridegroom had not attained his twenty first year when the marriage was celebrated, on the 3d of February, 1774. When Washington first learned of the attachment, and the engagement, he wrote a letter to the father of the young lady, from which we make the following extracts:

> "I write to you on a subject of importance, and of no small embarrassment to me. My son-in-law and ward, Mr. Custis, has, as I have been informed, paid his addresses to your second daughter; and, having make some progress in her affection, has solicited her in marriage. How far a union of this sort may be agreeable to you, you best can tell. But I should think myself wanting in candor, were I not to confess that Miss Nellie's amiable qualities are acknowledged on all hands, and that an alliance with your family will be pleasing to his.
>
> "This acknowledgment being made, you must permit me to add, sir, that at this, or in any short time, his youth, inexperience, and unripened education are, and will be, insuperable obstacles, in my opinion, to the completion of the marriage. As his guardian, I conceive it my indispensable duty to endeavor to carry him through a regular course of education, many branches of which, I am sorry to say, he is to day deficient in, and to guide his youth to a more advanced age, before an

event, on which his own peace, and the happiness of another, are to depend, takes place.

"If the affection, which they have avowed for each other, is fixed on a solid basis, it will receive no diminution in the course of two or three years, in which time he may prosecute his studies and thereby render himself more deserving of the lady, and useful to society. If, unfortunately, as they are both young, there should be an abatement of affection on either side, or both, it had better precede than follow marriage.

"Delivering my sentiments thus freely, will not, I hope, lead you into a belief that I am desirous of breaking off the match. To postpone it is all I have in view; for I shall recommend to the young gentleman, with all the warmth that becomes a man of honor, to consider himself as much engaged to your daughter as if the indissoluble knot were tied; and, as the surest means of effecting this, to apply himself closely to his studies, by which he will, in a great measure, avoid those little flirtations with other young ladies, that may, by dividing the attention, contribute not a little to divide the affection."

There was throughout the colonies a general combination against using tea, upon which Lord North had affixed a tax. The British merchants sent, to many of the American ports, ships laden with tea. At New York and Philadelphia, the people would not allow the tea to be landed; and the ships returned to London with their cargoes. At Charleston they landed the cargo and stored it in cellars, where it perished, as no purchasers could be found.

At Boston, a number of the inhabitants, disguised as Indians, boarded at night the tea ships which were, anchored in the harbor, and dashing the chests, emptied all the tea into the water. This event was popularly called The Boston Tea Party. The British Government was now thoroughly enraged. Its wrath was mainly directed against Boston. A bill was enacted by Parliament, known as the Boston Port Bill, closing the port against all commerce whatever, and transferring the Custom House to Salem. It was supposed that Boston would thus be punished by utter ruin.

As another vindictive measure, as exasperating as it was insulting, it was decreed that the people of Massachusetts should no longer have any voice in the choice of their rulers; but that all counsellors, judges, and magistrates should be appointed by the king of Great Britain, and should hold office during his royal pleasure.

Lord Dunmore, who had held the Government of New York, upon being appointed Governor of Virginia, repaired, after a little delay, to Williamsburg. A singular conflict appears to have taken place between the Governor and the powerful and patriotic aristocracy of Virginia. He did all in his power to win them over to the side of the crown, against the American people. His wife was an English lady of culture and high accomplishments. He had a numerous family of sons and daughters. Quite a brilliant court was established at Williamsburg. Magnificent balls and dinner parties were given. Very marked attention was paid to the opulent planters and their families, who constituted a sort of American nobility. On their vast estates, cultivated by hundreds of negro slaves, they occupied the position of the feudal barons of the European world. Regulations were drawn up, by order of the governor, and officially published, determining the etiquette to be observed at these grand receptions; and establishing the rank and precedence of all military and civil officers and their wives. Unwonted splendor embellished the streets of the capital. Gilded chariots and four, drawn by the most magnificent steeds richly caparisoned, almost crowded the streets of Williamsburg. It was indeed a glittering bribe which the governor pressed upon the aristocracy of the Ancient Dominion.

But these noble men wavered not in their advocacy of human rights. They stood as firm as their own Alleghanies. The advances of the governor were cordially met. They accepted the proffered hand of friendship. The parties of the governor were attended, and entertainments of equal splendor were given in return. But not one particle of principle was surrendered. Indeed, these nobles of the New World hoped that the Earl of Dunmore, like Lord Botetourt, might be led to appreciate the true posture of affairs, and to lend his influence to the cause of liberty, rather than to that of oppression.

Washington arrived at Williamsburg on the 15th of April, 1773. He immediately called upon the governor, to pay him his respects. The military and civil offices of Washington caused him to have a high position assigned him, in the court regulations. The House of Burgesses was opened with great pomp. The lady of the governor, having recently arrived, the Assembly voted to welcome her with a splendid ball, to be given on the 27th of the month.

Just then intelligence reached Williamsburg, of the vindictive acts of Parliament in closing the port of Boston, and in depriving the people of the choice of their own rulers. One general burst of indignation followed this announcement. A resolution of protest was promptly passed, and a day of fasting, humiliation, and prayer was appointed, that God would save the colonies from civil war; that He would interpose to protect their rights from destruction and that He would unite the hearts of all Americans, to oppose whatever encroachment might be attempted upon their liberties:

The anger of Lord Dunmore was aroused. The very next morning he summoned the Assembly to his council chamber, and, in laconic but excited speech, said.

> "Mr. Speaker and Gentlemen of the House of Burgesses: I have in my hand a paper, published by order of your House, conceived in such terms as reflect highly upon his majesty and the parliament of Great Britain, which makes it necessary for me to dissolve you; and you are dissolved accordingly."[73]

Thus the House of Burgesses was entirely broken up. It had no longer any legal existence. The members were sent to their homes. A new House of Burgesses must be formed, by another election.

This hostile act, on the part of the governor, excited, of course, great indignation. There was, in the vicinity, a public house which had long been known as the Old Raleigh Tavern. To a large hall in this house the members adjourned. They were now merely private citizens, with no official power. As a convention, however, they passed resolutions strongly denouncing the acts of parliament, recommending to all the colonies to desist from the use of tea, and all other European commodities, and

---

[73] "*To Dissolve*; to bring to an end by separating the parts or dispersing the members of; to terminate; to destroy; to cause to disappear; as, to *dissolve* parliament.

"*To Prorogue*; to continue from one session to another; to adjourn for an indefinite time; applied to the English Parliament."—*Webster.*

recommending the assembly of a General Congress, to be composed of deputies from the several colonies.

This all-important measure met with prompt concurrence, the 5th of September was appointed for the meeting of the first Congress in Philadelphia.

Still the gentlemen of Virginia remained on courteous terms with Lord Dunmore. The ball was attended with great spirit. It is said that the Earl was very marked in his attentions to Washington. He appreciated his lofty character, and the influence he was capable of exerting. On the very day when the governor dissolved the Assembly, Washington dined with him, and spent the evening in his company. The governor also soon accompanied Washington to Mount Vernon, breakfasted with him, and, by his side, rode over the splendid estate.

Two days after the ball, letters reached Williamsburg, from Boston, recommending a general league of the colonies and the suspension of all trade with Great Britain. Most of the members of the dissolved Assembly had returned to their homes. But twenty-five remained. They held a convention at which Peyton Randolph presided. It was voted to call a meeting of all the members of the late House of Burgesses, to take steps for the formation of such a league.

On the 1st of June the Boston Port Bill was to be enforced. The day was observed in Williamsburg and elsewhere as a season of fasting and prayer.[74] All business ceased. Flags were draped in crape, and hung at half-mast. Funeral bells were tolled. Less than three million of people were rising in opposition to the despotism of one of the most powerful empires on the globe. Every thoughtful man must have been pale with apprehension. The odds against the colonies were fearful. The king and his courtiers felt that they had but to close the hand that grasped the throat of the colonies, and inevitable strangulation would ensue. The awful cloud was growing blacker every day. There was no alternative for the Americans, but to bow their necks to the yoke of the cruel taskmaster, and surrender all their liberties, or to engage in a conflict where it would seem

---

[74] Washington's diary testifies that he fasted rigidly, and attended divine worship in the Episcopal Church. He still retained friendly intercourse with the Dunmore family.

that the chances were hundreds to one against them. Issues awful beyond conception were at stake. Solemnity sat on all countenances.

The king of England appointed General Thomas Gage to command the military forces in Massachusetts. The general had said to the king:

> "The Americans will be lions only so long as the English are lambs. Give me five regiments and I will keep Boston quiet."

Gage issued a proclamation denouncing the contemplated league as *traitorous*, and as consequently justly consigning all who should join it, to the scaffold. He ostentatiously encamped a force of artillery and infantry on the Common; and prohibited all public meetings, except the annual town meetings in March and May.

Washington returned to Mount Vernon the latter part of June. He presided at a convention of the inhabitants of Fairfax county, and was appointed chairman of a committee to express the sentiments of the meeting in view of the despotic acts of Parliament. The Fairfaxes, with their large wealth and their intimate associations with the British aristocracy, were exceedingly reluctant to break with the mother country. Bryan Fairfax, a very amiable man, with all of the gentle, and none of the stern attributes of humanity, occupied a beautiful mansion called Tarlston Hall, on an estate near Mount Vernon. He wrote to Washington, disapproving of the strong public measures which were adopted, and urging a petition to the throne. Washington replied:

> "I would heartily join you in your political sentiments, as far as relates to a humble and dutiful petition to the throne, provided there was the most distant hope of success. But have we not tried this already? Have we not addressed the Lords and remonstrated to the Commons? And to what end? Does it not appear clear as the sun in its meridian brightness, that there is a regular, systematical plan to fix the right and practice of taxation upon us?"

Washington, as chairman of the committee, drew up some admirable resolutions in entire accordance with the spirit of liberty which the Americans had thus far advocated. They were very forcibly expressed, and to them the king and Parliament could only reply with bayonets and bullets. The resolutions were promptly adopted, and Washington was chosen a delegate to represent the county at a general convention of the province of Virginia, to be held at Williamsburg, on the 1st of August, 1773.

Washington had strong hopes that the Non-Importation scheme would lead Parliament to a sense of justice, without an appeal to arms.

"I am convinced," he said, "that there is no relief for us but in their distress. And I think, at least I hope, that there is public virtue enough left among us, to deny ourselves everything but the bare necessaries of life to accomplish this."

Some suggested that the Americans should refuse to pay the debts which they owed the English merchants. To this proposition Washington indignantly replied:

> "While we are thus accusing others of injustice we should be just ourselves. And how this can be, while we owe a considerable debt, and refuse payment of it, to Great Britain is, to me, inconceivable. Nothing but the last extremity can justify it."

On the 1st of August the convention, composed of delegates from all parts of Virginia, met at Williamsburg. Washington presented the resolution he had been appointed to draft, in behalf of the citizens of Fairfax county. His feelings were so thoroughly aroused that he advocated them with a speech of remarkable eloquence. All were astonished; for Washington was not an eloquent man, but a man of calm judgment and deliberate speech. In the ardor of the moment, and fully prepared to fulfill his promise to the letter, he said:

"I am ready to raise one thousand men, subsist them at my own expense, and march, at their head, to the relief of Boston."[75]

The convention continued in session six days. George Washington, and six others, of the most illustrious sons of Virginia, were chosen to represent the province in the first colonial Congress. Soon after his return to Mount Vernon he received a letter from Bryan Fairfax, which throws much light upon the character of both of these estimable men. Mr. Fairfax wrote, in reference to the letter which he had previously sent to Washington, and which had not met with approval:

"I am uneasy to find that any one should look upon the letter as repugnant to the principles we are contending for. And therefore, when you have leisure I shall take it as a favor, if you will let me know wherein it was thought so. I beg leave to look upon you as a friend; and it is a great relief to unbosom one's thoughts to a friend. Besides, the information, and the correction of my errors, which I may obtain from a correspondence are great inducements to it. For I am convinced that no man in the colony wishes its prosperity more, would go greater lengths to serve it, or is, at the same time a better subject to the crown. Pray excuse these compliments. They may be tolerable from a friend."[76]

Washington was crowded with public and private affairs. He had no time to enter into a lengthy discussion. But in his brief reply he wrote:

"I can only, in general, add that an innate spirit of freedom first told me that the measures which the administration have for some time been, and now are violently pursuing, are opposed to every principle of natural justice; while much abler heads than my own have fully convinced me that they are not only repugnant to natural right, but subversive of the laws and constitution of Great Britain itself."

---

[75] See information given to the elder Adams, by Mr. Lynch of South Carolina.—*Adams' Diary*.
[76] "Washington's Writings," by Jared Sparks, vol. ii. p. 329.

The spirit of despotism held Boston in its own clutch. The port bill was enforced. No ships entered the harbor; the warehouses were closed; the streets were deserted; the rich were impoverished, and the poor were without employment and without food. A park of artillery was stationed upon the Common. Four large field pieces were planted, to sweep Boston Neck, the only approach to the town by land; a regiment of British regulars was encamped on Fort Hill. Boston bore the aspect of a city in military possession of the enemy. All hearts were moved with indignation, and yet there was a wonderful display of circumspection and sound judgment governing the indomitable courage of the inhabitants.

On the 5th of September, 1774, Congress assembled in a large building called Carpenter's Hall, in Philadelphia. Washington had made the journey there on horseback, from Mount Vernon, in the noble companionship of Patrick Henry and Edmund Pendleton. It was a solemn meeting of as majestic men as ever dwelt on this globe.[77]

All sectional and religious differences were merged in the one great object which absorbed their thoughts and energies. Patrick Henry expressed the common sentiment as, in a speech of eloquence such as has rarely been uttered from human lips, he exclaimed:

> "All America is thrown into one mass. Where are your landmarks, your boundaries of colonies? They are all thrown down. The distinctions between Virginians, Pennsylvanians, New Yorkers, and New Englanders are no more. I *am not a Virginian*, but an American."

Most of these men were imbued with deep religious feeling. Every man, of true grandeur of mind, must be awed by the tremendous mystery of this our earthly being—emerging from the sublime eternity of the past, to this brief, meteoric, tempestuous life, but again to plunge into the profundity of the eternity before us.

---

[77] "It is such an Assembly as never before came together, on a sudden, in any part of the world. Here are fortunes, abilities, learning, eloquence, acuteness, equal to any I ever met with in my life. Here is a diversity of religions, education, manners, interests, such as it would seem impossible to unite in one plan of conduct."—*Diary of John Adams.*

These patriots, moving amid solemnities of infinite moment, and threatened with the ruin of their own country and personal martyrdom, felt the need of the guidance and the aid of God. There were different religious denominations represented. Samuel Adams, one of Massachusetts' noble patriots, a strong Congregationalist, rose and said:

> "I can willingly join with any gentleman, of whatever denomination, who is a friend of his country. Rev. Mr. Duché, of this city, is such a man. I therefore move that he be invited to officiate as chaplain."

Mr. Duché was an eminent Episcopal clergyman. He appeared in his Episcopal robes, and read the impressive morning service, the clerk making the responses. On the 6th of September, a rumor, which afterward proved to be incorrect, reached Congress that the British were cannonading Boston. It so chanced that the Psalter for that day included the following verses from the 35th Psalm:

> "Plead my cause, O Lord, with them that strive with me. Fight against them that fight against me. Take hold of shield and buckler, and stand up for my help. Draw out also the spear, and stop the way of them that persecute me. Say unto my soul, I am thy salvation."

John Adams gave a very vivid description of the scene, in a letter to his wife. He wrote: "You must remember this was the morning after we heard the horrible rumor of the cannonade of Boston. I never saw a greater effect upon an audience. It seemed as if heaven had ordained that psalm to be read, on that morning.

> "After, this Mr. Duché unexpectedly struck out into an extempore prayer, which filled the bosom of every man present. Episcopalian as he is, Dr. Cooper himself never prayed with such fervor, such ardor, such earnestness and pathos, and in language so eloquent and sublime for America, for the Congress, for the province of Massachusetts Bay, and especially for the town of Boston."

Most of the members of Congress stood during this prayer. But it was observed that Washington threw himself upon his knees; and undoubtedly his devout spirit joined fervently in each petition. As the result of this session of Congress, it was resolved to recommend to decline all commercial relations with Great Britain. An address was prepared, to the people of Canada, urging the inhabitants there to make common cause with their brethren of the more southern colonies. A respectful but firm remonstrance was addressed to King George III and a statement of facts was presented to the people of Great Britain.[78]

The Congress remained in session fifty-one days. Patrick Henry, on his return home, was asked whom he considered the greatest man in Congress. He replied:

> "If you speak of eloquence, Mr. Rutlidge, of South Carolina, is by far the greatest orator. But if you speak of solid information, and sound judgment, Colonel Washington is unquestionably the greatest man on that floor."

Washington returned to Mount Vernon. Clouds of sorrow darkened his dwelling, Mrs. Washington was lonely and grief-stricken. Her beautiful, amiable, only daughter, was in the grave. Her only son was absent. Her noble husband had embarked in a cause which menaced him with the scaffold. Their much loved neighbor, George William Fairfax, whose friendship and intimacy had been one of their chief social joys, had left his estate at Belvoir, under the care of an overseer, and had returned to England, to enter upon the possession of large estates which had devolved upon him there. Washington, overwhelmed with immense national solicitudes, found his home enveloped in an atmosphere of loneliness and

---

[78] The illustrious William Pitt, Earl of Chatham, whose espousal, in the House of Lords, of the cause of the colonists has won for him the eternal gratitude of every American, said to the Lords, in Parliament:
"When your lordships look at the papers transmitted to us from America; when you consider their decency, firmness, and wisdom, you cannot but respect their cause, and wish to make it your own. For myself I must declare and avow that, in the master states of the world I know not the people or senate who, in such a complication of difficult circumstances, can stand in preference to the delegates of America assembled in General Congress at Philadelphia."

sadness. Such is human life. Such it has been from the days of the patriarchs:

> "A path it is of joys and griefs, of many hopes and fears,
> Gladdened at times by sunny smiles, but oftener dimmed by tears."

In March, 1774, Washington attended another Virginia Convention, at Richmond. Not one word of conciliation came from the British cabinet; but only insults and defiance, accompanied by acts of increasing outrage.

"It is useless," exclaimed Patrick Henry, "to address further petitions to the British government; or to await the effect of those already addressed to the throne. We must fight. I repeat it, we must fight. An appeal to arms, and to the God of Hosts, is all that is left to us."

Washington expressed full sympathy in these sentiments. He wrote to his brother Augustine, offering to take command of a company he was raising and disciplining. He added, "It is my full intention to devote my life and fortune to the cause."[79]

There were four thousand British troops in Boston. The province had a supply of military stores at Concord, distant about eighteen miles. On the night of the 18th of April, 1775, General Gage sent a detachment of about nine hundred men to capture and destroy the stores. The expedition was organized with the utmost secrecy. Boats, from the men-of-war anchored in the harbor, took the troops, from the foot of the Common, about ten o'clock at night, and carried them across the bay to Lechmere Point in Cambridge. Officers were stationed at all important points to prevent any intelligence of the expedition from being communicated to the people.

But eagle eyes were watching the movement, and couriers, on fleet horses were soon rushing, through the gloom of night, from farm-house to farm-house, with the alarming tidings. The bells in the village steeples sent forth their cry. And, through the night air, the booming of cannon was heard, proclaiming to the startled people that the detested foe was on the war-path.

---

[79] "Washington's Writings," by Jared Sparks, vol. ii. p. 405.

Colonel Smith, who led the British soldiers, was alarmed. He sent back to General Gage for reinforcements. At the same time he pushed Major Pitcairn forward with the advance, to seize the bridges at Concord, lest the Americans might attempt there to oppose his progress. Pitcairn captured every man he met or overtook. When he reached Lexington, about seventy or eighty of the people were huddled together on the green, near the church. They had sprung from their beds, half-dressed; some had guns in their hands, and some were unarmed, mere lookers-on, bewildered by a movement which signified they knew not what.

Pitcairn, splendidly mounted, and at the head of his strong array of British regulars, was approaching on the double-quick. As soon as he caught sight of the feeble band of citizens, he drew his sword, and shouted, with oaths which we need not record:

> "Disperse, you villains. Lay down your arms and disperse." Then turning to his men he added, with still other oaths, "Fire!"[80]

The soldiers were more humane than their commander. It seemed to them like murder, to be shooting these helpless citizens, who could offer no resistance to their march. The soldiers of the first platoon discharged their muskets; but took care to throw the bullets over the heads of those whom they were assailing. One or two muskets were discharged by the Americans as, in consternation, they turned and fled.[81] The British now

---

[80] It has generally been understood, as is stated here, that Major Pitcairn gave these orders. But Mr. Elias Phinney, in his very carefully prepared History of the Battle at Lexington, writes: "The British troops came up shouting, and almost upon the run, till within about ten rods of our line. Their commander, Lieutenant-Colonel Smith, advanced a few yards and exclaimed, 'Lay down your arms and disperse, you damned rebels!—Rush on, my boys. Fire!' The order not being instantly obeyed, he again called out brandishing his sword with great fury, 'Fire! God damn you, fire.' The first platoon then fired over the heads of our men. Colonel Smith repeating his order to fire, a general discharge, from the front ranks, was made directly into the American ranks. On receiving the fire of the first platoon, the Provincials imagined the regulars had fired nothing but powder, and did not offer to return it. But on the second discharge, seeing some of their numbers fall and others wounded, they no longer hesitated as to their right to resist, and some of them immediately returned the fire."—*History of the Battle of Lexington*, by Elias Phinney, p. 20.

[81] It is difficult to find any two narratives of these events which will agree in the minute details. It was a scene of awful confusion, and honest men would differ in the accounts they gave. But there can be no question whatever, that the all-important general facts are as here

opened a deadly fire. Eight of the Americans were killed, and ten wounded. The victorious British held the field. It was between four and five o'clock, of a September morning, and, in its dim light, objects at a distance could be but feebly discerned.

Two only of the British were wounded, one in the leg and one on the hand. In token of their victory the whole body fired a triumphant salute, and gave three cheers. They then marched, unopposed, six miles farther toward Concord. About seven o'clock they entered the town, in two divisions, by different roads. In the meantime many of the stores had been removed, so that the work of destruction, which was promptly commenced, proved not very successful.

By ten o'clock about four hundred armed Americans had assembled, in the vicinity, and the British commenced a retreat. The whole country was now alarmed. The farmers, with their rusty guns and rude accoutrements, were rushing, from all directions, to meet the foe. The highly disciplined regulars, in imposing battle array, but beginning to tremble, pressed along the road on their homeward route. The rustic marksmen, from behind rocks and trees and stumps and sheltering buildings, opened a straggling fire, which every moment seemed to increase in severity and deadliness.

Some of the British soldiers were shot dead; some were severely wounded, and had to be carried along by their comrades; and some dropped down, in utter exhaustion, by the way. While thus retreating, every hour added to their dismay, and the most ignorant soldier could see that they were in imminent danger of being entirely cut off by theirrapidly increasing foes. Their fears had now swollen to a panic.

About nine o'clock in the morning, General Gage had heard of the peril to which his troops were exposed, and he immediately despatched reinforcements, under Lord Percy, to their aid. The British Lord, as he commenced his march ordered his band, in derision of the Americans, to play "Yankee Doodle." His troops consisted of a brigade of a thousand men, with two field-pieces. This force he deemed invincible by any power

---

recorded.—See *History of the Battle of Lexington*, by Elias Phinney, and an admirable account of the expedition by Frederick Hudson in *Harper's Magazine*, vol. 50.

Massachusetts could bring against it. Hilariously he led his veterans over the Neck and through Roxbury, as if on a pleasure excursion.

About noon, to his surprise, he met the British regulars, in utter rout, flying as fast as terror could drive them, before the Massachusetts farmers. He opened his brigade to the right and left to receive the fugitives, and, planting his field-pieces on an eminence, held the Americans at bay.[82] A few moments were allowed for refreshment and repose, when the whole force resumed its humiliating flight. The enraged British soldiers behaved like savages. They set fire to the houses and shops by the way. Women and children were maltreated. The sick and helpless were driven from their flaming dwellings into the fields.

The Americans hotly pursued. They kept up a constant fire, from every available point. The British occasionally made a stand, and sharp skirmishes ensued. Every hour the march of the fugitives became more and more impeded by the number of their wounded. A bullet pierced the leg of Colonel Smith, and he sat upon his horse pallid and bleeding. A musket ball struck a button from the waistcoat of Lord Percy. One of his officers was so severely wounded that he had to be left behind, at West Cambridge. The ammunition of the British was failing them. Companies of the American militia were hurrying to the scene of battle, from Roxbury, Dorchester, and Milton. Colonel Pickering was approaching, with seven hundred of the Essex militia.

About sunset the wretched fugitives reached Charlestown Common, where they found rest under the protection of the guns of the British men-of-war. Gage was astounded at the disaster. The idea had not entered his mind that the unorganized farmers of Massachusetts would dare to meet, in hostile array, soldiers inured to war on the battle-fields of Europe. One of his officers had recently written to London, that the idea of the Americans taking up arms was ridiculous. He said:

---

[82] An eye-witness writes: "When the distressed troops reached the hollow square, formed by the fresh troops for their reception, they were obliged to lie down upon the ground, their tongues hanging out of their mouths like those of the dogs after the chase."

"Whenever it comes to blows the American that can run the fastest will think himself well off, believe me. Any two regiments here ought to be decimated if they did not beat, in the field, the whole force of the Massachusetts province."

Washington wrote: "If the retreat had not been as precipitate as it was—and God knows it could not well have been more so—the ministerial troops must have surrendered or been totally cut off."

In this memorable conflict, which ushered in the awful war of the Revolution, with its appalling catalogue of woes, the British lost, in killed, wounded, and missing, two hundred and seventy-one. Eighteen of their slain were officers. The loss of the Americans was forty-nine killed, thirty-nine wounded, and five missing.[83]

History records many atrocious crimes against the British court and cabinet. But perhaps there is none more unnatural, cruel, and criminal, than for that proud and powerful empire thus to attempt to rivet the chains of despotism upon her own sons and daughters, who were struggling, with the hardships of the wilderness, that they might enjoy civil and religious liberty.

This outrage roused all America. The tidings reached Virginia at a critical moment. Lord Dunmore, in obedience to a ministerial order which the king had sent to all the provincial governors, was then seizing upon the military munitions of the province. It was clear that the entire subjugation of the colonies was to be attempted. Every county in Virginia was crying "To Arms." Nearly all Virginians were looking to Washington to take command of the Virginia troops.

Washington was at Mount Vernon, preparing to leave for Philadelphia, as a delegate to the second Congress. Mr. Bryan Fairfax and Major Horatio Gage chanced to be his guests at that time. Washington wrote to his friend, George William Fairfax, then in England, in the following terms, alike characteristic of his humanity and his firmness:

---

[83] See minute and admirable account by Mr. Frederick Hudson, in *Harper's Magazine*, No. 300.

"Unhappy it is to reflect that a brother's sword has been sheathed in a brother's breast; and that the once happy and peaceful fields of America are either to be drenched with blood or inhabited by slaves. Sad alternative! But can a virtuous man hesitate in his choice."

It was now war. In all directions troops were mustering. A large camp of Americans held the British besieged in Boston. A heroic band, mainly of New Hampshire and Vermont men, under Ethan Allen, surprised and captured, without bloodshed, the old forts of Ticonderoga and Crown Point, where a large supply of military and naval stores was obtained.

The second Congress met, on the 10th of May, 1775. Peyton Randolph, of Virginia, was chosen president. Being obliged soon to return to Virginia, as speaker of the Virginia Assembly, John Hancock, one of the most illustrious sons of Massachusetts, succeeded him in the chair. There was still a lingering attachment for the mother country, which was ever affectionately called *Home*. All wished for reconciliation. Though a "humble and dutiful" petition to the king was moved and carried, many of the members regarded it as entirely futile, and somewhat humiliating. John Adams, of Massachusetts, vigorously opposed it as an imbecile measure.

A federal union was formed, which leagued the colonies together in a military confederacy. Each colony regulated its own internal affairs. The congress of their delegates was vested with the power of making peace or war, and of legislating on all matters which involved the common security. The enlistment of troops was authorized, forts were ordered to be reared and garrisoned, and notes, to the amount of three million dollars, were voted to be issued, on the pledged faith of the Confederacy, and bearing the inscription of "The United Colonies."

Washington was appointed chairman of the committee on military affairs. The infinitely important question agitated all hearts, Who should fill the responsible post of commander-in-chief of the united colonial armies?

General Charles Lee, an Englishman by birth, and a rough soldier, trained amid the rudeness of camps, was a prominent candidate. He was a veteran fighter, and had obtained great renown, for his reckless courage on some of the most bloody fields of European warfare. It does not seem, however, that Lee thought of seeking the office. When informed that his name had been proposed as a candidate, he wrote to Edmund Burke:

> "To think myself qualified for the most important charge that was ever committed to mortal man is the last stage of presumption. Nor do I think that the Americans would, or ought to confide in a man, let his qualifications be ever so great, who has no property among them. It is true I most devoutly wish them success, in the glorious struggle; that I have expressed my wishes both in writing and viva voce. But my errand to Boston was only to see a people in so singular circumstances."

It would seem, from John Adams' diary, that he was the first to propose Washington. There was an army of about ten thousand men encamped around Boston. They were nearly all New Englanders. It seemed a little discourteous to go to Virginia to find a commander. But Mr. Adams rose in his place and, in a few forcible words, proposed that Congress should adopt the army at Cambridge, and appoint George Washington, of Virginia, General-in-Chief.

"The gentleman," he said, "is among us, and is very well known to us all; a gentleman whose skill and experience as an officer, whose independent fortune, great talents, and excellent universal character would command the approbation of all America, and unite the cordial exertions of all the colonies better than any other person in the Union."

On the 15th of May the "Continental Army" was adopted by Congress. The pay of the commander-in-chief was fixed at five hundred dollars a month; and Washington received the unanimous vote, by ballot, for the all-important office. When the vote was formally announced, Washington rose, and in a brief speech, expressive of his high sense of the honor conferred upon him, said:

> "I beg it may be remembered by every gentleman in the room, that I this day declare, with the utmost sincerity, that I do not think myself equal to the command I am honored with. As to pay, I beg leave to assure the Congress that, as no pecuniary consideration could have tempted me

to accept this arduous employment, at the expense of my domestic ease and happiness, I do not wish to make any profit of it. I will keep an exact account of my expenses. Those, I doubt not, they will discharge; and that is all I desire."[84]

---

[84] John Adams wrote to a friend: "There is something charming to me in the conduct of Washington; a gentleman of the first fortunes on the continent, leaving his delicious retirement, his family and friends, sacrificing his ease, and hazarding all in the cause of his country. His views are noble and disinterested. He declared, when he accepted the mighty trust, that he would lay before us an exact account of his expenses, and not accept a shilling pay."

Chapter 7

PROGRESS OF THE WAR

Washington wrote in terms of great tenderness to his afflicted wife, whom he had no time to visit. We find the following expressions in his letter:

"My Dearest: I am now set down to write to you on a subject which fills me with inexpressible concern. And this concern is greatly aggravated and increased when I reflect upon the uneasiness I know it will give you.

"You may believe me, my dear Patty, when I assure you, in the most solemn manner, that, so far from seeking this appointment, I have used every endeavor in my power to avoid it; not only from my unwillingness to part with you and the family, but from a consciousness of its being a trust too great for my capacity. I should enjoy more real happiness in one month with you at home, than I have the most distant prospect of finding abroad, if my stay were to be seven times seven years.

"I shall rely confidently in that Providence which has heretofore preserved and been bountiful to me. I shall feel no pain from the toil or danger of the campaign. My unhappiness will flow from the uneasiness I know you will feel from being left alone. I therefore beg that you will summon your whole fortitude, and pass your time as agreeably as possible. Nothing will give me so much sincere satisfaction as to hear this, and to hear it from your pen."

Washington received his commission on the 20th of June. The next day he left Philadelphia for the army. He was then forty-three years of age, and in perfect health. His commanding stature, thoughtful countenance, and dignified demeanor arrested the attention and won the admiration of every beholder. He sat his horse with ease and grace rarely equalled and never surpassed.

Not quite four weeks before, several ships-of-war and transports, with large reinforcements, had entered Boston Harbor, from England. They brought also the distinguished generals, Burgoyne, Howe, and Clinton. There were, at that time, five thousand British regulars in the city. Ten thousand Americans held them in close siege. As Burgoyne stood upon the deck of his ship, and had the American's camp pointed out to him, he exclaimed, with surprise and scorn:

"What! ten thousand American peasants keep five thousand British shut up! Well, let us get in, and we will soon find elbow room."

Encouraged by these reinforcements, Gage issued a proclamation putting the province under martial law, threatening to punish, with death, as rebels and traitors, all who should continue under arms, but offering pardon to all who would return to their allegiance, excepting John Hancock and Samuel Adams. It was declared that their offences were "too flagitious, not to meet with condign punishment."

The threat exasperated the Americans, and the army was soon increased to about fifteen thousand. It was a motley assemblage of unorganized men under no one leader. There were four distinct and independent bodies. The Massachusetts troops were under General Artemas Ward; General John Stark led the New Hampshire men. The Rhode Islanders were under the command of General Nathaniel Greene. The impetuous and reckless Putnam was at the head of the Connecticut soldiers.

Intelligence, in those days, travelled slowly. On the 17th of June, 1775, the world-renowned battle of Bunker Hill was fought. But no rumor of the conflict had reached Philadelphia when Washington left for Cambridge, three days later. Washington was accompanied by Generals Lee and Schuyler, and a brilliant escort of Philadelphia troops. They had advanced but about twenty miles from the city, when they caught sight, in the distance, of a courier advancing, spurring his horse to his utmost speed. He brought despatches of the battle. Washington inquired, with almost breathless anxiety, into all the particulars. When told that the Americans stood their ground bravely, reserved their fire till they could take deliberate aim, and did not retreat until all their ammunition was expended, he exclaimed, with deep emotion, "The liberties of our country are safe."

We need not here enter into the details of this battle, as it was one in which Washington took no part. A general description of the wonderful event is however needful, that the reader may comprehend the transactions which soon ensued, resulting from it.

The American troops were kept together only by a general feeling of indignation against their oppressors. None of them were acquainted with the discipline of European armies. Most of them were without any uniform, or any soldierly accoutrements. The farmers and their boys had left the plough in the furrow, caught up the musket or the fowling-piece with the powder-horn, and, in their coarse, homespun clothes, without food, and with but the slightest supply of ammunition, had rushed to the field, to combat the veteran soldiers of Great Britain, under leaders who had already obtained renown in many a hard-fought battle.

There was a ridge of quite commanding heights, in the rear of the village of Charlestown, which overlooked the town and the shipping. Two of the most prominent of these eminences were called Bunker's Hill and Breed's Hill. A council of war decided to seize and occupy those heights. It was necessary that the enterprise should be undertaken with the utmost secrecy and caution; for the British men-of-war could open upon the works a deadly cannonade.

It was Friday night, the 16th of June. Just before sunset, about twelve hundred American soldiers, were assembled on Charlestown Common. None but the officers were aware of the expedition which was to be undertaken. President Langdon, of Harvard College, offered prayers. In the fading twilight they commenced their silent march. Though five of the

British ships-of-war were anchored, so as to bear, with their broadsides, upon the peninsula. The troops, in the darkness, and with careful tread, crossed the isthmus unseen.

Bunker Hill and Breed's Hill were so nearly connected as to be almost one. The lines, for the fortifications were marked out on Breed's Hill, and the American farmers, accustomed to the spade, went to work with a will. It was a warm summer night, and the serene, cloudless sky was brilliantly illumined with stars. From the shores of Boston the sentinel's cry of "All's well," floated over the silent waters.

As the day dawned, some sailors, on board one of the ships, espied the rising ramparts. The alarm was given. The ships promptly commenced their fire. Such thunders of war had never before been heard in that peaceful bay. All Boston was roused by the terrific cannonade. But the intrenchments were already so far advanced, as to afford the men protection from the iron storm with which they were assailed.

Gage called a council of war. From these heights, the Americans, should they hold them, could bombard Boston and the shipping. It was deemed necessary to dislodge them, at whatever cost. Twenty-eight large barges were crowded with the best of British troops, in their best equipments. Major-General Howe led them. It was not yet noon-day. The spectacle was sublime, as these veteran soldiers, in their scarlet uniforms, and with the brilliant sun of a June morning reflected from polished muskets and bayonets and brass field-pieces, were rowed across the placid waters in parallel lines.

They landed at Moulton's Point, a little north of Breed's Hill. Immediately every British ship in the harbor, and every battery which could bring its guns to bear upon the American works, opened fire. Not a cannon, not a musket, was discharged in return. Silence, as of the tomb, reigned behind the American intrenchments. The British soldiers, in military array, which they deemed irresistible, and which was truly appalling, commenced the ascent of the hill. The Americans, crouched behind their earthworks, took deliberate aim, and impatiently awaited the order to fire.

When the British were within thirty paces of the Americans there was a simultaneous discharge. The slaughter was awful. Every bullet hit its mark. Still the British troops, with disciplined valor characteristic of the nation, continued to advance notwithstanding an incessant stream of fire, which mowed down whole ranks. But soon the carnage became too deadly to be endured. The whole body broke and rushed precipitately down the hill in utter confusion. Thousand of spectators in Boston crowded the roofs, the heights, the steeples, watching this sublime spectacle with varying emotions. The British soldiers were astonished, and could hardly believe the testimony of their eye-sight, when they beheld the British regulars retreating in confusion before the American militia. But who can describe or imagine the emotions which agitated the bosoms of American wives and daughters, as they gazed upon the surges of the dreadful conflict, where their fathers, husbands, sons, and brothers were struggling in the midst of the awful carnage.

At the bottom of the hill, the troops were again marshalled in line, and, with reinforcements, commenced another ascent of the hill to storm the works. When within pistol-shot another series of volleys, flash following flash, was opened upon them. The ground was instantly covered with the dying and the dead. Again the bleeding, panic-stricken regulars, assailed by such a storm of bullets as they never had encountered before, recoiled and fled. Charlestown was now in flames, and a spectacle of horror was presented, such as even the veterans in European warfare were appalled to contemplate.

The case was becoming desperate. The British general, Burgoyne, was watching the scene, from one of the batteries in Boston, with mingled emotions of astonishment and anxiety. He wrote to a friend in London:

> "Sure I am, nothing ever has or ever can be more dreadfully terrible than what was to be seen or heard at this time. The most incessant discharge of guns that ever was heard by mortal ears; straight before, a large and noble town all in one great blaze, and the church steeples, being timber, were great pyramids of fire; the roar of cannon, mortars, and muskets to fill the ear, the storm of the redoubts to fill the eye; and the reflection that perhaps a defeat was a final loss of the British Empire in

America, to fill the mind, made the whole a picture and a complication of horror and importance, beyond anything that ever came to my lot to witness."[85]

Howe ordered a third attack. Many of the British officers remonstrated, saying that it would be downright butchery. General Clinton, who had been watching the action from Copp's Hill, hurriedly crowded some boats with reinforcements, and crossed the water to aid in a renewal of the battle. Accidentally it was discovered that the ammunition of the Americans was nearly expended. The neck of the peninsula was so swept by the cannonade from the ships, that no fresh supply of powder could be sent to them. Preparations were accordingly made by the British to carry the works by the bayonet.

The soldiers were exceedingly reluctant again to ascend the hill, in the face of the deadly fire which they knew awaited them. They were goaded on by the swords of the officers. Again the Americans reserved their fire till the assailants were within a few feet of the ramparts. A numerous volley of leaden hail fell upon them. Officers and men were alike struck down by wounds and death. General Howe was struck by a bullet on the foot.

But alas! the Americans had fired their last round. Their ammunition was exhausted. The British veterans, with fixed bayonets, rushed over the earthworks. A desperate fight now took place, hand to hand. Stones were hurled. Muskets were clubbed. Men clenched each other in the frenzied, deadly strife. The Americans, greatly outnumbered by their assailants, who had ammunition in abundance, were now compelled to retire. They cut their way through two divisions of the British, who were in their rear to intercept their retreat. As they were slowly retiring, disputing the ground inch by inch, they were assailed by a constant fire from the British. It was here that the patriot Warren fell. A musket ball passed through his head, and he dropped dead upon the spot. The retreating Americans crossed the neck, still exposed to a raging fire from ships and batteries. The bleeding, exhausted foe, did not venture to pursue. The victors took possession of

---

[85] "Soldier and Patriots," by F. W. Owen, p. 93; Irving's *Life of Washington*, vol. i. p. 478.

Bunker Hill, promptly threw up additional intrenchments, and hurried across, from Boston, that they might firmly hold the works.

The British admitted, in their returns of the battle, that out of a detachment of two thousand men they lost, in killed and wounded, one thousand and fifty four. This amounts to the astonishing proportion of more than one-half of the number engaged. The loss of the Americans did not exceed four hundred and fifty. Coolly the historian writes these numbers. Calmly the reader peruses them. But who can imagine the anguish which penetrated these American homes and those distant homes in England, where widows and orphans wept in grief which could not be allayed![86]

The Americans were defeated. But it was a defeat which exercised, over the public mind, the effect of a victory. The British were victors. But Britain admitted, that a few more such victories would bring the British empire in America to a close.

The news of the battle of Bunker Hill swept the land like a whirlwind. Washington was greatly encouraged, as he learned of the heroism with which the Americans had conducted the conflict. As he rapidly advanced, on his journey, escorted by his brilliant cavalcade, the inhabitants of all the towns and villages, on his way, crowded the streets to gaze upon him.

The Americans were exposed to great embarrassments. The governors of nearly all the provinces were Englishmen, and bitterly hostile to the American cause. They had great political power, and also much social influence over the most opulent and aristocratic portions of the community. In all the cities there were large numbers, of the higher classes, whose sympathies were earnestly with the crown of England. Many of these would shrink from no crime to thwart the plans of the Americans. It was therefore needful that Washington should travel with a strong guard.

Governor Tryon, of New York, was intense in his hostility to the "rebels," as he called all the Americans who were opposed to the despotism of Great Britain. He was then in England, but would soon

---

[86] The reader, who is interested in obtaining a more minute detail of the incidents of this momentous battle, will find them quite fully presented, in Mr. Irving's excellent *Life of Washington*.

return, with ships and armies, to hold New York bay, and the Hudson, in subserviency to the British. He might thus cut off all intercourse between the eastern and southern provinces. Anxiously General Washington discussed this matter, as he rode along, with his companions, Generals Lee and Schuyler.[87]

Washington decided to intrust the command of New York to General Schuyler. At Newark, New Jersey, a delegation met Washington to conduct him to the city of New York. They informed him that a ship had just arrived from England and that Governor Tryon, who was on board, was every hour expected to land. How would these antagonistic forces meet, at the same port—the British colonial governor, and the American military commander!

Washington reached the city first. The idea of American Independence of the British crown had not yet been uttered, if even it had occurred to anyone. It was evident that the authority of Congress and the authority of the British Crown would soon meet in conflict. What the result would be, no one could tell. Peter Van Burgh Livingston, president of the New York Assembly, addressing Washington in a very cautious speech of congratulation, said:

> "Confiding in you, sir, and the worthy generals immediately under your command, we have the most flattering hopes of success, in the glorious struggle for American liberty. And we have the fullest assurance that, whenever this important contest shall be decided, by that fondest wish of each American soul, *an accommodation with our mother country*, you will cheerfully resign the important deposit committed into your hands, and reassume the character of our worthiest citizen."

Washington, in entire harmony with these views, replied, "As to the fatal but necessary operations of war, when we assumed the soldier we did not lay aside the citizen. And we shall most sincerely rejoice, with you, in

---

[87] General Schuyler was a native-born American, descended from one of the most illustrious families. He had a large estate, near Saratoga, and was highly educated, particularly in all branches relating to military science. He was a tried patriot. In Congress and elsewhere he had proved himself the able and eloquent advocate of American rights. See Irving's *Life of Washington*, vol. i. (Mount Vernon Edition) p. 158.

that happy hour, when the establishment of American liberty, on the most firm and solid foundation, shall enable us to return to our private stations, in the bosom of a free, peaceful, and happy country."

Washington reached the city of New York about noon. Governor Tryon landed about eight o'clock in the evening. He was received with military honors, and by great demonstrations of loyalty by those devoted to the crown. The Mayor and Common Council received him respectfully. Any demonstrations of hostility would have been insane. A large British ship-of-war, Aria, then was at anchor opposite the city, ready, at any signal, with its terrible batteries, to open fire, which would inevitably lay every building in ashes. It was also rumored that a large British force was on the passage from England.

Washington pressed rapidly on toward the army in Cambridge. As he left General Schuyler behind, narrowly to watch the progress of affairs, he said to him:

> "If forcible measures are judged necessary respecting the Governor, I should have no difficulty in ordering them, if the Continental Congress were not sitting. But as that is the case, and the *seizing of a governor* quite a new thing. I must refer you to that body for direction."

Washington left New York on the 26th. General Lee accompanied him. He was escorted as far as Kingsbridge by several companies of militia, and a squadron of Philadelphia light horse. The Massachusetts Assembly was in session at Watertown. They were making vigorous preparations for the reception of the Commander-in-Chief. The residence of the president of the Provincial Congress, at Cambridge, was fitted up for his head-quarters.[88] As Washington pressed on his way, he was escorted from town to town by volunteer companies and cavalcades of gentlemen.

---

[88] The house stood on the Watertown road, about half a mile from the college. It subsequently was long known as the Cragie House. "The Cragie House is associated with American literature, through some of its subsequent occupants. Mr. Edward Everett resided in it the first year or two after his marriage. Later, Mr. Jared Sparks, during part of the time that he was preparing his collection of Washington's writings, editing a volume or two in the very room from which they were written. Next came Mr. Worcester, author of the pugnacious dictionary, and of many excellent books. And lastly, Longfellow, the poet, who purchased

On the 2d of July he reached Watertown, where he was greeted with the warmest congratulations, while, at the same time, he was told that he had come to take command of fragmentary bands of soldiers, poorly equipped, entirely unorganized, and quite ignorant of military discipline. It was three miles to the central camp in Cambridge.

Washington rode over, escorted by a troop of light horse and a cavalcade of citizens. His fame had preceded him. Officers, soldiers, and citizens were alike eager to see the man, in whose hands the destinies of our country seemed to be placed. No one was disappointed. Mrs. John Adams, one of the noblest of the patriotic women of America, witnessed the scene. She wrote to her husband, who had nominated him for this important post:

> "Dignity, ease, and complacency, the gentleman and the soldier, look agreeably blended in him. Modesty marks every line and feature of his face. These lines of Dryden instantly occurred to me.
>
> "'Mark his majestic fabric! He's a temple
> Sacred by birth, and built by hands divine;
> His soul's the deity that lodges there;
> Nor is the pile unworthy of the God.'"

Washington was fully awake to the fearful responsibilities now devolving upon him. General Gage held his head-quarters in Boston, sustained by a squadron of light horse and several companies of infantry and artillery. The bulk of his army had taken its stand on Bunker's Hill, where the troops were busy in strengthening their works, so as to render the position impregnable. Another strong party was on the neck of land between Boston and Roxbury. A deep intrenchment ran across the neck, which was bristling with cannon, and with the bayonets of the regular troops who guarded all the approaches. A fleet of British war ships was in the harbor.

---

the house of the heirs of Mr. Cragie, and refitted it."—Irving's *Life of Washington*, Mount Vernon Edition, vol. i. p. 167.

The American lines extended entirely around Boston and Charleston, from Mystic River to Dorchester. The distance was about twelve miles. Plain farmers, many of them in their working attire, had seized their muskets, and, in the month of June so important to all their agricultural interests, had abandoned their fields to engage in the revolting employments of war. They were gathering from Massachusetts, Connecticut, Rhode Island, and New Hampshire. From the far-away banks of the Potomac George Washington had come, to place himself at the head of the sons of New England, struggling in the defence of the dearest of all earthly rights.

On the morning of the 3d of July Washington took formal command of the army. It was a solemn hour. There was no boasting; no exultation. The troops were drawn up, upon Cambridge Common. An immense crowd of spectators had assembled from the country all around. Washington, as he rode upon the ground, was accompanied by General Lee and a numerous suite. He took his stand under the shade of a venerable elm, probably one of the primeval forest when he reviewed those heroic men, who had no love for war, whose hearts were yearning for their peaceful homes, but who were ready to sacrifice life itself rather than surrender their infant country to the despotism of its ruthless oppressor.

The British army in Boston amounted to eleven thousand five hundred men. They were in the highest state of discipline, under able and experienced generals, and abundantly supplied with all the best arms, ammunition, and material of war which Europe could afford. Washington had under his command, fit for duty, only fourteen thousand five hundred men, with no general organization, no supply of stores or clothing, no military chest, and but wretchedly supplied with arms and ammunition.[89] It is one of the marvels of history that this motley assembly of farmers and mechanics was not swept away, before the British regulars, like withered leaves before autumnal gales.

Washington convened a council of war. It was promptly decided, without a dissenting voice, that at the least twenty-two thousand men were

---

[89] Sparks' *Life of Washington*, p. 136.

needed, to hold the posts which the Americans then occupied. And those posts must be held, or British marauders would range the country, plundering villages and farm-houses.

Washington was appalled to find that there was not powder enough in the whole camp to supply nine cartridges to a man. Had the British known this, they might have marched from their intrenchments in Roxbury and Charlestown, and have utterly annihilated the American army, leaving not a vestige behind.

Washington rode to various eminences, from which he carefully reconnoitered the British posts. His military eye revealed to him the skill with which everything was conducted by his powerful foe. Of the troops under Washington's command, nine thousand were from Massachusetts. The remainder were from the other New England colonies. The encampment of the Rhode Island troops attracted the eye of Washington and won his admiration. General Nathaniel Greene led them. His soldiers were admirably drilled. Order and discipline prevailed, under his rule, unsurpassed in any of the British camps.[90]

The troops, in general, were destitute of suitable clothing. And there was no money in the military chest. A British soldier could be instantly recognized, by his brilliant scarlet costume. Washington showed his knowledge of human nature, by judging that any uniform, however simple in its nature, which at once revealed the American patriot, would prove a strong bond of union with the troops. He wrote to Congress, urging that ten thousand hunting shirts should be immediately sent to the army, as the cheapest dress which could be promptly furnished.

It is a little remarkable that the Massachusetts troops were the most destitute of all. The fact, as expressed by Washington, proved highly honorable to that heroic State. He wrote:

---

[90] "General Green was a son of Rhode Island, of Quaker parentage. He was a man of fine personal appearance, of excellent character, and of superior natural abilities. His thirst for knowledge led him to avail himself of every opportunity for mental improvement. He thus became an intelligent gentleman. His troops were pronounced to be the best disciplined and the best appointed in the army. He stepped at once into confidence of the Commander-in-Chief, which he never forfeited, but became one of his most attached, faithful, and efficient coadjutors."—*Soldiers and Patriots*, p. 96.

"This unhappy and devoted province has been so long in a state of anarchy, and the yoke has been laid so heavily on it, that great allowances are to be made, for troops raised under such circumstances. The deficiency of numbers, discipline, and stores can only lead to this conclusion, that *their spirit has exceeded their strength*."

The religious spirit which animated many of these patriots may be inferred from the following extract from a letter, written to General Washington at this time, by Governor Trumbull of Connecticut. "May the God of the armies of Israel shower down the blessings of divine providence on you; give you wisdom and fortitude; cover your head in the day of battle and danger; add success; convince our enemies of their mistaken measures, and that all their attempts to deprive these colonies of their inestimable constitutional rights and liberties are injurious and vain."

It was necessary for Washington, as Commander-in-Chief, to maintain considerable state. Every day some of his officers dined with him. Though naturally very social, his mind was so entirely engrossed by the vast responsibilities which rested upon him, that he had no time to devote to those social indulgences of the table of which many are so fond. He was extremely simple in his diet. Often his dinner consisted of a bowl of baked apples and milk. Having finished his frugal repast, he early excused himself from the table, leaving some one of his officers to preside in his stead.

His first aide-de-camp was Colonel Mifflin, a very accomplished gentleman from Philadelphia. His second was John Trumbull, who afterward obtained much renown as an historical painter. His noble father, Jonathan Trumbull, Governor of Connecticut, was one of Washington's most efficient cooperators. He was the only one of the colonial governors, appointed by the crown, who, at the commencement of the revolution, proved true to the cause of the Americans.[91] Colonel John Trumbull, in allusion to his appointment, wrote:

---

[91] Irving's *Life of Washington*, Mount Vernon Edition, vol. i. p. 166.

"I now suddenly found myself in the family of one of the most distinguished and dignified men of the age; surrounded, at his table, by the principal officers of the army, and in constant intercourse with them. It was further my duty to receive company, and to do the honors of the house to many of the first people of the country, of both sexes."

Mr. Joseph Reed, of Philadelphia, accepted the post of secretary to the Commander-in-Chief. He was a lawyer of high repute, having studied in America, and at the Temple, in London. His practice was extensive and lucrative; and his rank, culture, and refined manners rendered him a favorite in the highest circles in Philadelphia, where he was in intimate association with the families of British officers and other strong adherents of the crown.

Many of his friends considered it the height of infatuation that he, at thirty-five years of age, should abandon his young wife, his happy home, and his profession, in which he was rapidly accumulating wealth, for the hardships and perils of the Revolutionary Camp. To their remonstrances he replied:

"I have no inclination to be hanged for half-treason. When a subject draws his sword against his prince, he must cut his way through, if he means to sit down in safety. I have taken too active a part in what may be called the civil part of opposition, to renounce, without disgrace, the public cause, when it seems to lead to danger; and I have the most sovereign contempt for the man who can plan measures he has not the spirit to execute."

Washington, in the terrible hours which he was to encounter, needed a bosom friend, who could be in true sympathy with him, and to whom he could confide all his solicitudes. Such a friend, intelligent, courageous, warm-hearted, polished in manners, of pure life and pure lips, he found in Joseph Reed. Lee, Putnam, and Gates[92] were very efficient army officers,

---

[92] "Horatio Gates was an Englishman who adopted the cause of America. He had distinguished himself in the West Indies. But England did not recognize his claims, as much as he thought she ought to have done. He therefore went out to America and bought land in Virginia.

but they were not congenial heart-companions for Washington. The fearless, energetic Connecticut general was very popular with the soldiers. He was invariably called "Old Put." That nick-name alone sufficiently reveals his character. Washington highly prized his services. Whatever works he undertook were pushed forward with wonderful energy. Washington one day said to him:

> "You seem, General, to have the faculty of infusing your own spirit into all the workmen you employ."

The arrival of Washington infused astonishing energy into the army. His engineering skill enabled him to select the most important strategic points of defence. Every man was at work, from morning till night. All Cambridge and Charlestown were covered with camps, forts, and intrenchments. The line of circumvallation was so extended, that it soon became quite impossible for the British to cut their way through.

There were three grand divisions of the army. The right wing was stationed on the heights of Roxbury. The left wing was on Winter and Prospect Hill. The centre was at Cambridge. Fleet horses were kept at several points, ready saddled, to convey instant intelligence of any movement of the British. Washington was every day traversing these lines, and superintending all the works.

Each regiment was summoned every morning, to attend prayers. A day was appointed, by Congress, of fasting and prayer, to obtain the favor of Heaven. Washington enforced the strict observance of the day. All labor was suspended. Officers and soldiers were required to attend divine service. But they were all armed and equipped, ready for immediate action.[93]

Great commotion was excited, in the camp, one morning, when fourteen hundred sharpshooters came marching upon the ground, from

---

When the war began, he seemed to see in it a more secure means to self-advancement than he had found before, and therefore he joined in it."—*Soldier and Patriot*, p. 95.

[93] "Lee, we are told, scoffed with his usual profaneness. Heaven, he said, was ever found favorable to strong battalions. Lee was an Englishman by birth. The Indians called him, from his impetuosity, *Boiling Water*."—*Graydon's Memoirs*, p. 138.

Pennsylvania, Maryland, and Virginia. They were all tall men, and made a very imposing appearance, in their picturesque costume, of fringed hunting shirts and round hats. It was said that, while on the rapid march, these men could hit a mark seven inches in diameter, at the distance of two hundred and sixty yards.[94]

The British were in entire command of the sea. They were continually landing, from their ships, at unprotected points, and inflicting a vast amount of injury. It was impossible to prevent this. The ocean was, to these foes, what the forest had been to the savage. One or two ships would suddenly appear, send an armed party on shore in their boats, plunder, burn, and kill at their pleasure, and long before any military force could be assembled to resist them, their marauding fleet would have disappeared beyond the horizon of the sea.

Washington had soon cut off all possible communication between the British, in Boston, and the back country. He ordered all the livestock, on the coast, to be driven into the interior, beyond the reach of plundering parties from the men-of-war's boats. Famine began to prevail in Boston. But the position of the American army was still perilous in the highest degree. They were, notwithstanding Washington's most intense endeavor, almost without ammunition. The supply was reduced, as we have said, to nine cartridges to a man. And thus for a fortnight they boldly faced the well-supplied armies of Great Britain. At length a partial supply from New Jersey put an end to this fearful risk.

General Gage was treating his American prisoner as outlaws, throwing them indiscriminately into common jails, and treating them with the utmost barbarity. Washington was personally acquainted with Gage. He had led the advance-guard in Braddock's defeat. Washington wrote to him, in respectful but earnest terms, remonstrating against this inhumanity, and stating that, if it were continued, he should be under the very painful necessity of retaliating.

Gates returned a defiant and insolent reply, in which he spoke of the American patriots as rebels who, by the laws of England, were "destined to

---

[94] Thatcher's "Military Journal," p. 37.

the cord, and that he acknowledged no rank which was not derived from the king."[95]

Washington restrained his indignation, and again wrote to his unmannerly foe, in the courteous language of a gentleman. In this admirable letter he said:

> "I addressed you, sir, on the 11th instant, in terms which gave the fairest scope for that humanity and politeness which were supposed to form a part of your character.
>
> "Not only your officers and soldiers have been treated with the tenderness due to fellow-citizens, but even those execrable parricides, whose counsels and aid have deluged their country with blood, have been protected from the fury of a justly enraged people.
>
> "You affect, sir, to despise all rank not derived from the same source with your own. I cannot conceive one more honorable than that which flows from the uncorrupted choice of a brave and free people, the purest source and original fountain of all power.
>
> "I shall now, sir, close my correspondence with you, perhaps forever. If your officers, our prisoners, receive a treatment from me different from that I wish to show them, they and you will remember the occasion of it."[96]

In conformity with these views Washington issued orders that the British officers who were at large on parole, should be confined in Northampton jail. But his humane heart recoiled from punishing the innocent for the crimes of the guilty. The order was revoked, and they remained at large, as before.[97]

---

[95] "These principles set at naught all the rules of honorable warfare; and indicated that the highest officers in the American army, if captured, would be treated as culprits."—Sparks' *Life of Washington*, p. 142.
[96] See this correspondence, more fully given in Irving's *Life of Washington*, vol. i. Mount Vernon edition, p. 172, 173.
[97] "The order was countermanded while the prisoners were on the road to Northampton. 'The General further requests,' wrote his secretary Colonel Reed, 'that every other indulgence, consistent with their security, may be shown to them. The general does not doubt that your conduct toward them will be such as to compel their grateful acknowledgments that Americans are as merciful as they are brave.'"—Sparks' *Life of Washington*, p. 142.

Ethan Allen and Benedict Arnold urged very strenuously upon Congress the importance of an expedition for the conquest of Canada. There were about seven hundred British regulars occupying different posts in that province. The Indians generally loved the French. But they hated the English, who had always treated them with contempt, which they keenly felt. Many of these chiefs were now eager to join the Americans against the English, though the rich government of Great Britain could offer them far higher bribes. A delegation of the highest chiefs, from several of the important tribes on the St. Lawrence, visited Washington at Cambridge. They were received with those tokens of respect which their rank, character, and mission demanded.

Washington invited them all to dine with him and his leading officers. It was remarked that in dignity of demeanor and propriety of deportment they conducted themselves like men who from infancy had been accustomed to the usages of good society. A council was held. The chiefs offered, in behalf of their several tribes, to cooperate in any movement for the invasion of Canada.

It was an embarrassing offer. Congress had voted not to enter into any alliance with the Indians unless the British should call the savages to their aid. But the chief of the St. Francis Indians declared that Colonel Guy Carleton, who commanded the British forces in Canada, had offered them large rewards if they would take up arms against the Americans. An express was sent to General Schuyler at Albany, to ascertain whether the British were endeavoring to enlist the Indians on their side. It so happened that General Schuyler was then attending a conference of the chiefs of the Six Nations. He declared that there was no question whatever that General Carleton and his agents were attempting to rouse the Indian tribes.

It was decided that while General Schuyler should conduct troops, by the way of Ticonderoga upon Montreal, General Arnold should lead an expedition, of about twelve hundred men, up the valley of the Kennebec, in Maine, to make an assault upon Quebec.

Chapter 8

THE SIEGE OF BOSTON

Several weeks passed away, while Washington vigorously prosecuted the siege of the British troops in Boston. Having strengthened his intrenchments, and obtained a sufficient supply of ammunition, he was quite desirous of inciting them to make an attack upon his lines. A rumor reached him, the latter part of August, that General Gage, annoyed by the scarcity of provisions, was preparing for a sortie, in great strength. Washington endeavored to provoke the movement by offering a sort of challenge.

He accordingly, one night detached fourteen hundred men, to seize upon an eminence within musket shot of an important part of the British lines upon Charleston Neck. He hoped that the enemy, upon discovering the movement, would immediately advance to drive them back; and that thus a general engagement might be brought on.

The task was executed with great secrecy and skill. With the earliest dawn, the British, to their great surprise, saw the eminence crowned with quite formidable ramparts. But Gage had learned a lesson at Bunker Hill. He knew Washington, and was well aware that he was a foe to be feared. The proud Englishman did not venture to accept the challenge. It must have been to him a great humiliation. He kept his troops carefully sheltered behind their works, and contented himself with a bombardment, from his heavy guns, which did but little injury. The Americans completed and held possession of this advanced post.

Figure 3. House Where Lee Was Captured.

Washington found it difficult to account for the fact that the British officers, at the head of their large and well-appointed troops, allowed themselves to be hedged in by undisciplined bands of American farmers, of whose military prowess they had loudly proclaimed their contempt. He wrote:

> "Unless the ministerial troops in Boston are waiting for reinforcements, I cannot devise what they are staying there for, nor why, as they affect to despise the Americans, they do not come forth and put an end to the conflict at once."

It is probable that Gates imagined that Washington's troops, composed of men who loved their homes, and who, as he knew, had enlisted only till the 1st of January, would, as soon as the snows and storms of winter came, disperse. He could then, with his fresh troops, sweep the province of Massachusetts at his will.[98]

The country could not understand the reason for the apparent inactivity of the American army. Washington was very desirous for a battle. But a decisive defeat would prove the entire ruin of the national hopes. Still some active movement seemed essential to reanimate the people. After revolving the circumstances in his mind very carefully, he summoned a council of war, and proposed that a simultaneous attack should be made upon the enemy in Boston, by crossing the water in boats, and, at the same time, impetuously assailing their lines on the Neck. This was indeed a very bold measure. Washington must have had great confidence in his men, to advance, with inexperienced militia, against British regulars behind their ramparts. But it is very certain that he had weighed all the chances, and that he had made every possible preparation to guard against a decisive disaster.

"The success of such an enterprise," he said, "depends, I well know, upon the all-wise Disposer of events; and it is not within the reach of human wisdom to foretell the issue. But if the prospect is fair the undertaking is justifiable."

The council was held on the 11th of September. Eight generals were present. They unanimously decided that the project was too hazardous to be undertaken, at least for the present.[99] Washington now turned his attention to the expedition into Canada. Eleven hundred men were detached, for the purpose, and encamped on Cambridge Common. Aaron Burr, then a brilliant young man of twenty years, volunteered for the service. Thus he entered upon his varied, guilty, and melancholy career.

---

[98] "In fact they (the British) never meditated an attack, unless reinforcements should arrive. General Gage wrote to Lord Dartmouth, that such an attempt, if successful, would be fruitless, as there were neither horses nor carriages for transportation, and no other end could be answered than to drive the Americans from one stronghold to another."—Sparks' *Life of Washington*, p. 146.

[99] "The enterprise," Washington wrote, "was thought too dangerous. Perhaps it was. Perhaps the irksomeness of my situation led me to undertake more than could be warranted by prudence. I did not think so. And I am sure yet that the enterprise, if it had been undertaken with resolution, must have succeeded. Without it, any would fail."—Sparks' *Life of Washington*, p. 160.

Benedict Arnold, whose reputation for valor was established, was intrusted with the command. The instructions which Washington gave are characteristic of that noblest of men. The following extracts will show their spirit:

> "I charge you, and the officers and soldiers under your command, as you value your own safety and honor and the favor and esteem of your country, that you consider yourselves as marching, not through the country of an enemy, but of our friends and brethren; for such the inhabitants of Canada and the Indian nations have approved themselves, in this unhappy contest between Great Britain and America; and that you check, by every motive and fear of punishment, every attempt to plunder or insult the inhabitants of Canada.
>
> "Should an American soldier be so base and infamous as to injure any Canadian or Indian, in his person or property, I do most earnestly enjoin you to bring him to such severe and exemplary punishment as the enormity of the crime may require. Should it extend to death itself, it will not be disproportioned to its guilt, at such a time and in such a cause.
>
> "I also give in charge to you, to avoid all disrespect to the religion of the country and its ceremonies. While we are contending for our own liberty, we should be very cautious not to violate the rights of conscience in others; ever considering that God alone is the judge of the hearts of men, and to Him only, in this case, are they answerable.[100]
>
> "If Lord Chatham's son should be in Canada, and, in any way, fall into your power, you are enjoined to treat him with all possible deference and respect. You cannot err in paying too much honor to the son of so illustrious a character and so true a friend to America."

On the 13th of September, Arnold struck his tents and commenced his long march through the almost unbroken wilderness. We have not space here to detail the sufferings and romantic incidents of this unsuccessful expedition. Though wisely planned, and energetically executed, untoward circumstances, which could not have been foreseen, prevented its success.

---

[100] As Canada was originally settled by the French, the Roman Catholic religion almost universally prevailed there.

The conduct of Arnold was approved by Washington and applauded by the country generally.[101]

The time was rapidly approaching when the Americans must enlist a new army. The Connecticut and Rhode Island troops were engaged to serve only till the month of December. None were enlisted beyond the 1st of January. Thus Washington would find himself entirely without troops, unless new levies could be raised. The British, in Boston, cut off from supplies by land, were fitting out small armed vessels to ravage the coasts. Newport, Rhode Island, was the rendezvous of a strong fleet of the enemy. Stonington was cannonaded. There was everywhere distress and consternation. The British treated the Americans as if they were criminals beyond the reach of mercy.

To check these marauding expeditions, Massachusetts, Rhode Island, and Connecticut, each fitted out two armed vessels. They cruised along the whole coast of New England, to the waters of the St. Lawrence. Portland, then called Falmouth, was one of the most heroic of the New England seaports. Its sturdy inhabitants, by their proclaimed patriotism, had become especially obnoxious to the enemy. Several armed vessels were sent to lay the defenceless town in ashes. Two hours were given to remove the sick and the infirm. Lieutenant Mount, in command of this cruel expedition, entirely unauthorized by the rules of civilized warfare, announced that he was instructed to burn down every town between Boston and Halifax, and that New York, he supposed, was already destroyed.[102]

The terrific bombardment was commenced about half-past nine o'clock, on the morning of the 12th of October. One hundred and twenty-

---

[101] General Schuyler wrote to Washington, "I wish I had no occasion to send my dear general this melancholy account. My amiable friend, the gallant Montgomery, is no more. The brave Arnold is wounded; and we have met with a severe check in our attack upon Quebec. May Heaven be graciously pleased that this misfortune terminate here. I tremble for our people in Canada."

[102] "The British ministry have, in latter days, been exculpated from the charge of issuing such a desolating order as that said to have been reported by Lieutenant Mount. The orders, under which that officer acted, we are told, emanated from General Gage and Admiral Graves."—Irving's *Life of Washington*, vol. i. p. 188.

nine dwelling-houses, and two hundred and twenty-eight stores, were burned.[103] In view of this barbarism Washington wrote:

> "The desolation and misery, which ministerial vengeance had planned, in contempt of every principle of humanity, and so lately brought on the town of Falmouth, I know not how sufficiently to commiserate; nor can my compassion for the general suffering be conceived beyond the true measure of my feelings."

General Greene wrote, "O, could the Congress behold the distress and wretched condition of the poor inhabitants, driven from the seaport towns, it must, it would, kindle a blaze of indignation against the commissioned pirates and licensed robbers. People begin heartily to wish a declaration of independence."

Though a hundred years have passed away since these deeds of wanton and demoniac cruelty, the remembrance of them does now, and will forever excite the emotion of every human heart against the perpetrators of such crimes. The families of every town on the coast were in terror. Mothers and maidens, pale and trembling, feared every morning that, before night, they might hear the bombardment of those dreadful guns.

And these were the crimes which the government of Great Britain was committing, that it might compel the Americans to submit to any tax which Great Britain might impose upon them. There was no mystery about this war. "Submit yourselves to us to be taxed as we please," said England. "If you do not we will, with our invincible armies, sweep your whole country with fire and blood."

At Portsmouth, which was daily menaced, there was a fortification of some strength. Washington sent General Sullivan there to assist the inhabitants in their defence. Washington wrote:

> "I expect every hour to hear that Newport has shared the same fate of unhappy Falmouth."[104]

---

[103] *Holmes' Annals*, vol. ii. p. 220.
[104] "American Archives," vol. iii. p. 1145.

Gage was recalled by the British government. The battle of Bunker Hill and the siege of their troops, in Boston, mortified the English.[105] A committee of Congress visited Cambridge to confer with Washington. The British in Boston could be bombarded, but not without danger of laying the city in ashes. After several conferences, reaching through four days, it was decided that an attack upon Boston would be inexpedient. Congress had, however, voted to raise a new army, of a little over twenty-two thousand men, for one year. Mr. Reed, Washington's highly valued and beloved secretary, found that his private concerns demanded his return to Philadelphia.

General Howe succeeded General Gage in Boston. He was instructed, by his government, that he was commissioned to quell the rebellion of traitors, who merited the scaffold. In accordance with these principles he conducted the war. Great contempt was manifested by the British officers, for every form of religion, excepting that of the church of England. The Old South Church was converted into a riding school, for Burgoyne's light dragoons. The North Church was torn down, for fuel. Howe denounced the penalty of death upon any one who should attempt to leave Boston without his permission. The inhabitants were commanded to arm themselves, under British officers, to maintain order.

Throughout the country the tories were becoming more and more defiant, and open in their opposition to the American cause. The ice of winter would soon so bridge the bays, that the British troops, in Boston, could, unimpeded, march from their warm barracks, to assail any portion of the extended American lines. The annoyances of Washington were indescribable. It was very difficult to find men ready to enlist. The sentiment of patriotism, as it glowed in the bosom of George Washington, was a very different emotion from that which glimmered in the heart of the poor, obscure farmer's boy, who was to peril life and limb upon the field of battle, and who, if he fell, would soon be as entirely forgotten as would be the cart-horse he might be driving.

---

[105] "Poor Gage is to be the scapegoat, for what was a reason against employing him—incapacity."—*Horace Walpole.*

Amid these scenes of toil, trouble, and grief, the American schooner Lee, under Captain Manly, which had been sent out by Washington, entered Cape Ann. It had captured a large and richly freighted English brigantine. Indescribable was the joy, when a large and lumbering train of wagons, in apparently an interminable line, came rumbling into the camp of Cambridge. The wagons were decorated with flags, and bore a vast quantity of ordnance and military stores.

There were two thousand stand of arms, one hundred thousand flints, thirty thousand round shot, and thirty-two tons of musket balls. Among the ordnance there was a huge brass mortar, of a new construction. It weighed three thousand pounds. The army gazed upon it with admiration. Putnam christened it. Mounting the gun, he dashed a bottle of rum upon it, and shouted its new name of Congress. The cheers which rose were heard in Boston, and excited much curiosity there to learn what could be the occasion for such rejoicing in the American camp.

Soon after this Washington learned that Colonel Ethan Allen had been captured near Montreal, and had been thrown, by the British General Prescott, into prison fettered with irons. He could not have been treated more brutally had he been the worst of criminals.

Washington immediately wrote a letter of remonstrance to General Howe. In this letter he said:

> "I must take the liberty of informing you that whatever treatment Colonel Allen receives, whatever fate he undergoes, such exactly shall be the treatment and fate of Brigadier Prescott, now in our hands. The law of retaliation is not only justifiable in the eyes of God and man, but is absolutely a duty, in our present circumstances, we owe to our relations, friends, and fellow-citizens.
>
> "Permit me to add, sir, that we have all the highest regard and reverence for your great personal qualities and attainments; and the Americans in general esteem it as not the least of their misfortunes, that the name of Howe, a name so dear to them, should appear at the head of

the catalogue of the instruments employed by a wicked ministry for their destruction."[106]

Nothing can show more impressively the arrogant air assumed by these haughty British officers, than Howe's reply to this letter. Having curtly stated that he had nothing to do with affairs in Canada he wrote:

> "It is with regret, considering the character you have always maintained among your friends as a gentleman, that I find cause to resent a sentence, in the conclusion of your letter, big with invectives against my superiors and insulting to myself, which should obstruct any farther intercourse between us."

The humane Americans could not carry out their threat. Prescott was taken to Philadelphia, and thrown into jail, though not put in irons. As his health seemed to be failing he was released on his parole. Thomas Walker, a merchant of Montreal, wished to ascertain how he was situated.

> "To his great surprise he found Mr. Prescott lodged in the best tavern of the place; walking or riding at large through Philadelphia and Bucks counties, feasting with gentlemen of the first rank in the province, and keeping a levee for the reception of the grandees."[107]

Colonel Allen was held in close confinement and chains, until finally he was exchanged for a British officer. Washington was indefatigable in strengthening his old posts, and seizing new ones which would command portions of the enemy's lines. General Putnam was exceedingly officious in these operations. The labors of the soldiers, in throwing up these

---

[106] William Howe was a man of fine presence and of winning manners. He was brother of Lord Howe, who fell on the banks of Lake George, in the French war. He was one of the most attractive of young men, and had secured, to a wonderful degree, the affection of the American people. A sorrowful feeling pervaded the country when it found that General William Howe was fighting against the Americans at the battle of Bunker's Hill. In an address from Congress to the people of Ireland it was said, "America is amazed to find the name of Howe on the catalogue of her enemies. She loved his brother."

[107] "American Archives," 4th series, vol. iv. p. 1178.

redoubts, were often carried on under a continual cannonade from the British ships.

The British became much alarmed. A battery was raised on Phipps farm, where the great mortar, the Congress, was mounted. A British officer wrote:

> "If the rebels can complete their battery, this town will be on fire about our ears a few hours after; all our buildings being of wood or a mixture of wood and brick-work. Had the rebels erected their battery on the other side of the town, at Dorchester, the admiral and all his booms would have made the first blaze, and the burning of the town would have followed.[108] If we cannot destroy the rebel battery by our guns, we must march out and take it sword in hand."

One very great embarrassment was the want of powder. Washington found it necessary often, to submit to a severe cannonading from the foe, without returning the fire. Prudence required that the small amount of powder the Americans had, should be reserved to repel direct attacks. The winter fortunately proved to be one of unusual mildness. One of the Americans officers wrote:

> "Everything thaws here except old Put. He is still as hard as ever, crying out for powder, powder, powder; ye gods, give us powder."

There was great suffering in Virginia. The British governor, Lord Dunmore, held the province under military rule. Many feared that he would send a detachment and lay Mount Vernon in ashes. Lady Washington was advised to seek a retreat beyond the Blue Ridge. But the armed patriots were on the alert. Washington had left the management of the large estate under the care of Mr. Lund Washington, in whose integrity and ability he had entire confidence.

---

[108] From the heights of Dorchester the admiral's fleet, riding at anchor in the harbor, could be bombarded, and destroyed. Then the British army might be captured. But this would probably be at the expense of laying the whole town in ashes. Lord Admiral Howe was brother of Sir William.

To his agent Washington wrote, "Let the hospitality of the house, with respect to the poor, be kept up. Let no one go hungry away. If any of this kind of people should be in want of corn, supply their necessities, provided it does not encourage them to idleness. And I have no objection to your giving my money in charity, to the amount of forty or fifty pounds a year, when you think it well bestowed. What I mean by having no objections is, that it is my desire that it should be done. You are to consider that neither myself nor wife is now in the way to do these good offices."[109]

Mrs. Washington was very lonely, very anxious, very sad. By invitation of her husband she visited him at Cambridge. Her son accompanied her, and she travelled with her own horses and carriage. She took easy stages, as Washington was very careful of his horses, which were remarkable for their beauty.

The pageantry of aristocratic England pervaded the higher classes in this country, at that time, much more than at the present day. Lady Washington was escorted from town to town by guards of honor. At Philadelphia she was received like a princess, and was detained several days by the hospitalities of the patriotic inhabitants. The whole army greeted her arrival at Cambridge with acclaim. She entered the camp in a beautiful chariot, drawn by four horses. Her black postilions were quite gorgeously dressed, in liveries of scarlet and white. This was the usual style of the magnates of Virginia at that day.

The presence of Mrs. Washington was of great assistance to her husband. She presided over his household, and received his guests with great dignity and affability. Family prayers were invariably observed, morning and evening. On the Sabbath Washington punctually attended the church, in which he was a communicant.

A party of Virginia riflemen came to the camp. They were a strange looking set of men, in half-savage equipments, with deer-skin hunting shirts, fringed and ruffled. As they were strolling about, they met a party of Marblehead fishermen. To the Virginians, the costume of the fishermen was grotesque, with tarpaulin hats, flowing trousers, and round jackets.

---

[109] Sparks' *Life of Washington*, p. 155.

The two parties began to banter each other. There was snow upon the ground; and snow-balls began to fly thickly. The contest grew warm. It was a battle between Virginia and Massachusetts. Both sides were reinforced. Angry feelings were excited. From snow-balls they proceeded to blows. It became a serious tumult, in which more than a thousand were engaged.

At this moment Washington appeared, mounted, and followed by a single servant. There was something in his majestic frame and commanding air which impressed the common mind with awe. He sprang from his horse, plunged into the thickest of the mêlée, and seizing two of the most brawny Virginians, held them at arm's length, as though they had been children, while he administered a very severe reproof. The other combatants instantly dispersed. In three minutes there was not one left upon the ground.[110]

In December a vessel was captured, which was conveying supplies, from Lord Dunmore, in Virginia, to Boston. In a letter to General Howe, found in the vessel, Lord Dunmore urged that the war should be transferred from New England to the southern States. He said that by liberating and arming the negroes, their force could be greatly augmented, consternation could be thrown into all the southern provinces, and victory would thus be speedy and sure. The despatch alarmed Washington. He said:

> "If this man is not crushed, before spring, he will become the most formidable enemy America has. His strength will increase as a snow ball."

This proposition of Dunmore, and the barbarous treatment, by the British officers, of the American prisoners of war, roused the indignation of General Charles Lee to the highest pitch. He wrote:

> "I propose to seize every governor, government man, placeman, tory, and enemy to liberty on the continent, and to confiscate their estates; or at least lay them under heavy contributions for the public. Their persons

---

[110] Memoranda by Hon. Israel Trask.

should be secured in some of the interior towns, as hostages for the treatment of those of our party, whom the fortune of war shall throw into their hands."[111]

Had these decisive measures been adopted, it would probably have saved many American captives from an untold amount of misery. The month of December was, to Washington, a period of great anxiety and perplexity. The troops, whose time of service had expired, were rapidly leaving, and but few came to occupy their places.

On the 1st of January, 1776, the army besieging Boston did not exceed ten thousand men. These troops had no uniform, were wretchedly supplied with arms, and there was a great destitution of ammunition in the camp. The genius of Washington, in maintaining his post under these circumstances, led even Frederick of Prussia to pronounce him the ablest general in the world. It was indeed evident, during those perilous months, that the aid of heaven was not always with the heaviest battalions. Washington wrote to Congress:

> "Search the volumes of history through, and I much question whether a case similar to ours is to be found: namely, to maintain a post, against the power of the British troops, for six months together; without powder; and then to have one army disbanded and another raised within musket-shot of a reinforced enemy. How it will end, God, in His great goodness, will direct. I am thankful for His protection to this time."

Again he wrote, in strains which excite alike our sympathy, our reverence, and our love:

> "The reflection on my situation, and that of this army, produces many an unhappy hour, when all around me are wrapped in sleep. Few people know the predicament we are in, on a thousand accounts. I have often thought how much happier I should have been if instead of accepting the command, under such circumstances, I had taken my musket on my shoulder, and entered the ranks; or, if I could have justified

---

[111] Letter of Charles Lee to Richard Henry Lee.—*Am. Archives*, 4th series, vol. iv. p. 248.

the measure to posterity and my own conscience, had retired to the back country and lived in a wigwam. If I shall be able to rise superior to these, and many other difficulties which might be enumerated, I shall most religiously believe that the finger of Providence is in it, to blind the eyes of our enemies."

General Henry Knox had been sent to Ticonderoga, at the head of Lake George, to transport cannon and ordnance stores to the camp at Cambridge.[112] With marvelous energy he had surmounted difficulties, apparently insurmountable. On the 17th of December he wrote to Washington:

"Three days ago it was very uncertain whether we could get them till next spring. Now, please God, they shall go. I have made forty-two exceedingly strong sleds, and have provided eighty yoke of oxen, to drag them as far as Springfield, where I shall get fresh cattle to take them to camp."

Early in January there was great commotion in Boston, visible from the heights which the Americans held. A fleet of war-ships and transports, crowded with troops and heavily laden with munitions of war, was leaving the harbor, on some secret expedition.

The plan had been formed, by the British ministry, to take military possession of New York, Albany, and the Hudson river; to treat as rebels all who would not join the king's forces; to station men-of-war, with armed sloops, so as to cut off all communication between the southern and the northern provinces.

Colonel Guy Johnson was to raise as large a force as possible, of Canadians and Indians, and ravage the provinces of Massachusetts, New Hampshire, and Connecticut. "This," it was said, "would so distract and divide the Provincial forces as to render it easy for the British army, at

---

[112] "Knox was one of those providential characters which spring up in emergencies, as if they were formed by and for the occasion. A thriving bookseller in Boston, he had thrown up business, to take up arms for the liberties of his country. He was one of the patriots who fought on Bunker Hill; since when, he had aided in planning the defences of the camp before Boston."—Irving's *Life of Washington*, vol. i. p. 190.

Boston, to defeat them, break the spirit of the Massachusetts people, depopulate their country, and compel the absolute subjection to Great Britain."[113]

Sir Henry Clinton[114] was in command of this naval expedition. The fleet entered the harbor of New York on a morning of the Sabbath. The whole city was thrown into consternation. Many of the inhabitants immediately began to move their effects back into the country. Through all the hours of the day, and of the ensuing night, the rumbling of carts was heard in the streets, and boats were passing up the North and the East rivers, heavily laden with goods and merchandise.[115]

Clinton professed to be very much surprised at the alarm of the inhabitants. He said that he came with no hostile intent, but merely to pay a short visit to his friend Governor Tryon.

General Lee, dispatched by Washington, was already in the city, with a small escort. Quite an enthusiastic army hastily collected in Connecticut, was ready and eager to march for the defence of the place. Clinton could, with perfect ease, lay the city in ashes. But there were perhaps as many tories as patriots in the city; and the tories constituted the most opulent portion of the inhabitants. A general conflagration would consume their mansions and property.

It is also said that General Lee, whose eccentricities, seemed, at times, almost to amount to insanity, sent the menace to Colonel Clinton, that if he, by a bombardment, set a single house on fire, one hundred of Clinton's most intimate friends should be chained by the neck, to the house, and there they should find their funeral pyre. Colonel Clinton knew well the

---

[113] "American Archives," 4th series, iii. 1281.

[114] General Henry Clinton was grandson of the Earl of Lincoln, and son of George Clinton, who had been the crown-appointed governor of New York, for ten years from 1743.—Irving's *Life of Washington*, vol. i. p. 163.

[115] "General Lee was despatched, with instructions from the Commander-in-Chief, to raise volunteers in Connecticut, hasten forward to New York, call to his aid other troops from New Jersey, put the city in the best posture of defence which his means would permit, disarm the tories, and other persons inimical to the rights and liberties of America, and guard the fortifications on Hudson river."—Sparks' *Life of Washington*, p. 157.

character of General Lee, and that he probably would not hesitate to execute his threat.[116]

The Duke of Manchester, alluding to this event, in the House of Lords, said:

> "My Lords: Clinton visited New York. The inhabitants expected its destruction. Lee appeared before it with an army too powerful to be attacked; and Clinton passed by without doing any wanton damage."

The fleet disappeared, sailing farther south. Lee commenced, with great energy, arresting the tories and raising redoubts for the defence of the city. It would seem that Governor Tryon took refuge on board the Asia, which was anchored between Nutten and Bedlow's Islands.

The British, in Boston, continued, during the remainder of the winter, within their tents. Gradually the American army augmented its forces. Notwithstanding all the efforts of the British officers to find amusement, their condition daily became more melancholy. Fuel was scarce; food still more so; sumptuous feasting impossible. The small-pox broke out. Poverty and suffering caused houses to be broken open and plundered. Crime was on the increase, which the sternest punishment could not arrest. The hangman was busy. The whipping post dripped with blood. Four, six, even a thousand lashes were inflicted on offenders. A soldier's wife was convicted of receiving stolen goods. She was tied to a cart, dragged through the streets, and a hundred lashes laid on her bare back.

The situation of Washington was dreadful. He could not reveal his weakness; for that would invite attack, and sure destruction. It was loudly proclaimed that he had twenty thousand men, well-armed, well disciplined, behind impregnable ramparts, and abundantly supplied with the munitions of war. These representations alarmed the British, and saved him from assaults which he could not repel. But the country clamored loudly, "Why did he not then advance upon the foe?" To his friend, Mr. Reed, he wrote:

---

[116] "American Archives," 5th series, iv. 941.

"I know the unhappy predicament I stand in. I know that I cannot be justified to the world, without exposing my weakness. In short my situation has been such that I have been obliged to use art to conceal it from my own officers."[117]

At length Colonel Knox arrived, from Ticonderoga, with his long train of sledges, bringing more than fifty cannon, mortars, and howitzers, with other supplies. Powder was also brought to the camp from several quarters, and ten regiments of militia came in.

On Monday night, the 4th of March, Washington commenced, from several points, a heavy cannonading of the British breastworks. The fire was tremendous. Mrs. Adams, describing the scene to her husband, wrote:

"I could no more sleep than if I had been in the engagement. The rattling of the windows, the jar of the house, the continual roar of twenty-four-pounders, and the bursting of shells, gave us such ideas, and realized a scene to us, of which we could scarcely form any conception."

Under cover of this fierce bombardment, a working party, of about two thousand men, with intrenching tools and a train of three hundred wagons, in silent and rapid march reached, unseen, the eminences of Dorchester Heights, which commanded the harbor. It was eight o'clock in the evening. They knew well how to use the spade, and vigorously commenced fortifying their position. They worked with a will. Skilful engineers guided every movement. Not a moment was lost. Not a spadeful of earth was wasted. They had brought with them a large supply of fascines and bundles of screwed hay.

Before the morning dawned a very formidable fortress frowned along the heights. Howe gazed, appalled, upon the spectacle. He saw, at a glance,

---

[117] To while away weary hours the spirit of gambling was prevailing ruinously in the camp. Clouds of gloom were settling down over the public mind. Washington, who felt most deeply the need of Divine favor, by an order of the day, issued on the 26th of February, forbade these demoralizing practices. He wrote:
"At this time of public distress, men may find enough to do in the service of God and their country, without abandoning themselves to vice and immorality."
Six days after the issue of this order, Washington's batteries were planted triumphantly on Dorchester Heights.—Irving's *Life of Washington*, vol. i. p. 220.

that the Americans must be dislodged, or his doom was sealed. He exclaimed, in his astonishment:

> "The rebels have done more in one night, than my whole army would have done in one month."

Another British officer wrote, "This morning, at daybreak, we discovered two redoubts on Dorchester Point, and two smaller ones on their flanks. They were all raised, during the last night, with an expedition equal to that of the genii belonging to Aladdin's wonderful lamp. From these hills they command the whole town, so that we must drive them from their place or desert the post."

Washington was watching, with intense anxiety, the effect which the discovery of the operation would have upon the British. The commotion, in the city, was very visible. Instantly the shipping in the harbor, and every battery which could be brought to bear upon the works, commenced the fiercest bombardment. All the hills around were covered with spectators, witnessing the sublime and appalling spectacle. The patriot soldiers were now familiar with cannon-shot, and paid little heed to balls and shells, as they stood behind their ramparts, every hour adding to their strength. Washington was in the midst of his troops, encouraging them; and he was greeted with loud cheers as he moved from point to point.

Howe kept up the unavailing bombardment through the day, preparing to make a desperate night-attack upon the works, with a strong detachment of infantry and grenadiers. In the evening twenty-five hundred men were embarked in transports. But God did not favor the heavy battalions. A violent easterly storm arose, rolling such surges upon the shore that the boats could not land. It was necessary to postpone the attack until the next day. But still the storm continued to rage, with floods of rain. It was the best ally the Americans could have. It held the British in abeyance until the Americans had time to render their works impregnable.

The fleet and the town were at the mercy of Washington. Howe, intensely humiliated, called a council of war. It was decided that Boston must immediately be evacuated. Howe conferred with the "select men" of

Boston, and offered to leave, without inflicting any harm upon the place, if permitted to do so unmolested. Otherwise the town would be committed to the flames, and the troops would escape as best they could. The reply of Washington was, in brief:

> "If you will evacuate the city without plundering, or doing any harm, I will not open fire upon you. But if you make any attempt to plunder, or if the torch is applied to a single building, I will open upon you the most deadly bombardment."

The correspondence in reference to the evacuation continued for several days. General Howe behaved like a silly boy. His fancied dignity, as an officer of the crown, would not allow him to recognize any military rank on the part of the Americans. He therefore indulged in the childishness of sending an officer, with memoranda written upon pieces of paper, addressed to nobody, and signed by nobody.[118]

The exasperated British soldiers committed many lawless acts of violence, which General Howe, in vain, endeavored to arrest. Houses were broken open and furniture destroyed. These depredations imperilled the life of the army. Washington, if provoked to do so, could sink their ships. General Howe issued an order that every soldier, found plundering, should be hanged on the spot. An officer was ordered to perambulate the streets, with a band of soldiers and a hangman, and immediately, without farther trial, to hang every man he should find plundering.

At four o'clock in the morning of the 17th of March, 1776, the embarkation began, in great hurry and confusion. There were seventy-eight ships and transports in the harbor, and about twelve thousand, including refugees, to be embarked in them. These refugees were the friends of British despotism, the enemies of free America. As they had manifested

---

[118] "Washington consulted with such of the general officers as he could immediately assemble. The paper was not addressed to him, nor to any one else. It was not authenticated by the signature of General Howe. Nor was there any other act obliging that commander to fulfil the promise asserted to have been made by him."—Irving's *Life of Washington*, vol. i. Mount Vernon edition, p. 223.

more malignity against the American patriots than the British themselves, they did not dare to remain behind. Washington wrote, respecting them:

> "By all accounts there never existed a more miserable set of beings than those wretched creatures now are. Taught to believe that the power of Great Britain was superior to all opposition, and that foreign aid was at hand, they were even higher and more insulting in their opposition than the regulars. When the order was issued, therefore, for embarking the troops in Boston, no electric shock, no sudden clap of thunder, in a word, the last trump, could not have struck them with greater consternation. They were at their wits' end, and chose to commit themselves, in the manner I have above described, to the mercy of the waves, at a tempestuous season, rather than meet their offended countrymen."[119]

Again he wrote, as he entered the town and beheld the ruin around him: ordnance with trunnions knocked off, guns spiked and cannons thrown from the wharves:[120]

> "General Howe's retreat was precipitate beyond anything I could have conceived. The destruction of the stores at Dunbar's camp, after Braddock's defeat, was but a faint image of what was to be seen in Boston. Artillery carts cut to pieces in one place, gun-carriages in another, shells broke here, shots buried there, and everything carrying with it the face of disorder and confusion, as also of distress."[121]

While the British were thus hurriedly embarking, the Americans stood by the side of their guns, gazing upon the wondrous spectacle with unutterable joy, and yet not firing a shot. A British officer afterward wrote:

---

[119] Letter to John A. Washington.—*Am. Archives*, v. 560.
[120] A British officer wrote, in reference to this scene, so joyful, yet so sad. "The confusion, unavoidable to such a disaster, will make you conceive how much must be forgot, where every man had a private concern. The necessary care and distress of the women, children, sick and wounded, required every assistance that could be given. It was not like breaking up a camp, where every man knows his duty. It was like departing from your country, with your wives, your servants, your household furniture and all your incumbrances. The officers, who felt the disgrace of their retreat, did their utmost to keep up appearances."— *Remembrancer*, vol. iii. p. 108.
[121] Lee's Memoirs, p. 162.

"It was lucky for the inhabitants now left in Boston, that they did not. For I am informed that everything was prepared to set the town in a blaze, had they fired one cannon."

Chapter 9

THE WAR IN NEW YORK

By ten o'clock on the morning of the 18th of February, 1776, the British troops were all embarked, and the humiliated fleet was passing out of the harbor. At the same time a division of the American troops, under General Putnam, with flying colors and triumphant martial strains, entered and took possession of the recaptured city. From a thousand to fifteen hundred tories had fled with the British. Houseless, homeless, in the depth of poverty, to be fed and clothed by charity, their situation was truly heart-rending. There were among them, affectionate fathers, loving mothers, amiable sons and daughters. They were the victims of circumstances and not of intentional wrong. War is indeed cruelty. Who can refine it?

Nearly two thousand members of patriot families returned with the conquering army. Weary months of destitution and suffering had been theirs, because they adhered to their country in dark hours of adversity. "It was truly interesting to witness the tender interviews and fond embraces of those who had been long separated under circumstances so peculiarly distressing."[122]

When we consider the feeble resources of Washington's **command**, the powerful forces he had to resist, and the obstacles to be surmounted, it must be admitted that the triumphant result of this campaign places

---

[122] Thatcher's "Military Journal," p. 50.

Washington in the highest rank of military commanders. The annals of war may be searched in vain for a more brilliant achievement. No language can express the astonishment and chagrin with which these tidings were heard in England.[123]

It was expected that the British would make an attack upon New York. Washington reached the city on the 13th of April. Soon a patriot army, amounting in all to about eight thousand men, was distributed at various points in the city of New York and its environs. Governor Tryon was still on board one of the ships of war, about twenty miles below the city. He was keeping up an active correspondence with the tories. Arduous duties engrossed every moment of the time of General Washington and his officers. Lady Washington was there, with several other distinguished ladies. One of them wrote:

> "We all live here like nuns, shut up in a nunnery. No society with the town, for there are none there to visit. Neither can we go in or out, after a certain hour, without the countersign."

England, greatly exasperated, was redoubling her efforts for the subjugation of America. She hired four thousand three hundred troops, from the Duke of Brunswick in Germany, and thirteen thousand from the Prince of Hesse. Thus seventeen thousand Germans were hired by England, to aid in rivetting the chains of slavery upon the necks of the children of her own sons and daughters.

The remnants of Arnold's army were still in Canada. And, strange to say, they were besieging Quebec, with a force not equal to one-half of the British garrison, in that almost impregnable fortress. The British general, Carleton, was not a heroic soldier. Perhaps he acted humanely in keeping, with his men, behind their ramparts, where they were safe from harm. After sundry wild adventures, the little army found it necessary to retreat.

---

[123] General Charles Lee was in Virginia, when he heard of the evacuation. The following characteristic letter was from his pen. "My dear General: I most sincerely congratulate you. I congratulate the public on the great and glorious event. It will be a most bright page in the annals of America; and a most abominable one in those of the beldam Britain. Go on, my dear general. Crown yourself with glory; and establish the liberties and lustre of your country on a foundation more permanent than the Capitol rock."

Just then five British ships arrived, bringing a reinforcement of about one thousand men. As the Americans could not muster three hundred, they retired as rapidly as possible. Montreal was in the hands of the Americans. They reached their friends in that vicinity without much molestation.

The latter part of May, Washington repaired to Philadelphia, to confer with Congress respecting the next campaign. General Putnam was left in command, at New York, during his absence. The spirit of Washington infused new energy into Congress. He assured them that all hope of reconciliation with implacable England was at an end; that America must summon all its energies, and submit the question to the deadly arbitration of battle.

Congress promptly voted to hire soldiers for three years. A bounty of ten dollars was offered each recruit. About thirteen thousand militia were to be sent, at once, to New York. Gun-boats and fire-ships were to be built, to prevent the British fleet from entering the harbor. Ten thousand militia were to be stationed in the Jerseys. The British were engaging a large force of Indians, on the Mohawk, to descend that valley, and ravage the upper banks of the Hudson with the torch and the scalping knife. Washington wrote to his brother Augustine:

> "We expect a bloody summer in New York and Canada. And I am sorry to say that we are not, either in men or arms, prepared for it. However, it is to be hoped that, if our cause is just, as I most religiously believe, the same Providence which has, in many instances, appeared for us, will still go on to afford us its aid."

It was now the great object of the British to get possession of New York. A powerful armament was daily expected. The tories had extensively entered into a conspiracy to unite with them. Extravagant reports were in circulation respecting their diabolical plans of assassination and plunder. The plot, infamous in all its aspects, was traced, by a committee of Congress, of which John Jay was chairman, distinctly to Governor Tryon, who, from his safe retreat on a British man-of-war, was acting through his agents. David Mathews, the tory mayor of the city, was deeply implicated in the plot. Mathews was residing at Flatbush. He was arrested, with many others. This threw the tories into the greatest dismay. Conscious of guilt, many fled into the woods. It was proved that Tryon had offered a bounty of five guineas to everyone who would enlist in the service of the king, with the promise of one hundred acres of land for himself, one hundred for his wife, and fifty for each child.[124]

On the 28th of June, four British ships-of-war appeared off the Hook. The next morning forty vessels were in sight. They came from Halifax, bringing about ten thousand troops. Most of them were soldiers who had been expelled from Boston. The alarm was great. The conspiracy had undefined limits. It was reported that it extended into the American camp; and that men were bribed to spike the guns of the batteries as soon as the ships approached. Soon other vessels arrived, swelling the number of ships-of-war and transports, in the harbor, to one hundred and thirty. They did not attempt to ascend the Hudson, but landed their troops on Staten Island. The heights were soon whitened with their tents.

General Howe came to Staten Island in one of these ships. He wrote, to the British government:

> "There is great reason to expect a numerous body of the inhabitants to join the army from the province of York, the Jerseys, and Connecticut, who, in this time of universal oppression, only wait for opportunities to give proofs of their loyalty and zeal."

What is now called "The Park," upon which the City Hall stands, was then a field, at some distance out of town. General Greene was crossing the field one day, when a company of American artillery were there on drill. Their commander was almost girlish, of fragile and graceful stature, but exercised wonderful powers of command and discipline. He seemed to be but about twenty years of age. It was Alexander Hamilton, whose renown subsequently filled the land, but whose heroic life was sullied with many a

---

[124] "A deep plot, originating with Governor Tryon, was defeated by timely and fortunate discovery. His agents were found enlisting men in the American camp, and enticing them with rewards. It was a part of the plot to seize General Washington, and carry him to the enemy."—Sparks' *Life of Washington*, p. 169.

stain. He was a native of one of the West India Islands, and from his youth, was inspired with the intense desire to make for himself a name in the world.[125]

It is a melancholy fact that the inhabitants of Staten Island were bitter foes of the American cause. They received the British with rejoicing. Such was the alarming state of affairs when the Congress, at Philadelphia, was discussing, with closed doors, the question whether the united colonies should declare themselves free and independent States. The resolution passed unanimously on the 2d. On the 4th, the sublime *Declaration* was adopted.

John Adams, the renowned patriot of Massachusetts, wrote, "This will be the most memorable epoch in the history of America. I am apt to believe that it will be celebrated by succeeding generations as the great anniversary festival. It ought to be commemorated, as the day of deliverance, by solemn acts of devotion to Almighty God. It ought to be solemnized with pomp and parade, with shows, games, sports, guns, bells, bonfires and illuminations, from one end of this continent to the other, from this time forth forevermore."

Washington, who had long been convinced that the British Government would never relinquish its claim to tax the Americans at its pleasure, hailed this event with joy. At the same time no one foresaw, more clearly than he did, the terrible ordeal of blood and suffering through which the Americans must pass, before their powerful and haughty foe would recognize their independence.

On the 9th of July the Declaration was read, at the head of each brigade in the army. Most of the tories had fled from New York, and the remaining inhabitants were patriotic in the highest degree. Their joy amounted almost to frenzy. There was a leaden statue of their implacable oppressor, George III., in the Bowling Green. They hurled it from its pedestal and ran it into bullets.

---

[125] While a lad, in a counting house at Santa Cruz, he wrote, "I contemn the grovelling condition of a clerk, to which my fortune condemns me. I would willingly risk my life, though not my character, to exalt my station. I mean to prepare the way for futurity. I am no philosopher, and may justly be said to build castles in the air. I wish there was a war."

Washington disapproved of the act. It too much resembled lawlessness and riot. He could not denounce the very natural event with severity, but in words characteristic of this best of men, he wrote:

> "The General hopes and trusts that every officer and man will endeavor to live and act as becomes a Christian soldier, defending the dearest rights and liberties of his country."[126]

The British were now in their ships in the lower harbor, and troops were landed, in large force, on Staten Island. The Americans were in the city, watching the foe with spy glasses, and adopting every precaution to guard against surprise. An engagement was expected every day.

On the 12th of July, about three o'clock in the afternoon, two ships-of-war, mounting together sixty guns, came rapidly up the bay, favored by both wind and tide. The batteries opened fire upon them. But they swept by unharmed. It was their object to take possession of the river above the city, and rally the tories around them. That same evening Admiral Lord Howe arrived, and was greeted with a sublime salute from the fleet. Thus the two brothers were in command, for the attack upon New York. Lord Howe led the ships, and Sir William the land troops.

These haughty men, declaring the Americans to be rebels, refused to recognize their officers by any military title. Admiral Howe sent a flag of truce with a letter, which Lieutenant Brown, the carrier, said was directed to Mr. Washington. As this was intended as an indignity, Colonel Reed, Washington's adjutant-general, declined receiving the document, saying that he knew of no such person in the American army. Upon producing the letter it was found to be directed to George Washington, *Esquire*.

Colonel Reed, who, it will be remembered, was Washington's former secretary and intimate friend, was a polished gentleman. He knew well how to unite mildness of demeanor with firmness of action. Very courteously he dismissed Lieutenant Brown, assuring him that no such communication could be conveyed to the Commander-in-Chief of the armies of America.

---

[126] Orderly Book, July 9; Sparks iii. 456.

Lieutenant Brown was greatly agitated and embarrassed. On the 19th General Howe sent an aide, with a flag, to inquire if Colonel Patterson, the British adjutant-general, could be admitted to an interview with *General Washington*. Colonel Reed assured him that there could be no difficulty, and that he would pledge his honor for the safety of Colonel Patterson.

The next morning Colonel Reed and another officer met the flag, in the harbor, and took Colonel Patterson into their barge. A cheerful and friendly conversation was maintained on the way, as they conveyed the officer to Washington's head-quarters, Washington received them with much ceremony. The Commander-in-Chief was in full dress, and his guards were in attendance in military array. Colonel Patterson was either in some degree overawed by the imposing scene, to which he was introduced, or native politeness restrained him from the rudeness of which his superior officers were guilty.

After addressing Washington as "Your Excellency," which title he had probably studiously adopted, as not involving any military rank, he presented him with a document, which Sir William Howe had insolently addressed to "George Washington, Esquire, &c., &c., &c." He suggested that the *et cetera*, might imply anything which Washington could wish it to imply.

Patterson was courteously informed that no such communication could be received; and after a brief, desultory conversation, the conference terminated.[127]

The ships-of-war, which had ascended the river, cast anchor in Haverstraw Bay and Tappan Sea. Their boats were exploring the river above. One of the tenders approached within long shot of Fort Montgomery. A thirty-two pounder was brought to bear, and a shot was plunged through her quarter. The British commander, in revenge, ran around Dunderberg, landed a boat's crew, plundered the house of a poor farmer, and applied the torch to all his buildings. The marauders were

---

[127] "Washington received the applause of Congress and of the public, for sustaining the dignity of his station. His conduct, in this particular, was recommended as a model to all American officers in corresponding with the enemy. And Lord Howe informed his government that thenceforth, it would be polite to change the superscription of his letters."—Irving's *Life of Washington*, vol. i. 248.

punished severely by rustic sharpshooters, who, from the shore, assailed them with a deadly fire as they returned to their ship.

Vigorous precautions were adopted to prevent the passage of the hostile ships farther up the river. The wreck of the American army, which had invaded Canada, was now at Crown Point, in a state of great destitution and suffering. In the motley army assembled around Washington, very unhappy jealousies existed between the officers and troops from the different provinces.

It will be remembered that Sir Henry Clinton had entered New York harbor with his fleet, and had again suddenly disappeared, sailing south. Much anxiety was felt to know where he would next attempt to strike a blow. He looked in upon Norfolk. But the energetic General Lee was prepared to meet him. Again he spread his sails and soon appeared before Charleston, South Carolina. Here he was fated to meet with a humiliating repulse. Six miles below the city a strong fort had been built, on the southwest point of Sullivan's Island. It mounted twenty-six guns, was garrisoned by about four hundred men, and was commanded by Sir William Moultrie, of South Carolina, who had planned and superintended the works.

On the 28th of June, Clinton commenced an attack upon this fort, by both fleet and army. One of the most furious cannonades was opened, which had ever been heard on these shores. Lee, a veteran soldier in the wars of Europe, who was present, wrote, "It was the most furious fire I ever heard or saw."

For twelve hours the bombardment continued. The British were bloodily repulsed, and, with their fleet much cut up, withdrew. A British officer, who took part in the engagement, wrote:

> "In the midst of that dreadful roar of artillery, they (the Americans) stuck with the greatest constancy and firmness to their guns; fired deliberately and slowly, and took a cool and effective aim. The ships suffered accordingly. They were torn almost to pieces. The slaughter was dreadful. Never did British valor shine more conspicuous; and never did

our marine, in an engagement of the same nature, with any foreign enemy, experience so rude an encounter."[128]

One hundred and seventy-five men were killed on board the fleet, and about the same number wounded. Many of these wounds were awful, tearing off legs and arms, and proving, to the sufferers, a life-long calamity.

This conflict was deemed one of the most memorable and hotly contested of the war. The Americans lost, in killed and wounded, but thirty-five. The shattered fleet put to sea, and returned to the north, to unite with the squadron in New York Bay. General Washington, in announcing this gratifying victory to the army, on the 21st of July, said:

> "With such a bright example before us, of what can be done by brave men fighting in defence of their country, we shall be loaded with a double share of shame and infamy, if we do not acquit ourselves with courage, and manifest a determined resolution to conquer or die."

General Putnam projected a plan to obstruct the channel of the Hudson, so as to prevent the passage of the British ships up the river. Fire-ships were also constructed. Putnam wrote to General Gates:

> "The enemy's fleet now lies in the bay close under Staten Island. Their troops possess no land here but the island. Is it not strange that those invincible troops, who were to lay waste all this country, with their fleets and army, dare not put their feet on the main?"

In the course of a few days a hundred additional British vessels arrived, bringing large supplies of those mercenary troops who were hired from princes of Germany, and who were called Hessians. There was something in the name of Hessian rather appalling to the popular mind. There was a general impression that a Hessian was a sort of human bloodhound, whom nothing could resist.

---

[128] "History of the Civil War in America," Dublin, 1779; "Annual Register."

It was evident that England, chagrined by defeats, was rousing all her energies for the subjugation of the colonies. Her troops, as they arrived, were disembarked on Staten Island. They had learned to respect the prowess of the Americans; for, numerous as was their host, and though the island was guarded by their majestic fleet, they still deemed it necessary to throw up strong intrenchments upon the hills, to guard against attack.

Ships-of-war continued to arrive, bringing Hessians and Scotch Highlanders. Early in August, Sir Henry Clinton entered the bay, with his battered fleet, from Charleston. He brought with him Lord Cornwallis and three thousand troops.

The British accumulated a force of thirty thousand men in the vicinity of New York; while Washington had but about twenty thousand, dispersed at various posts which were exposed to attack. The prospects of the Americans were dark indeed. There was much sickness in the American army in consequence of the general destitution. It was at this time that Washington issued his celebrated order of the day, entreating both officers and men to refrain from the "foolish and wicked practice of profane cursing and swearing, as tending to alienate God from our cause." In this same order he said:

> "That the troops may have an opportunity of attending public worship, as well as to take some rest after the great fatigue they have gone through, the general, in future, excuses them from fatigue duty on Sunday, except at the ship-yard, or on special occasions, until further orders."[129]

Many of Washington's hastily levied troops had no weapons but a shovel, spade, or pick-ax. It was evident that the British were preparing for some very decisive movement. On the 17th of August many thousands were seen crowding into the transports. No one knew where the blow would fall. The anxiety of Washington was manifest in the orders he issued, entreating every officer and every man to be at his post, ready for instantaneous action. His benevolent heart was deeply moved, in view of

---

[129] Orderly Book, Aug. 3, 1776. *Writings of Washington*, vol. xiv. p. 28.

the woes which he knew must ensue. To the New York Convention he wrote:

> "When I consider that the city of New York will, in all human probability, very soon be the scene of a bloody conflict, I cannot but view the great numbers of women, children, and infirm persons remaining in it, with the most melancholy concern. Can no method be devised for their removal."[130]

The two British ships which had ascended the river, were so annoyed by the menaces of fire-ships, and by having their boats fired upon whenever they attempted to land, that on the 18th of August they spread their sails, and sought refuge with the rest of the fleet. Had they remained two days longer, Putnam's obstructions would have been so far completed that their retreat would have been cut off, and they would have been captured.

The British landed on Long Island, and advanced in great strength, to take possession of Brooklyn Heights which commanded the city of New York. Twenty thousand men were embarked on this expedition. Fifteen thousand were detached to create a diversion, by an attack upon Elizabethtown Point, and Amboy. Washington sent to General Greene, at Brooklyn, six battalions.[131] Not another man could be spared; for the next tide would undoubtedly bring the British fleet to attack the city. To human vision the doom of Washington was sealed. Certainly there was no hope if God should lend His aid to the "heavy battalions."

Nine thousand British troops, with forty pieces of cannon, were landed without molestation. Sir Henry Clinton led the first division. Lord Cornwallis, one of his associates in command, led a corps of Hessians.

---

[130] History cannot record, neither can imagination conceive the woes of these households. Husbands and fathers were slain. They were without employment, in abject poverty, and driven houseless, foodless, clothesless, from their homes. In view of these awful tragedies of this sad world, which have continued through dreary centuries, one is led to exclaim, in anguish, "O Lord! how long! how long!"

[131] Anticipating this movement Washington had stationed a body of troops there and thrown up breastworks. General Greene was placed in command. Falling sick of a fever he was succeeded by General Sullivan, who was succeeded by General Putnam.

While others were landing, they rapidly advanced to seize the Heights. Should they succeed, New York would be entirely at their mercy. The panic in the city was dreadful.

The genius of General Greene had well-fortified the Heights and established strong outworks. The British were assailed on their march with shot and shell, and the deadly fire of sharp-shooters. They soon found it necessary to advance slowly and with caution. It was quite amusing to contrast the boasting of the British and their assumed contempt for the Americans armed with scythes, pitchforks and shot-guns, with the exceeding circumspection they used in approaching those Americans on the field of battle.

The British commenced landing on the 21st of August. Overpowering as were their numbers they found it necessary to fight every step of their way. The rattle of musketry and the thunder of artillery, during this almost continuous battle of seven days' duration, rolled their echoes over the city of New York, creating intense solicitude there. There were some scenes of awful slaughter when the outnumbering Hessians plied the bayonet with the fury of demons. There were glorious victories and awful defeats. As Washington gazed upon one of these scenes, where a detachment of his heroic troops was literally butchered by the plunges of Hessian bayonets, he wrung his hands in agony, exclaiming, "O good God, what brave fellows I must this day lose."[132]

In this engagement fifteen thousand British troops attacked five thousand Americans. The Americans lost in killed, wounded and captured, about twelve hundred. General Sullivan and Lord Stirling were among the prisoners.

On the 28th the British army encamped within a mile of the American lines on the Heights. Their number and armament were such, that there was no doubt of their being able to carry the works. The British fleet had entire command of the water, so as apparently to preclude the possibility of escape. There were nine thousand American soldiers on the Heights. The broad flood of East River flowed between them and New York. The British

---

[132] "American Archives," 5th series ii. 108.

sentries were so near that they could hear every blow of the pickax. How was escape possible!

Chance, says the atheist, God, says the Christian, sent a fog, so dense that no object was visible at the distance of a boat's length. The rain fell dismally. At the same time a gentle breeze sprang up to waft the boats across to the New York shore. To add to the wonder, the atmosphere was clear on the New York side of the river.

Aided by the darkness of the night and the fog, the troops were all embarked, with the guns and ammunition, and before the morning dawned they were safe on the New York shore. Scarcely a musket or a cartridge was left behind. Their escape was like that of the Israelites, across the Red Sea, pursued by the enslaving hosts of Pharaoh. This extraordinary retreat was one of the most signal achievements of the war. Exceeding great was the surprise and mortification of the British, in finding that the Americans had thus escaped them. Though British sentries were within a few yards of the American lines, the last boat was crossing the river before the retreat was discovered.[133]

The British were now in full possession of Long Island. They could lay New York in ashes. But it is said a majority of the inhabitants of that rich and commercial city were tories. The conflagration would lay their possessions low. This arrested the torch. As the British would make its comfortable dwellings their headquarters during the winter, and as these dwellings were generally the property of the enemies of free America, the question was seriously discussed, whether Washington, in his retreat, should commit the city to the flames.[134]

The British immediately commenced vigorous measures to cut off the retreat of the Americans at King's Bridge. Intense activity prevailed in

---

[133] "This retreat, in its plan, execution and success, has been regarded as one of the most remarkable military events in history, and as reflecting the highest credit on the talents and skill of the commander. So intense was the anxiety of Washington, so unceasing his exertions that, for forty-eight hours, he did not close his eyes, and rarely dismounted from his horse."—Sparks' *Life of Washington*, p. 179.

[134] Washington wrote to Congress, "If we should be obliged to abandon the town, ought it to stand as winter quarters for the enemy. They would derive great convenience from it, on the one hand, and much property would be destroyed on the other. At the present, I dare say the enemy mean to preserve it if they can."

both camps. Random blows were struck and returned. The sick and wounded, with such military stores as were not immediately needed, were sent by Washington to Orangetown, New Jersey. The troops were much disheartened. The most unintelligent could see that there was nothing before them but retreat. This led to alarming desertions. Washington could make humane allowances for these desertions. He wrote:

> "Men, just dragged from the tender scenes of domestic life, and unaccustomed to the din of arms, totally unacquainted with every kind of military skill, are timid and ready to fly from their own shadows. Besides, the sudden change in their manner of living brings on an unconquerable desire to return to their homes."[135]

Admiral Lord Howe, was a personal friend of Franklin. He seemed really desirous of promoting reconciliation, and suggested an unofficial meeting with some of the prominent American gentlemen, to talk the matter over. John Adams, Edward Rutledge and Benjamin Franklin were appointed on this mission. The conference was fruitless. Lord Howe was not authorized to propose any terms but the return of America to subjection to the British crown. This proposition could only be peremptorily rejected.[136]

The whole British force, excepting a small garrison of four thousand men, left on Staten Island, was removed to Long Island. Their plan was to surround the Americans with fleet and army, on Manhattan Island, and

---

[135] In a somewhat similar strain of sympathy General Greene wrote: "People coming from home, with all the tender feelings of domestic life, are not sufficiently fortified with natural courage, to stand the shocking scenes of war. To march over dead men, to hear without concern the groans of the wounded—I say few men can stand such scenes, unless steeled by habit or fortified by military pride."

[136] On the 30th of July, 1776, Colonel Palfrey went on board Lord Howe's ship to negotiate an exchange of prisoners. The noble Admiral was careful to speak of the American Commander-in-Chief as *General* Washington; he declared that he held his person and character in the highest esteem, and that his heart was deeply touched by the affectionate allusion of Washington and of Congress, to his elder brother Lord George, who fell at Ticonderoga. With a moistened eye he alluded to the fact that the province of Massachusetts had erected a monument to his brother in Westminster Abbey. In closing the interview he sent his kind regards to Washington, and added, "I hope that America will one day or other be convinced that, in our affection for that country, we are also Howes."

thus compel their surrender or cut them to pieces. Congress, by a vote passed on the 10th of September, left the fate of the city in the hands of General Washington. A council of war unanimously decided that the evacuation of the city was necessary. There were daily shots exchanged. Ships were moving up both rivers. At times there were very heavy exchanges of bombardments, rolling their portentous reverberations along the shores.

Washington established his head-quarters at King's Bridge. On the retreat, some of the troops were thrown into a panic, and displayed the most shameful cowardice. The disgust of Washington was so great that, for a few moments, he seemed quite in despair. "Are these the men," he vehemently exclaimed, "with whom I am to defend America?"

Soon, however, he regained that self-control which he so seldom lost. The city was finally abandoned, in such haste, being attacked by both the fleet and the army, that most of the heavy cannon, and a considerable amount of military stores were left behind. Washington won the admiration of his officers by the coolness and efficiency he manifested during this dreadful retreat. It was a day of burning, blistering heat. The terror, confusion and suffering were dreadful. The army was encumbered with women and children, tottering along, moaning, crying, faint, thirsty, exhausted and in unutterable woe. Colonel Humphreys wrote:

> "I had frequent opportunities that day, of beholding Washington issuing orders, encouraging the troops, flying on his horse covered with foam, wherever his presence was most necessary. Without his extraordinary exertions, the guards must have been inevitably lost, and it is possible the entire corps would have been cut in pieces."

On the upper part of Manhattan Island there is a neck of land several miles long, and but about one mile wide. Here Washington established his fortified camp. About a mile below him, the British lines extended, across the island, in an encampment about two miles in length. The flanks were strongly covered by the fleet. In throwing up the fortifications here the youthful Alexander Hamilton arrested the attention, and secured the warm attachment, of Washington by the science and skill he displayed.

The British the next day attacked a redoubt, with overpowering numbers, and, after a severe conflict drove off the brave defenders. With characteristic boastfulness, they insultingly sounded their bugles, as usual after a fox-chase. The next day Washington avenged the insult by sending troops to attack one of the posts of the British. The British were met in the open field, and driven before the impetuous assault. This victory though unimportant, greatly revived the desponding spirit of the army.[137]

The next night there was a destructive conflagration in the city. A large portion of the buildings were laid in ashes. Whether this were the result of accident, or the work of incendiaries, has never been known. The British began to land their heavy cannon in preparation for an attack upon the American camp. Still their caution was inexplicable to Washington. They had vastly superior numbers, were thoroughly disciplined, had an abundance of the best weapons and munitions of war, and a powerful fleet to cooperate with the land troops; and yet, day after day, they sheltered themselves behind their ramparts, not venturing upon an attack.

Three ships-of-war ascended the river. "They broke through the vaunted barriers as through a cobweb." The Hudson was at their control. They began to plunder and to burn. The Tories flocked to the British camp eager to enlist. Many felt that the whole lower part of the river must be abandoned to the foe. John Jay wrote to the Board of War:

> "I wish our army well-stationed in the Highlands, and all the lower country devastated. We might then bid defiance to all further efforts of the enemy in that quarter."

---

[137] It would seem that God must have stricken the British leaders with gross incapacity, else with such a powerful fleet and with such a numerous highly-disciplined, and thoroughly equipped army, the feebleness of half-starved, half-clothed, and not half-equipped American farmers would have been entirely crushed out in a week. No one familiar with military affairs can examine these operations without *amazement* that the Americans could have maintained so unequal a conflict. There is nothing to be compared to it in all the annals of warfare. For be it remembered that neither the British officers nor soldiers were cowards. Men more reckless of danger never stormed a battery.

The British were establishing strong fortifications in the rear of the American army to cut off its supplies. Its majestic fleet of men-of-war and gunboats could crowd the waters of the North River and the East River, and, encircling the island, could reach every spot with its terrific bombardment of round-shot and shell.

A council of war decided that the island of Manhattan was no longer tenable; and that it must be immediately abandoned. In good order the troops retired, a new position having been selected on the mainland. Washington established his head-quarters at White Plains in a fortified camp. Several skirmishes ensued, in which the British were taught the necessity of continued caution in approaching the American works.

The latter part of October the British made their appearance, in two solid columns, to attack the encampment at White Plains. The conflict lasted several hours, without any decisive result. About four hundred were struck down on each side. During the night the two armies lay opposite each other, within cannon shot. It was clear and cold. But fuel was abundant; and the soldiers on each side were struck with the sublime spectacle which the gloomy camp-fires presented. A British officer, writing to a friend in London, gives the following account of the condition of the American troops at this time:

> "The rebel army are in so wretched a condition, as to clothing and accoutrements, that I believe no nation ever saw such a set of tatterdemalions. There are few coats among them but such as are out at elbows, and, in a whole regiment, there is scarce a pair of breeches. Judge, then, how they must be pinched by a winter's campaign. We, who are warmly clothed and well-equipped, already feel it severely; for it is even now much colder than I ever felt it in England."

Under these circumstances there can be no question that, in generalship, Washington was far the superior of the British officers who were arrayed against him. And it is probably the unanimous voice of those skilled in the art of war, that there was not another general in the American army who could have filled the place of Washington.

A higher compliment to American valor could hardly be paid than the announcement, that the next morning, when General Howe saw the arrangements Washington had made to receive him, he did not venture to attack the American lines. On the night of the 31st Washington retired, with his main army, a distance of about five miles, to the high, rocky hills about North Castle. Here again he rapidly intrenched himself with spade and mattock. It must have been a deep humiliation for the haughty General Howe with his magnificent army to find all his plans thwarted by this feeble band of "tatterdemalions." He made no attempt to dislodge Washington.

At midnight, on the 4th of November, Howe commenced withdrawing his troops, as though he were a vanquished foe, retreating before his victors. Soon the whole force disappeared from White Plains. The plan of the British general was soon made manifest. He encamped his army on Fordham Heights, near King's Bridge, in preparation for an attack upon Fort Washington. He invested the fort and, on the 15th, sent a summons to surrender, with a barbaric threat, if he was forced to carry the works by assault. Washington hastened to the beleaguered fortress, which he reached in the gloom of a cold November evening. Colonel Magaw, who was in command, had nearly three thousand men. As the fort itself could not contain more than one thousand, the others were stationed at the outposts.

General Howe planned for four simultaneous attacks. The assault was a series of complicated battles, some at the distance of two and a half miles from the fort, and some within cannon shot of its walls. Washington witnessed one of those awful conflicts, where the Hessians rushed like fiends over the ramparts of a battery, and bayoneted the young Americans begging for life. It is said that his sympathies were so moved by the demoniac scene, that he wept with the tenderness of a child.[138]

The redoubts were captured and the retreating troops so crowded the fort, that the men could scarcely move about. The British could throw in a

---

[138] It requires a heart hardened by the horrors of war to see, unmoved, an overpowering band of soldiers, maddened by the conflict, plunging their bayonets into the faces, bosoms, and bowels of farmers, boys, crying for mercy, and who have but just come from their peaceful firesides.

shower of shells and balls, which would cause awful carnage. A capitulation could not be avoided.

Washington stood upon a neighboring eminence, and saw the American flag fall and the British flag rise in its place. The loss was a severe one. Washington had recommended, not ordered, that the fort should be evacuated, and the men and stores removed to a place of safety.[139] But some of his more sanguine generals were confident that they could hold the place. Deep as was his grief, he did not reproach them. The impetuous General Lee wrote to Washington; "Oh, General, why would you be overpersuaded by men of inferior judgment to your own? It was a cursed affair."

Colonel Tilghman wrote on the 17th to Robert R. Livingston, of New York: "We were in a fair way of finishing the campaign with credit to ourselves and I think to the disgrace of Mr. Howe. And had the general followed his own opinion, the garrison would have been withdrawn immediately upon the enemy's falling down from Dobbs Ferry."

The captives, amounting, according to General Howe's returns, to two thousand eight hundred and eighteen, were marched off, at midnight, to the awful prison hulks of New York, where they endured sufferings which must forever redound to the disgrace of the British government.

---

[139] Washington wrote to General Greene, on the 8th of November: "I am inclined to think that it will not be prudent to hazard the men and stores at Mount Washington. But, as you are on the spot I leave it to you to give such orders, as to evacuating Mount Washington, as you may judge best; and so far revoking the orders given to Colonel Magaw, to defend it to the last."

Chapter 10

THE VICISSITUDES OF WAR

Washington removed the most of his army across the Hudson, a little below Stony Point, that he might seek refuge for them among the Highlands. General Heath was entrusted with the command. As the troops crossed the river, three of the British men-of-war were seen a few miles below, at anchor in Haverstraw Bay. Fort Lee, on the Jersey shore, was now useless, and was promptly abandoned. On the 20th the British army crossed the river in two hundred boats. It is remarkable that their fears were such that they took the precaution of crossing, as it were by stealth, in a dark and rainy night.

A corps of six thousand men under Cornwallis, was marshaled about six miles above the fort, under the towering Palisades. The troops, retreating from Fort Lee, about three thousand in number, were at Hackensack, without tents or baggage, and exceedingly disheartened. Still the British were in great strength on the east of the Hudson. They could concentrate their forces and make a resistless raid into New England, or, with their solid battalions march upon Philadelphia and the opulent towns in that region. It soon became evident that the British were aiming at Philadelphia. Washington endeavored to concentrate as many as possible of his suffering troops at Brunswick. It makes one blush with indignation to remember that a loud clamor was raised against Washington for his continual retreat.

It would have been the act of a madman to pursue any course different from that which Washington was pursuing. His feelings were very keenly wounded, by seeing indications of this spirit of ignorant censure, on the part of some whom he had esteemed his firmest friends. There were others, however, and among them many of the very noblest in the land, who appreciated the grandeur of Washington's character and the consummate ability with which he was conducting as difficult a campaign as was ever intrusted to mortal guidance.

Washington, with a feeble, disheartened band, in a state of fearful destitution, lingered at Brunswick until the 1st of December. The haughty foe, in solid columns was marching proudly through the country, with infantry, artillery and cavalry, impressing horses, wagons, sheep, cattle and everything which could add to the comfort of his warmly clad and well fed hosts.[140]

The chill winds of winter were moaning over the bleak fields, and ice was beginning to clog the swollen streams. About twelve hundred men were stationed at Princeton, to watch the movements of the enemy. On the 2d his harassed army reached Trenton. In that dark hour, when all hearts began to fail, Washington remained undaunted. He wrote to General Mercer:

> "We must retire to Augusta county, in Virginia. Numbers will repair to us for safety. We will try a predatory war. If overpowered, we must cross the Alleghanies."

In these hours of despondency and dismay, Admiral Howe and his brother the general, on the 30th of November, issued a proclamation, offering pardon to all who, within thirty days, should disband and return to

---

[140] "The people of New Jersey beheld the commander in chief retreating through their country, with a handful of men, weary, way-worn, dispirited, without tents, without clothing, many of them barefooted, exposed to wintry weather, and driven from port to port, by a well clad, triumphant force tricked out in all the glittering bravery, of war."—Irving's *Life of Washington*, p. 304.

their homes. Many, particularly of those who had property to lose, complied with these terms. On the 2d of December a British officer wrote to a friend in London:

> "The rebels continue flying before our army. Washington was seen retreating with two brigades to Trenton, where they talk of resisting. But such a panic has seized the rebels that no part of the Jerseys will hold them; and I doubt whether Philadelphia itself will stop their career. The Congress have lost their authority. They are in such consternation that they know not what to do. However, should they embrace the inclosed proclamation, they may yet escape the halter."[141]

Congress hastily adjourned to meet at Baltimore on the 20th of December. It was really a flight from Philadelphia. Washington had but five thousand five hundred men. It is difficult to account for the conduct of General Lee, upon any other plea than that of insanity. He turned against Washington, assumed airs of superiority, and was extremely dilatory in lending any cooperation. Washington wrote to him:

> "Do come on. Your arrival may be the means of preserving a city, (Philadelphia,) whose loss must prove of the most fatal consequence to the cause of America."

Lee was loitering at Morristown, with about four thousand men. He was an Englishman by birth, and a man of undoubted military ability, but coarse and vulgar in dress, mind, language, and manners. His ordinary speech was interlarded with oaths. On the 12th of December Lee was at a tavern at Baskenridge, not far from Morristown. There was no British cantonment within twenty miles. He was naturally an indolent man, and was entirely off his guard.

At eight o'clock in the morning he came down to breakfast, in his usually slovenly style, apparently unwashed and uncombed, in slippers, with linen much soiled, collar open, and with a coarse, war-worn blanket

---

[141] American Archives, 5th series, iii. 1037.

overcoat. Suddenly a party of British dragoons surrounded the house, seized him, forced him instantly on a horse, bare-headed, and in his slippers and blanket coat, and upon the full gallop set off with their prize for Brunswick. It was a bold movement, and heroically was it achieved. In three hours the heavy booming of guns at Brunswick, announced the triumph of the English.[142]

Though the British were very exultant over this capture, and the Americans felt keenly the disgrace and the loss, it is by no means improbable that, had not Lee thus been captured, he would have proved the ruin of the country. He was a reckless, dashing man, destitute of high moral qualities, was plotting against Washington, and would unquestionably have sacrificed the army in some crushing defeat had he been intrusted with the supreme command. There were not a few who, disheartened by defeat, were in favor of trying the generalship of Lee.[143]

Washington combined in his character, to an astonishing degree, courage and prudence. It is doubtful whether there was another man on the continent who could have conducted his retreat through the Jerseys.[144] With a mere handful of freezing, starving, ragged men, he retreated more than a hundred miles before a powerful foe, flushed with victory and strengthened with abundance. He baffled all their endeavors to cut him off, and preserved all his field-pieces, ammunition, and nearly all his stores. There was grandeur in this achievement which far surpassed any ordinary victory.[145]

---

[142] American Archives, 5th series, iii. 1265. Letter of Joseph Trumbull to Governor Trumbull.

[143] From the tavern at Baskinridge Lee wrote to General Gates: "The ingenious manœuvre at Fort Washington has completely unhinged the goodly fabric we had been building. There never was so damned a stroke. *Entre nous* (between us) a certain great man is damnably deficient."

[144] In 1676, the present territory of New Jersey was set off in two great divisions called East and West Jersey. Each belonged to different proprietors. In the year 1702, the two provinces were united. But still, in all the early annals, the province was spoken of as "the Jerseys."

[145] Washington, ever magnanimous, comments as follows on the capture of Lee, who he knew was trying to supplant him. He wrote to his brother Augustine, "This is an additional misfortune and the more vexatious as it was by his own folly and imprudence, and without a view to effect any good, that he was taken. As he went to lodge three miles out of his camp, a rascally tory rode in the night, to the enemy, who sent a party of light horse, that seized him and carried him off with every mark of indignity and triumph."

In this emergency Congress invested Washington with almost dictatorial authority. It was voted that "General Washington should be possessed of all power to order and direct all things relative to the department and to the operations of war."[146] General Sullivan hastened to join him with Lee's troops. They were in a deplorable state of destitution. In ten days several regiments would have served out their term. Washington would then be left with but fourteen hundred men. General Wilkinson writes:

> "I saw Washington in that gloomy period: dined with him and attentively marked his aspect. Always grave and thoughtful, he appeared at that time, pensive and solemn in the extreme."

Washington crossed the Delaware, destroyed the bridges, and seized all the boats for a distance of seventy miles up and down the river. These he either destroyed, or placed under guard, on the west bank. Here he stationed his troops with the broad river between him and his foes. He had then about five or six thousand men. Cornwallis continued his troops, mostly Hessians, on the east bank of the Delaware, facing the American lines. The idea of his being attacked by Washington was as remote from his thoughts as that an army should descend from the skies.

There were three regiments at Trenton. The weather was intensely cold. Vast masses of ice were floating down the river. In a few days it would be frozen over, so that the British could pass anywhere without impediment. The energies of despair alone could now save the army. But Washington guided those energies with skill and caution, which elicited the wonder and admiration of the world.

He knew that on Christmas night the German troops, unsuspicious of danger, would be indulging in their customary carousals on that occasion. Their bands would be in disorder, and many would be intoxicated. He

---

[146] The Committee of Congress who communicated to Washington the vote conferring upon him these powers, added: "Happy is it for our country that the general of their forces can safely be intrusted with the most unlimited power, and neither personal security, liberty nor property, be in the least degree endangered thereby."—*American Archives*, 5th series, iii. 1510.

selected twenty-five hundred of his best troops with a train of twenty pieces of artillery. With these feeble regiments, he was to cross the ice-encumbered river, to attack the heavy battalions of the foe. One can imagine the fervor with which he pleaded with God to come to the aid of his little army. Defeat would be ruin—probably his own death or capture. The British would sweep everything before them; and then all American rights would be trampled beneath the feet of that despotic power.

The wintry wind was keen and piercing as, soon after sunset, the thinly clad troops entered the boats to cross the swollen stream. Washington passed over in one of the first boats, and stood upon the snow-drifted eastern bank, to receive and marshal the detachments as they arrived. The night was very dark and tempestuous, with wind, rain and hail, compelling the British sentinels to seek shelter. It was not until three o'clock in the morning that the artillery arrived.

The landing was effected nine miles above Trenton. The storm was raging fiercely, driving the sleet with almost blinding violence into the faces of the troops. They advanced, in two divisions, to attack the town at different points. Washington led one division, Sullivan the other. At eight o'clock, enveloped in the fierce tempest, they made a simultaneous attack. The conflict was short and the victory decisive. The British commander—Colonel Rahl—a brave and reckless soldier, like Lee, but a poor general, lost all self-possession, and was soon struck down by a mortal wound. The Hessians, thrown into a panic, and having lost their commander, threw down their arms.

Under the circumstances, it was a wonderful and glorious victory. A thousand prisoners were captured, including twenty-three officers. Six brass field pieces, a thousand stand of arms, and a large supply of the munitions of war were also taken. It was comparatively a bloodless victory. The Americans lost but four. Two were killed and two frozen to death. Lieutenant Monroe, afterward President of the United States, was wounded. The British lost in killed, between twenty and thirty.[147]

---

[147] It is not strange that the soldiers should have been disposed to revile the Hessian captives for having hired themselves to aid the British to rob the Americans of their liberties. One of the Hessian soldiers wrote in his journal:

Washington, aware that an overpowering force might soon come down upon him, recrossed the Delaware the same day, with his prisoners, and with the artillery, stores and munitions of war which were of such priceless value to the army at that time.

Washington had made arrangements for another division of his troops to cross the river a little below Trenton, to aid in the attack. But the ice and the storm delayed them, so that they could take no part in the heroic enterprise. A general panic pervaded the scattered cantonments of the British. It was reported that Washington was marching upon them at the head of fifteen thousand troops. Many posts were abandoned, and the troops sought refuge in precipitate flight. The tories were alarmed, and began to avow themselves patriots. The patriotic Americans were encouraged, and more readily enlisted. And though there was many a dreary day of blood and woe still to be encountered, this heroic crossing of the Delaware was the turning point in the war. The midnight hour of darkness had passed. The dawn was at hand, which finally ushered in the perfect day.[148]

Washington gave his brave and weary troops a few days of rest, and again, on the 29th, crossed over to Trenton. It was mid-winter, and the roads were in a wretched condition. But it was necessary to be regardless of cold and hunger, and of exhaustion, in the endeavor to reclaim the Jerseys from the cruel foe. Not a Briton or a Hessian was to be seen. The enemy had drawn off from their scattered cantonments, and were concentrating all their forces at Princeton.

Lord Cornwallis, greatly chagrined at the defeat, rallied about eight thousand men at Princeton. General Howe was on the march to join him,

---

"General Washington had written notices put up in town and country, that we were innocent of this war, and had joined in it not of our free will but through compulsion. We should therefore not be treated as enemies but as friends. From this time things went better with us. Every day many came out of the towns, old and young, rich and poor, and treated us with kindness and humanity." *Tagebuch des corporals Johannes Reuber.*

[148] When General Howe, in New York, heard of the affair at Trenton, he raised his hands in amazement, exclaiming: "Is it possible that three veteran regiments of the British army, who make war their profession, can have laid down their arms to a ragged and undisciplined militia, with scarcely any loss on either side."

with an additional body of a thousand light troops which he had landed at Amboy, with abundant supplies.

Washington posted his troops on the east side of a small stream called the Assumpink. Cornwallis with nearly his whole force, approached about mid-day. He made repeated attempts to cross the stream, but was driven back by the well posted batteries of Washington. It was impossible for the Americans to retreat, for the broad Delaware, filled with floating ice, was in their rear. As night came on Cornwallis decided to give his troops some sleep, and await the arrival of his rear-guard. He said, "Washington cannot escape me. I will bag the fox in the morning."

Again Washington performed one of those feats of skill and daring, which has never perhaps been surpassed in the achievements of war. In the gloom of that wintry night he piled the wood upon his watchfires, left sentinels to go their rounds, employed a band of sappers and miners to work noisily in throwing up trenches; and then in a rapid, silent march, with all his remaining force, by a circuitous route, passed round the British encampment, and when morning dawned had reached Princeton undiscovered, many miles in the rear of the foe. Here he attacked three British regiments and put them to flight, killed one hundred of the enemy, captured three hundred, and replenished his exhausted stores from the abundant supplies which the British had left there under guard.

Should Cornwallis continue his march to Philadelphia, Washington would immediately advance upon Brunswick, and seize all his magazines. The British commander was therefore compelled to abandon that project and retreat, with the utmost precipitation, to save his stores. The battle at Princeton was fiercely contested. Washington plunged into the thickest of all its perils. But the victory, on the part of the Americans, was decisive. The foe was routed and scattered in precipitate flight. One of the British officers who fell on this occasion was Captain Leven, son of the wealthy and illustrious Earl of Leven. He seems to have been a gallant and amiable young man. His death was sincerely deplored by his comrades. It is often said that bayonets must not think; that it is their sole function to obey. But those who guide bayonets are culpable, in the highest degree, if they direct the terrible energies of those bayonets against the right and for the wrong.

History must record that the prospective Earl of Leven fell, ignobly fighting to rivet the chains of an intolerable despotism upon his fellow-men. It is well that the woes of cruel war penetrate the castle as well as the cottage.

It is said that when Cornwallis awoke in the morning, and heard the heavy booming of cannon far away in his rear, he was lost in astonishment, being utterly unable to account for it. And when he learned that, during the night, his victims had escaped, and that Washington was cutting down his guard, and seizing his magazines, he could not refrain from expressing his admiration of the heroism of his foe.

Greatly humiliated, he marched at the double quick, to save, if possible, the large supplies at Brunswick, compelled to admit that he had been completely foiled and outgeneraled.

Washington, thus gloriously a victor, thought it not prudent to advance upon Brunswick, as a strong guard was left there, and it was certain that Cornwallis would come rushing down upon him at the double quick. He therefore continued his march, which may be truly called a victorious retreat, to the mountainous region of Morristown. Here he established his winter quarters, in strong positions which the British did not venture to assail.

Washington, while on the march, wrote to General Putnam: "The enemy appear to be panic-struck. I am in hopes of driving them out of the Jerseys. Keep a strict watch upon the enemy. A number of horsemen, in the dress of the country, must be kept constantly going backward and forward for this purpose."

To General Heath, who was stationed in the Highlands of the Hudson, he wrote: "The enemy are in great consternation. As the panic affords us a favorable opportunity to drive them out of the Jerseys, it has been determined, in council, that you should move down toward New York, with a considerable force, as if you had a design upon the city. That being an object of great importance, the enemy will be reduced to the necessity of withdrawing a considerable part of their force from the Jerseys, if not the whole, to secure the city."

Washington reinforced his little band at Morristown, and, keeping a vigilant watch upon the movements of the British, so harassed them, that Cornwallis was compelled to draw in all his outposts, and his land communication with New York was entirely cut off. The whole aspect of the war, in the Jerseys, was changed. The grand military qualities of Washington were generally recognized. Alexander Hamilton wrote:

> "The extraordinary spectacle was presented of a powerful army, straitened within narrow limits, by the phantom of a military force, and never permitted to transgress those limits with impunity."[149]

The British had conducted like savages in the Jerseys, burning, plundering and committing all manner of outrages, often making no discrimination between friends and foes. Thus the whole country was roused against them. The American troops speedily erected a village of log huts in a sheltered valley covered with a dense forest.

General Howe, in New York, was a gamester, a wine-bibber, and a fashionable young man of pleasure. He and his officers spent the winter in convivial and luxurious indulgence. The American prisoners were treated with barbarity which would have disgraced the Mohawks. General Lee was held in close confinement, Howe affecting to regard him as a deserter, as he had once been an officer in the British army.[150]

Washington had but a very feeble force with him at Morristown. He however succeeded in impressing the British with the conviction that he had a powerful army quite well equipped. He wrote: "The enemy must be ignorant of our numbers and situation, or they would never suffer us to remain unmolested."

---

[149] The Italian historian *Botta*, in his admirable story of the American War writes, "Achievements so astonishing, gained for the American commander a very great reputation, and were regarded with wonder by all nations, as well as by the Americans. All declared him to be the saviour of his country; and proclaimed him equal to the most renowned commanders of antiquity."—*Storia della Guerra dell' Independenza degli Stati Uniti d'America*, Tom. ii. lib. 7.

[150] The officers and soldiers were confined in the hulks of old ships which were anchored in the harbor, and which were, not inappropriately, called *floating-hells*. They were destitute of every comfort. A dreadful malady broke out among them, and they perished by hundreds.

The fame of the great struggle for American independence had now pervaded the civilized world. Everywhere, the hearts of the lovers of freedom throbbed in sympathy with the American cause. Many foreign officers came, and applied for service in the patriot army. One of the most illustrious of these was the Polish general, Thaddeus Kosciusko.[151]

Toward the end of May, Washington broke up his camp at Morristown, and advanced to Middlebrook, about ten miles from Brunswick. His entire force consisted of seven thousand three hundred men. The whole country was smiling in the beautiful bloom of spring. A fleet of a hundred crowded British transports left New York. Great was the anxiety to learn where the blow was to fall. At the same time, Sir William Howe took up his headquarters at Brunswick. He soon drew out his forces upon the Raritan, and by plundering and burning private dwellings, endeavored to provoke Washington to descend from his strong position, and attack him. Failing in this, and finding that he could not advance upon Philadelphia with such a foe in his rear, he broke up his camp, and abandoning the Jerseys, returned with all his troops to New York.

Washington having thus driven the foe from the Jerseys, awaited, with great anxiety, tidings of the British fleet. Its destination, whether south or east, was matter only of conjecture. The ships contained quite a formidable army of eighteen thousand thoroughly equipped soldiers. They were capable of striking very heavy blows. Circumstances inclined him to the opinion that it was the aim of the fleet to capture Philadelphia. He therefore moved his army in that direction, and encamped at Coryell's Ferry, about thirty miles from the city. General Gates was stationed at Philadelphia, with a small force. On the 30th of July, Washington wrote to General Gates:

> "As we are yet uncertain as to the real destination of the enemy, though the Delaware seems the most probable, I have thought it prudent

---

[151] Kosciusko brought a letter from Franklin to Washington. "What do you seek here;" inquired the commander-in-chief. "To fight for American independence," was the reply. "What can you do?" said Washington. "Try me," was the simple response. There was something in the bearing of the man which won the confidence of Washington. He received him as an aide-de-camp. In the hour of trial, he was never found wanting.

to halt the army at this place, at least till the fleet actually enters the bay, and puts the matter beyond a doubt.

"That the post in the Highlands may not be left too much exposed, I have ordered General Sullivan's division to halt at Morristown, whence it will march southward, if there should be occasion, or northward upon the first advice that the enemy should be throwing any force up the North river."

The next day Washington received intelligence that the British fleet of two hundred and twenty-eight sail, had appeared off the Capes of Delaware. He immediately advanced to Germantown, but six miles from the city. The next day, however, the fleet again disappeared and the embarrassments of Washington were renewed. He feared that the appearance of the fleet in the Delaware was a mere feint, and that its destination might be to get entire possession of the Hudson River.

Several days passed, when, on the 10th of August, tidings reached him that, three days before, the fleet was seen about fifty miles south of the Capes of Delaware. During his encampment Washington repeatedly visited the city to superintend operations for its defence.

On one occasion he dined in the city with several members of Congress. One of the guests was a young nobleman from France, the Marquis de Lafayette. This heroic man, whose memory is enshrined in the heart of every American, had left his young wife, and all the luxurious indulgence of his palatial home, that he might fight in the battles of American patriots against British despotism. In his application to Congress for employment Lafayette wrote:

"After many sacrifices I have the right to ask two favors. One is to serve at my own expense; the other to commence serving as a volunteer."

The commanding air yet modest bearing immediately attracted the attention of Washington, and a life-long friendship was commenced. He said to the rich young nobleman who was familiar with the splendid equipments of the armies of Europe:

"We ought to feel embarrassed in presenting ourselves before an officer just from the French army."

The reply of Lafayette, alike characteristic of him and of the polite nation, was:

"It is to learn, and not to instruct, that I came here."[152]

For the defence of Philadelphia the militia of Pennsylvania, Delaware and Northern Virginia were called out. Washington with his troops marched through the city, and established his headquarters at Wilmington, at the confluence of the Brandywine and Christiana Creek. There were many tories in Philadelphia. Washington wished to make such a display of his military power as to overawe them.

He rode at the head of the army accompanied by a numerous staff. Lafayette was by his side. They marched, with as imposing array as possible, down Front and up Chestnut street.

"The long column of the army, broken into divisions and brigades, the pioneers, with their axes, the squadrons of horse, the extended train of artillery, the tramp of steed, the bray of trumpet, and the spirit-stirring sound of drum and fife, all had an imposing effect on a peaceful city, unused to the sight of marshaled armies."[153]

While Philadelphia was thus imperiled, General Burgoyne was advancing upon the Hudson from Canada, with a strong and well-conditioned army.[154] The tories were flocking to his standard. A large band

---

[152] "Lafayette from the first attached himself to Washington with an affectionate reverence which could not be mistaken; and soon won his way into a heart which, with all its apparent coldness, was naturally confiding and required sympathy and friendship."—Irving's *Life of Washington*, vol. i. p. 375.

[153] Irving's *Life of Washington*, vol. i., p. 396.

[154] General Burgoyne was a natural son of Lord Bingley. He was of active mind, and ready wit, and as a man of fashion, in all convivial scenes, stood preëminent. Gambling was then the common vice of the British aristocracy. But Junius accuses Burgoyne of cheating at cards. Both Washington and Napoleon endeavored to drive the foul practice of gambling from

of northern Indians accompanied him. There was a very beautiful girl, Jane McCrea, the daughter of a New Jersey clergyman, who was visiting a family on the upper waters of the Hudson.

Her lover, to whom she was engaged to be married, was a tory, and was in the British army. Under these circumstances she felt no anxiety, in reference to her personal safety, from the approach of Burgoyne's troops. Still, at the urgent solicitation of some of her friends, she decided to embark in a large bateau, with several other families, to descend the river to Albany.

On the morning of the intended embarkation, suddenly the hideous yell of the savage was heard. A demoniac band surrounded the house, and Miss McCrea was seized as a captive. A quarrel arose among the savages as to who was entitled to the prize. In the fray an Indian, maddened probably with rum as well as rage, buried his tomahawk in her brain. He then stripped off her scalp, and her gory body was left unburied.

Burgoyne was naturally a humane man. He was horror-stricken in view of this deed. But the murderer was a renowned chief and warrior. At any attempt to punish him, all the Indians would desert his camp. Consequently the crime was unpunished. The manifest displeasure of Burgoyne exasperated the Indians, and they soon all disappeared, carrying with them all the plunder they could obtain.[155]

The British troops were rendezvoused at Fort Edward, not far from Crown Point. The British had large forces in this region. They were able to detach seventeen hundred men to besiege Fort Schuyler, formerly called Fort Stanwix, on the right bank of the Mohawk River, at the head of navigation. Colonel St. Leger had command of this force. He had gathered a large band of savages. From behind the forest trees they kept up a constant fire upon any of the garrison who exposed themselves to repair

---

their armies. But for this vice, the brave and able General Arnold would probably now be enrolled among the most prominent of American patriots.

[155] "Lieutenant Jones is said to have been completely broken in spirit by the shock of her death. Procuring her scalp, with its long silken tresses, he brooded over it in anguish, and preserved it as a sad, but precious relic. Disgusted with the service, he threw up his commission and retired to Canada; never marrying, but living to be an old man, taciturn and melancholy and haunted by painful recollections." Irving's *Life of Washington*, vol. i., p. 378.

the parapets when injured by shot or shell. At night the woods were filled with their fiend-like yells and howlings.

A party of eight hundred men was sent to the rescue of the garrison. One of the most desperate and bloody battles of the Revolution took place. Both parties suffered terribly. Each side lost about four hundred in killed and wounded. Still the loss was by no means equal. The British regulars were generally the offscouring of the cities of Europe. But the Americans who fell were among the most worthy and intelligent of husbands and sons in the farm-houses of the valley of the Mohawk. Neither party admitted a defeat, and neither claimed a victory. The Americans still held the fort.[156]

The German troops were very reluctant to recognize the Indians as their allies. One of the Hessian officers wrote:

> "These savages are heathens, huge, warlike, and enterprising, but wicked as Satan. Some say they are cannibals; but I do not believe it. Though, in their fury, they will tear the flesh of the enemy with their teeth."[157]

Burgoyne was encamped east of the Hudson, near Saratoga. A bridge of boats crossed the river. Colonel Baum was despatched by him to Bennington, with five hundred men, to seize a large amount of American stores, which were deposited there. The Americans mustered from all quarters to repel them, under the rustic but heroic General Stark. Riding at the head of his troops, he exclaimed as soon as the British appeared in sight:

---

[156] "Old neighbors met in deadly feud; former intimacy gave bitterness to present hate; the bodies of combatants were afterward found, on the field of battle, grappled in death, with the hand still grasping the knife plunged in a neighbor's heart.

"The very savages seemed inspired with unusual ferocity, by the confusion and deadly struggle around them, and the sight of their prime warriors and favorite chiefs shot down. In their blind fury they attacked the white men indiscriminately, friend or foe. So that in this chance medley fight many of Sir John's greens were slain by his own Indian allies." Irving's *Life of Washington*, vol. i. p. 380.

[157] The British officers did not very highly esteem their German allies. "The very hat and sword of one of them," it was said, "weighed nearly as much as the whole equipment of a British soldier. The worst British regiment in the service would march two miles to their one."

"Now my men! There are the red-coats. Before night they must be ours or Molly Stark will be a widow."

The clouds of a drenching storm had passed away, and a serene morning of surpassing loveliness dawned upon the landscape, when five hundred British and Hessian regulars met, face to face, seven hundred American farmers, many of whom had rushed from their firesides, seizing their ordinary firelocks without bayonets.

The battle was fought, on both sides, with equal desperation. Baum had artillery well posted. Stark had none. The Americans made the assault in front, flank, and rear. The British with stolid bravery stood to their guns in resistance. After a battle of two hours, during which the roar of the conflict resembled an incessant clap of thunder, the foe was utterly routed. Many were killed, more wounded, and more taken prisoners.

Just then a strong, well-armed reinforcement came to the aid of the British, when the Americans, disorganized by victory were, in broken ranks, plundering the British camp. In vain Stark endeavored to rally them. An awful defeat threatened to follow their signal victory, when, very opportunely, Colonel Seth Warner arrived with fresh American troops from Bennington.

It was four o'clock in the afternoon. Another battle was fought with renewed ferocity. Again the American farmers put the British regulars to flight. Night alone enabled the fugitives to escape. It was a grand victory, both in its immediate achievements and its remote results. Four brass field-pieces, a thousand stands of arms, and four wagons of ammunition fell into the hands of the Americans. They also captured thirty-two officers, and five hundred and sixty-four privates. The number of the British who were slain is not known. The battle spread far and wide through the forest, and there was probably many an awful tragedy as poor wounded soldiers, in those gloomy depths, slowly perished of starvation and misery. The Americans lost one hundred in killed and wounded.

Language can hardly describe the exultation with which the American farmers learned that they could meet the British regulars, in the open field, and at disadvantage, and yet beat them. From all quarters, the young men seized their guns and rushed to the American camp. They surrounded Burgoyne. They cut off his supplies. They drove back his foraging parties. Burgoyne became alarmed. He was far removed from any reinforcements. He soon awoke to the terrible apprehension, that he might be reduced to the humiliation of surrendering his whole army to farmers' boys, whose soldierly qualities he had affected so thoroughly to despise.

Washington was at Wilmington, near Philadelphia, when he heard the tidings of this great victory. He was watching the British fleet which, conveying an army of nearly twenty thousand men, was evidently directing its course toward Philadelphia. He wrote to General Putnam:

> "As there is not now the least danger of General Howe's going to New England, I hope the whole force of that country will turn out, and by following the great stroke struck by General Stark, near Bennington, entirely crush General Burgoyne, who, by his letter to Colonel Baum, seems to be in want of almost everything."

The British troops, who had been sent, under St. Leger, to capture Fort Stanwix, and ravage the valley of the Mohawk, broke up the camp in a panic, and fled to Saratoga. They took to flight in such a hurry that they left behind them their tents, artillery, ammunition, stores, and most of their baggage. A detachment from the garrison harassed them in their flight. But they received more severe and richly merited punishment from their savage allies, who plundered them mercilessly, massacred all who lagged in the rear, and finally disappeared in the forest laden with spoil.

The battle at Bennington took place on the 16th of August. Nine days after this, on the 25th of August, General Howe began to land his army from the fleet, in Elk river, near the head of Chesapeake Bay, about six miles below the present town of Elkton. He was then seventy miles from Philadelphia. After sundry marchings and countermarchings, with various skirmishes, the two armies met, on the opposite banks of a small stream called the Brandywine, which empties into the Delaware, about twenty-five miles below Philadelphia.

It was the 8th of September. Washington had eleven thousand men he could lead into the field. They were but poorly armed and equipped. General Howe had eighteen thousand Regulars; fifteen thousand of whom he brought into action. His troops were in the finest condition, both as to discipline and armament.

General Howe had learned to respect his foe. He advanced with great caution, and displayed much military ability in his tactics. It was not until the 11th, that the battle took place. It was fought with desperation. Lafayette conducted with great heroism, and was wounded by a bullet passing through his leg. The Americans, after a very sanguinary conflict, were overpowered, and were driven from the field. General Howe did not venture to pursue them. At Chester, twelve miles from the field of battle, the defeated army rallied, as the shades of night were deepening around them.

Dreadful was the consternation, in Philadelphia, when the tidings of the disastrous battle reached the city. The field of conflict was distant about twenty-five miles. Through the day the roar of this awful tempest of war had been heard, like the mutterings of distant thunder. Patriots and tories, with pale faces and trembling lips, met in different groups, crowding the streets and squares. Toward evening a courier brought the intelligence that the American army was in full retreat. Many of the patriots, in their consternation, abandoned home and everything, and fled with their families to the mountains. Congress adjourned to Lancaster and subsequently to Yorktown. Washington was invested with dictatorial powers, for a distance of seventy miles around his headquarters, to be in force for sixty days.[158]

Notwithstanding the defeat of the Americans, General Howe followed the retreating army slowly and with great caution. He had not forgotten Washington's crossing of the Delaware, and had learned to respect the military ability of his foe. He spent the night after the battle, and the two

---

[158] Washington has been censured, by foreign writers, for fighting this battle under such disadvantages. But Congress and the country were clamorous for a battle. Had he surrendered Philadelphia to the English without firing a gun, it would have been the ruin of his reputation. The defeat was certainly less injurious upon the public mind than a continued retreat would have been.

following days, on the battle-field. Washington quietly retired across the Schuylkill to Germantown, but a short distance from Philadelphia. His troops were not disheartened. Overpowered by numbers, they regarded their repulse as a check rather than a defeat.

General Howe reported his loss to be ninety killed, six hundred wounded, and six missing. He gave the American loss at three hundred killed, six hundred wounded and four hundred taken prisoners. His estimate of the American loss must have been entirely conjectural; since General Washington made no return of his loss to Congress.[159]

---

[159] In reference to this conflict, Washington wrote to the President of Congress, "But though we fought under many disadvantages, and were, from the causes above mentioned, obliged to retire, our loss of men is not, I am persuaded, very considerable. I believe much less than that of the enemy. We have lost seven or eight pieces of cannon, according to the best information I am able, at present, to obtain. The baggage having been previously moved off, is all secure, saving the men's blankets, which, being at their backs, many of them are doubtless lost. Divers officers were wounded, and some slain; but the number of either cannot now be ascertained."

Chapter 11

THE LOSS OF PHILADELPHIA, AND THE CAPTURE OF BURGOYNE

Washington took advantage of the dilatoriness of Howe to prepare to attack him again. The two armies were often face to face. Washington, with his feeble force, could only harass the foe and retard his march. At length, Howe encamped, with the main body of his army, at Germantown, but a short distance from Philadelphia, and sent Cornwallis, with a brilliant staff, and a very magnificent array of troops, to take formal possession of the city. Washington was by no means in despair. He wrote to Governor Trumbull:

> "This is an event which we have reason to wish had not happened, and which will be attended with several ill consequences. But I hope it will not be so detrimental as many apprehend; and that a little time and perseverance will give us some favorable opportunity of recovering our loss, and of putting our affairs in a more flourishing condition."

In the meantime, prosperity was smiling upon the American cause. A noble spirit of patriotism imbued the hearts of the people. Burgoyne complained bitterly that the farmers were all rebels; that at an hour's warning they would abandon their plows by thousands, take their own subsistence with them, and, having achieved any enterprise for which they were called forth, would return to their farms. Several fierce battles were fought, in none of which did Burgoyne gain any advantage, and in all of which his plans were thwarted.

The Americans were rapidly encircling his army in folds from which escape would be difficult, if not impossible. Famine began to threaten him. He tried to retreat, but the Americans hedged up his way, and fought with bravery which the British regulars had never seen excelled. Washington sent a band of Morgan's riflemen to their aid. The scene of conflict was over hills and dales, covered with a dense forest. In this warfare Morgan's men were far superior to the trained soldiers of England and Germany. Their well-aimed bullets produced fearful havoc. The shrewd Indians saw that the tides of war were turning against them. They never loved the English. Without any leave-taking, they disappeared, carrying with them all the plunder they could seize. The Canadians deserted by hundreds.[160]

Burgoyne struggled with the energies of desperation. But all his efforts to escape were in vain. The impetuosity with which the Americans rushed upon the cannon of the foe, in the face of murderous discharges of grape-shot, excited the astonishment of both the British and Hessian officers. Many heroic and pathetic scenes occurred which we have not space here to record. After a bloody battle and a disastrous defeat, Burgoyne made another attempt to escape from his terrible foe. The night was dark even to blackness. The rain fell in torrents. The gale, chill and piercing, penetrated the clothing of the shivering soldiers, and moaned its saddest requiems through the gloom of the forest.

On the 9th, they reached Saratoga. A detachment of Americans had preceded them, and were throwing up intrenchments. Burgoyne set fire to farm-houses, mansions, granaries, mills. He himself estimated the value of the property destroyed at fifty thousand dollars. He excused himself for the

---

[160] Burgoyne wrote: "From the 20th of September to the 7th of October, the armies were so near that not a night passed without firing, and sometimes concerted attacks on our pickets. I do not believe that either officer or soldier ever slept, in that interval, without his clothes; or that any general officer or commander of a regiment passed a single night without being constantly upon his legs, occasionally at different hours, and constantly an hour before day light."—*Burgoyne's Expedition*, p. 166.

act on the plea of self-preservation. But generally, friend and foe alike condemned the cruel deed.

The sufferings of the British soldiers were awful. Drenched with rain, numb with cold, and exhausted by their toilsome march, they had no strength to cut wood for camp-fires. They sought such repose as could be found on the wet ground. Burgoyne could retreat no farther. He was surrounded. There was no escape. A deadly cannonade was opened upon his despairing troops. Scenes of horror ensued which could hardly have been surpassed in the realms of Pandemonium. One of the British generals exclaimed:

"I would not for ten thousand guineas see this place again. I am heart-broken with what I have seen."

Burgoyne was in despair. A council of war was held. They had food, upon short allowance, but for three days. The cannonade continued. Shot were striking all around. While they were deliberating, an eighteen-pound ball passed through the tent, and swept the table at which they were convened. All concurred that surrender was inevitable. The articles were signed on the night of the 16th of October, 1777.

Burgoyne's army was reduced from nine thousand men to five thousand seven hundred and fifty-two. The Americans, under General Gates, numbered ten thousand five hundred and fifty-four men on duty. The trophies of this great victory, left in the hands of the Americans, were a fine train of artillery, seven thousand stand of arms, and a large supply of clothing, tents, and military stores.

The British troops were marched to a particular spot, where they grounded their arms. They were allowed a free passage to Europe, being pledged not to serve again during the war. Gates and Burgoyne met at the head of their respective staffs. The British general was in rich, royal uniform. Gates appeared in a plain blue frock.

"The fortune of war," said Burgoyne, "has made me your prisoner."

Gates replied: "I shall always be ready to testify that it has not been through any fault of your Excellency."

Burgoyne and all his officers bore unequivocal and constant testimony to the extraordinary humanity and politeness with which all the captives were treated.[161]

Washington was at this time not far from Germantown, with a force, including militia, of about eleven thousand men. The British fleet could not ascend the Delaware to Philadelphia, in consequence of obstructions which had been placed in the river. Washington wrote to Congress:

> "If these can be maintained, General Howe's situation will not be the most agreeable. For if his supplies can be stopped by water, it may easily be done by land, and I am not without hopes that the acquisition of Philadelphia may, instead of his good fortune, prove his ruin."[162]

No one familiar with military affairs can critically examine the record of these events without the conviction that neither the campaigns of Napoleon I., nor of Frederic, called the Great, exhibit any more consummate generalship than the commander-in-chief of the American armies displayed through these trying scenes. Washington was head and shoulders above any of his generals. There was no one of them whom the voice of impartial history pronounces to be, in any respect, his rival. There was probably not one but he, who could have carried our country successfully through the terrible ordeal.

A large force of the British was encamped at Germantown, a small village but a few miles out from Philadelphia. The settlement consisted of a single street, about two miles long, running north and south. The houses were generally one story, sometimes of stone, standing apart from each other, surrounded with yards and gardens.

Washington, as bold as he was cautious, ever watching for an opportunity to strike a blow, and ever avoiding to strike where he would receive a heavier blow in return, formed the plan to attack the foe by surprise. The plan was admirably arranged and heroically executed. It

---

[161] The surrender of Burgoyne, though mainly the result of Washington's far-seeing plans, had suddenly trumped up Gates into a *quasi* rival.—*Irving's Life of Washington*, Vol. II., Mount Vernon edition, p. 429.

[162] *Letters to the President of Congress.—Sparks' Correspondence, Vol. V.*, p. 71.

would have proved a signal success but for one of those accidents which no human foresight can foresee.

In the gathering darkness of the evening of the 2d of October, he commenced a march of fifteen miles, over roads so rough that the morning was beginning to dawn gloomily through clouds and a dense fog, when he approached the British encampment. The British sentries gave the alarm. The roll of drums and bugle-peals rap sublimely along the extended lines of the foe, rousing the sleepers to battle. Washington hurled his troops upon them, with the impetuosity which ever characterized his attacks.

Wayne led. The British broke and fled. Hotly they were pursued. The fugitives, reaching reinforcements, rallied, and for a short time fought bravely. But again they broke in a panic, and ran, abandoning their artillery. All were mingled in the flight and the pursuit. The Americans, exasperated by many cruel deeds of the English, plied the bayonet ferociously. The slaughter was dreadful. The officers found it very difficult to restrain their fury towards those who threw down their arms and cried for quarter. In the terrific excitement of such scenes, even the most humane men often lose their self-possession, and conduct with frenzy which is truly maniacal.

The fog was now so dense that objects could with difficulty be discerned at the distance of one hundred feet. It was dangerous to use cannon or musketry, for in several cases friends had been mistaken for enemies. The Americans, in the full tide of victory, were attacking the British in front and on the flanks. Two or three times they had unfortunately exchanged shots, friend against friend. The British had probably done the same. It was a frenzied scene of obscurity, tumult, and terror. But the British were routed. They fled from their camping-ground, abandoning tents and baggage.

As the Americans rushed forward, they came suddenly upon a large body of troops, rapidly approaching, like specters, through the fog upon their flank. Shots were exchanged. The British had already been driven a distance of three miles. The troops thus mistaken for the British, were in reality some regiments of the Jersey and Maryland militia.

The appearance of this apparently strong reinforcement of the foe checked the pursuit. Alarm was created. The cry arose, "We are being surrounded, and cut off from retreat." A panic ensued; and the victorious troops broke and ran. No appeals can arrest the steps of a panic-stricken army. The gloom, created by fog and smoke, was almost like midnight darkness. The fugitives soon came upon another division of the Americans, pressing forward in the flush of victory.

These troops also mistook the fugitives rushing down upon them for the foe, and, in their turn, fell into confusion. The British, thus unexpectedly rescued from destruction, rallied. Lord Cornwallis arrived from Philadelphia with a squadron of light horse. The rising sun dispelled the fog.

The victory of the Americans was turned into a defeat. They retired in good order, taking with them all their wounded and their baggage. For about five miles a running fight was kept up. The British admitted a loss of seventy-one killed, and four hundred and twenty-nine wounded and missing. The Americans lost one hundred and fifty killed, five hundred and twenty-one wounded, and four hundred taken prisoners.[163]

In reference to this battle General Sullivan wrote: "I saw, with great concern, our brave commander-in-chief, exposing himself to the hottest fire of the enemy, in such a manner that regard for my country obliged me to ride to him and beg him to retire. He, to gratify me and some others, withdrew to a small distance; but his anxiety for the fate of the day soon brought him up again, where he remained till our troops had retreated."

The battle of Germantown, notwithstanding its unfortunate issue, exerted a good effect upon the public mind. It convinced the community that our army was not disheartened, and that it was still in a condition to

---

[163] In Washington's account of the battle he wrote: "Had it not been for a thick fog, which rendered it so dark at times, that we were not able to distinguish friend from foe at the distance of thirty yards, we should, I believe, have made a decisive and glorious day of it. Providence designed it otherwise. For after we had driven the enemy a mile or two, after they were in the utmost confusion, and flying before us in most places, after we were upon the point, as it appeared to everybody, of grasping a complete victory, our own troops took fright, and fled with precipitation and disorder."

take the field.[164] The Count de Vergennes, in Paris, conferring with the American Commissioners, in reference to a treaty of alliance, said:

> "Nothing has impressed me so deeply, as General Washington's attacking and giving battle to General Howe's army. To bring an army raised within a year, to do this, promises everything."

Washington having received considerable reinforcements, took up a new position at White Marsh, about fourteen miles from Philadelphia. Here he threw up such intrenchments as to be able to challenge the British to attack him. He was also in a condition to cut off their foraging parties, and to prevent the tories from conveying into the city any provisions.

There were two American forts, commanding obstructions on the Delaware, which prevented any vessels from ascending with supplies. These were called Mifflin and Mercer. Howe concentrated all the energies of fleet and army for the destruction of Mifflin. The conflict was terrible; American valor never shone more brightly than in the defense against fearful odds. Several times the advancing columns of the British were repulsed with great slaughter. In one attack they lost, in killed and wounded, four hundred men; while the Americans lost only eight killed, and twenty-nine wounded.

Three British war vessels attempted to anchor, so as to open fire upon the fort. The *Augusta* had sixty-four guns, the *Roebuck* forty-four—both frigates. The *Merlin* was a sloop of war, eighteen guns. There was also a well-armed galley. Many other vessels of the fleet were co-operating. Together they could throw a storm of iron hail upon the fort, which it would seem that nothing could resist.

In struggling through the lower line of chevàux-de-frise, the *Augusta* and *Merlin* ran aground. A red-hot shot, from the American battery, set the *Augusta* on fire. In a terrible panic the crew rushed to the boats. With a volcanic explosion, whose thunders seemed to shake the hills, the

---

[164] A British officer wrote: "In this action the Americans, though repulsed, showed themselves a formidable adversary, capable of charging with resolution and retreating in good order. The hope, therefore, of any action with them as decisive, and likely to put a speedy termination to the war, was exceedingly abated."—*Civil War in America*, Vol. I., p. 269.

magazine of the majestic fabric exploded. Several of the crew had not escaped. No fragments of their mangled bodies were ever found.

There was no escape for the *Merlin*. The British themselves applied the torch. The remaining vessels dropped down the river.

This discomfiture led Howe to redouble his efforts for the removal of those obstructions which imperiled the very existence of his army. Gigantic efforts were made. Batteries were reared, which threw eighteen and twenty-four pound shot. A large Indiaman was cut down to a floating battery, armed with the heaviest guns.

At a concerted signal the fire was opened. It was terrific. Ships, forts, gondolas, and floating batteries, opened their thunders at once. This tempest of war raged with deafening roar, such as never before had been heard on the shores of the New World. Hour after hour, through the long day, shot and shell fell like hailstones. Guns were dismounted, palisades shivered, parapets beaten down to the ground, and the slaughter of the heroic garrison was awful. Nearly every man of a company of artillery was killed. Most of the officers were wounded.

Night came, with its gloom and horror. Ruins, wounds, blood, death were everywhere. The moans of the dying floated away sadly on the night air. Tidings of woe were on the way to many a farm-house. The fort could no longer be held. Fire was applied to all that was combustible of the smoldering ruins, and the surviving officers and men retired, by the light of the flames, taking with them their wounded and such articles as could be removed. A more heroic resistance history has not recorded. Under the circumstances, the defeat gave the renown of a victory.[165]

The British now established themselves in Philadelphia, for their winter quarters. Weary of fighting, and some of them ashamed of the infamous cause in support of which they were filling a once happy land with death and woe, they devoted their time to gambling, drinking, carousing, and all those associate vices which have generally attended the encampment of an army. The patriotic citizens were subjected to every indignity. Some were driven from their houses, that the British might

---

[165] *Life of Talbot*, by Henry T. Tuckerman, p. 31.

occupy them. Upon some, soldiers were quartered, to be fed and housed. Some were plundered. When food was scarce, the inhabitants were left to hunger, that the soldiers might have abundance.

As wintry blasts began to sweep the fields, it was necessary for Washington to find shelter for his troops. About twenty miles from Philadelphia there was a glen, densely wooded and well watered, called Valley Forge. This spot Washington selected for the winter home of his heroic little band. The forest resounded with the blows of the ax, as the gigantic trees were felled, and there rapidly arose a large town, of comfortable log houses, scientifically arranged. The settlement was designed to accommodate about eleven thousand men. Each hut was fourteen feet by sixteen, and accommodated twelve soldiers. The whole encampment was so well protected by earth-works, that the carousing British did not deem it expedient to leave the firesides of Philadelphia to make an attack. The streets and avenues were neatly arranged, and the large military town presented quite a picturesque and cheerful aspect.

But the suffering here, during the winter of 1777 and 1778, was very severe. In consequence of inexperience in military affairs, and the incompetency of the commissariat department, the troops were left in a state of great destitution. They suffered for food and clothing. At times they were so destitute of arms and ammunition that they could present feeble resistance to an enterprising foe.

Washington was in a state of terrible embarrassment. He could not loudly make his wants known without proclaiming his destitution to the enemy and inviting attack. He was therefore compelled, while his men were freezing and starving, to let the impression go abroad, that his troops were rejoicing in abundance, and were ready, at any moment, to meet the British on the battle-field. From sickness and suffering the army dwindled down to five thousand men. On one occasion he wrote:

> "A part of the army has been a week without any kind of flesh, and the rest three or four days. Naked and starving as they are, we cannot enough admire the incomparable patience and fidelity of the soldiers, that

they have not been ere this, excited by their suffering to a general mutiny and desertion."

Figure 4. The Capitulation at Yorktown.

Chapter 12

Concluding Scenes

The dreary winter passed slowly away, while Washington was making vigorous preparations for opening the campaign in the spring. Immense embarrassments arose from the fact that Congress did not represent a *nation*, but merely a *confederacy* of independent states. Each state decided the pay it would offer the troops, and claimed the right to retain them at home or to send them abroad at its pleasure. These difficulties subsequently led the United States to organize themselves into a *nation*.

No man can be in power without being denounced. Washington was assailed most cruelly. He wrote to the President of Congress:

> "My enemies know I cannot combat their insinuations however injurious, without disclosing secrets it is of the utmost moment to conceal. But why should I expect to be exempt from censure, the unfailing lot of an elevated station? Merit and talent which I cannot pretend to rival, have ever been subject to it."

In these dark hours France generously came to the aid of the patriots, struggling for freedom in America against such desperate odds. The tidings of the French Alliance awoke new emotions of joy in the weary hearts at Valley Forge. The British army in Philadelphia amounted to not less than thirty thousand men. They were greatly alarmed. The danger was imminent that a French fleet might appear in the Delaware and cut off their retreat by water, while the American farmers, thus encouraged, would rise *en masse* and prevent their escape by land. This doubtless would have been their doom but for a succession of storms which delayed the French fleet.

With precipitation, the British evacuated Philadelphia. Their heavy material of war was shipped to New York. The troops marched very cautiously through New Jersey. Washington followed closely in their rear. The 28th of June was a day of intense heat. The British were at Monmouth. The march of another day would unite them with the troops in New York. They would then be safe from attack. Washington was extremely anxious that they should not escape without receiving at least one heavy blow.

Lee was in the advance with five thousand men. Washington ordered him to make an impetuous assault, promising to hasten to his support. Instead of obeying orders this strange man, of undoubted abilities but of inexplicable eccentricity, commenced a retreat. Intense, beyond the power of utterance, was the chagrin of Washington as he met Lee, at the head of his troops, in this retrograde movement. In tones of anguish he exclaimed: "What means this ill-timed prudence?" Lee instantly replied:

> "I know of no man blessed with a larger portion of that rascally virtue than your Excellency."

There was no time for altercation. Lee's men felt humiliated. As soon as they caught sight of Washington they greeted him with cheers. Promptly they wheeled around at his command, and rushed upon the foe. A bloody battle ensued with all its ordinary complications of uproar, tumult, woe and death.

The British were routed and driven from the field. The Americans, exhilarated by their success, slept upon the field with their arms by their side, and impatiently awaited the morning, eager to renew the battle. Signal as had been their success, it would have been far more decisive had General Lee obeyed orders. General Washington wrapped himself in his cloak, and slept in the midst of his soldiers.

In the night the vanquished British silently stole away. In the morning no foe was to be seen. There were left three hundred of the mutilated bodies of their dead unburied upon the plain. Sixty prisoners were taken, and six hundred deserted the ranks, and scattered through the country. They were disgusted with the infamous service into which they had been driven by kings and courts, and were kindly received by the American farmers. At Middletown the remains of the fugitive army, protected by the guns of the fleet, embarked and were conveyed to New York.

Thus another summer passed away of marches, countermarches and skirmishes, many of them bloody and woeful, but without any decisive results. The inhuman court of England, disheartened by the wholesale desertion of troops, both English and German, and disappointed in their inability to enlist Tories for the war, redoubled their efforts to summon the demoniac savages to their aid. Loud were the remonstrances against this atrocious conduct by many of the noblest men of England, both in the Commons and in the House of Lords. But the King and the Court declared, that in order to subdue America they had a right to use whatever instruments God and nature had placed in their hands. The British sent agents to the cruel savages of the Mohawk to rouse the fierce warriors of the Six Nations against the feeble villages of the frontier. It was a demoniac deed. Scenes of horror were witnessed too awful for recital. The annals of our globe contain scarcely any tragedies more awful than the massacres of Cherry Valley and Wyoming. The narrative of these deeds sent a thrill of horror not only throughout France and America, but into multitudes of humane hearts in England. Some Englishmen pleaded earnestly for us, like Lord Chatham, in the House of Lords. We shall never forget his words as he exclaimed, in view of these outrages:

"Were I an American as I am an Englishman, I would never lay down my arms, never—*never*—NEVER."

Washington sent four thousand men to defend, as far as possible, the poor, helpless pioneers from the torch and the scalping-knife. Hundreds of lowly homes were laid in ashes. Hundreds of families, parents and children, were butchered, before the savages were driven from their murderous work. They fled at length to Niagara, where the British received their allies into their fortresses.

The American army, feeble in numbers, and suffering from cold and hunger, were led by Washington into winter quarters, mainly on the Hudson, near West Point. The British remained within their lines in the city of New York. Their fleet gave them command of the ocean, and they reveled in abundance. It would seem that both officers and men were a godless set, dead to humanity, and still more dead to religion. None but the worst of men would engage in so foul an enterprise. They spent the winter in dancing, gambling, drinking, and every species of dissolute carousal.

Alarmed by the tidings that France was coming to the aid of America, British pride and rage were roused to intensity. The spring campaign opened with renewed devastation and plunder. Lord George Germain had the effrontery to say in Parliament, in view of these scenes of massacre and brutal treatment of prisoners:

> "A war of this sort will probably induce the rebellious provinces to return to their allegiance."

The sky was reddened with the wanton burning of villages. Women and children were driven, houseless and without food, to perish in the fields. Fairfield and Norwalk, Connecticut, and many other towns were laid in ashes.

While the British were thus ravaging defenseless regions, Washington had no power to face their concentrated armies, yet he was eagerly watching for every opportunity to strike a blow, where there was good prospect of success. To subject his troops to almost certain defeat, would not only be cruel, in the slaughter which would ensue, but disheartening and ruinous to the cause.

The British had an important fortress at Stony Point on the Hudson. General Washington sent General Wayne to take it. With great gallantry he conducted the enterprise. Sixty-three of the British were killed, five hundred and forty-three were taken prisoners, and all the military stores of the fortress were captured. Many similar enterprises were conducted. With skill, which now seems supernatural, this wonderful man, thoughtful, prayerful, and confident of final success, held the fleets and armies of the empire of Great Britain at bay, thwarted all the efforts of their ablest generals, and closed the campaign unvanquished. We know not where to look for a record of greater military genius, of more self-denying patriotism, of higher nobility of soul, than is here displayed.

Again, as the wintry winds of 1779 swept the field, both armies retired to winter quarters, preparing to renew the conflict. With the early spring, the British troops were sent abroad in detachments to carry on their work of conflagration, blood, and misery. Sir Henry Clinton, then in command of the British forces, was anxious to crush the Americans before the fleet and army which France was so generously organizing should reach these shores.

In July, twelve French vessels of war with a supply of arms and ammunition, and an army of five thousand soldiers arrived. But England had by this time concentrated a far more formidable fleet in our waters, and had greatly increased her armies. Thus many felt that even the aid of France could be of no avail. Years of war and woe had filled some of even the stoutest hearts with despair. Many of the truest patriots urged that it was madness longer to continue the conflict; that it was in vain for these feeble colonies in their utter impoverishment, any longer to contend against the richest and most powerful monarchy on the globe.

General Arnold was in command at West Point. He was one of the bravest of soldiers, but a ruined gambler. Napoleon I. declared that he would never appoint any gambler to any post of responsibility. Arnold was overwhelmed with these so-called debts of honor. He saw no hope for his country. He could turn traitor, and barter West Point for almost boundless quantities of British gold. The gambler became a traitor. The treason was detected. The traitor escaped, but young Andrè, who allowed himself to act the part of a spy in this foul deed, perished upon the scaffold. He was very young. He was surrounded by influences which perverted his judgment and deadened his conscience. Consequently, great sympathy was felt for him, and many tears were shed over his untimely end.

Britain proudly proclaimed that with her invincible fleet she ruled supreme over the wild waste of waters. The whole ocean she regarded as her undisputed domain. Lord Cornwallis was sent with a powerful army to overrun North and South Carolina. He had a numerous fleet to co-operate with him. The vigilant eye of Washington was fixed everywhere upon the foe, striving to ward off blows, and to harass the enemy in his movements.

Thus the dreary summer of 1780 lingered away, over our war-scathed, woe-stricken land. There were many bloody conflicts, but no decisive battles. Still Washington was victorious; for he thwarted all the herculean endeavors of the British to enslave our land.

In the opening spring of the year 1781, the British turned their main energies of devastation and ruin against the South. Richmond, in Virginia, was laid in ashes. With their armed vessels they ravaged the shores of the Chesapeake and the Potomac. They landed at Mount Vernon, and would have applied the torch to every building, and trampled down all the harvests, had not the manager of the estate ransomed the property by bringing in a large quantity of supplies. When Washington heard of this he was much displeased. He wrote to his agent:

> "It would have been a less painful circumstance to me to have heard that in consequence of your non-compliance with their request, they had burned my house and laid the plantation in ruins. You ought to have considered yourself as my representative, and should have reflected on the bad example of communicating with the enemy, and of making a voluntary offer of refreshments to them with a view to prevent the conflagration."

Still the prospects of the country were dark. The army dwindled away to three thousand men. There was no money in the treasury. The paper money issued by Congress had become quite valueless. The British, exasperated by defeats, and humiliated in seeing their fleets and armies held at bay so long by a foe so feeble, were summoning their mightiest energies to close the war as with a clap of thunder.

Cornwallis was now with a well-equipped army at Yorktown, in Virginia. There was no foe to oppose him. Washington made a secret movement, in conjunction with our generous allies, for his capture. He deceived the British by making them believe that he was preparing for the siege of New York. One bright and sunny morning in September, Cornwallis was surprised, and quite astounded in seeing the heights around him glistening with the bayonets and frowning with the batteries of the Americans. And at the same time a French fleet was ascending the bay, and casting anchor before the harbor. The British general was caught in a trap. A few days of hopeless despairing conflict ensued, when famine and the carnage of incessant bombardment compelled him to surrender. It was the 19th of October, 1781.

Awful was the humiliation of Cornwallis. Seven thousand British regulars threw down their arms. One hundred and sixty pieces of cannon graced this memorable triumph. The noble Washington, as the British troops were marching from their ramparts to become captives of war, said to the Americans:

> "My brave fellows, let no sensation of satisfaction for the triumphs you have gained induce you to insult your fallen enemy. Let no shouting, no clamorous huzzaing increase their mortification. Posterity will huzza for us."

The next day he issued the following characteristic order to the army:

> "Divine service is to be performed to-morrow, in the several brigades and divisions. The commander-in-chief earnestly recommends that the troops not on duty should universally attend, with that seriousness of deportment and gratitude of heart which the recognition of such reiterated and astonishing interpositions of Providence demand of us."

It was midnight when the rapturous tidings reached Philadelphia. A watchman traversed the streets shouting at intervals, "Past twelve o'clock, and a pleasant morning. Cornwallis is taken."

These words startled the slumbering citizens, almost like the "trump which wakes the dead." Candles were lighted, windows thrown up, figures in night robes and caps bent eagerly out to catch the thrilling sound.

Citizens rushed into the streets half clad; they wept, they laughed, they shouted, they embraced each other; the bells were rung, the booming of cannon and the rattle of musketry were heard in all directions, as men and boys, in the joyful salute, endeavored to give expression to their inexpressible joy.

The news flew upon the wings of the wind, over the mountains and through the valleys, no one could tell how. The shout of an enfranchised people rose like a roar of thunder from our whole land. The enthusiasm of the Americans was roused to the highest pitch. It was now clear, that, aided by the French fleet and the French army, and with such supplies of money, arms, and ammunition as France was generously affording, the British government could not enslave our land. The British were disheartened. Though they continued their menaces of hostility, it was evident that they considered the question as settled. Both parties retired to winter quarters. During the winter no movements were made by either party calling for record. Another summer came and went. There were marchings and counter-marchings, while neither the English nor the Americans seemed disposed to crimson the soil with the blood of a general conflict.

On the night of the 19th of April, 1783, the joyful tidings were communicated to the American army that a treaty of peace had been signed in Paris. It was just eight years from the day when the awful conflict commenced on the plain at Lexington. No one but God can know the amount of misery caused by those long years of battle. Thousands had perished amidst the agonies of the various fields of conflict; thousands had been beggared; millions of property had been destroyed; mothers and maidens whose numbers cannot be estimated had been dragged into captivity, a thousand-fold worse than death; and widows and orphans had been consigned to life-long poverty and grief.

Such was the vengeance which the powerful government of Great Britain wreaked upon these feeble colonies for their refusal to submit to intolerable despotism. The writer would not wish to perpetuate the remembrance of these wrongs, still it is not the duty of the historian to attempt to conceal or palliate atrocious outrages against the rights of human nature. It is difficult to find in all the records of the past, deeds more inexcusable, more wicked, more infamous, than this effort of Great Britain, to enslave these infant colonies.

Late in November, the British embarked in their fleet in New York, and sailed for their distant island. At the same time Washington, marching with his troops from West Point, entered the city. America was free and independent, and Washington was the universally recognized saviour of his country. There was no longer any foe. The army was disbanded on the 4th of December. Washington took leave of his companions in arms. His voice trembled with emotion as he said:

> "With a heart full of love and gratitude, I now take leave of you. I most devoutly wish that your latter days may be as prosperous and happy as your former have been glorious and honorable. I cannot come to each of you to take my leave, but shall be obliged if each of you will come and take me by the hand."

Tears blinded his eyes, and he could say no more. One after another, these heroic men grasped his hand in parting. Not a word was spoken. Slowly he journeyed towards Mount Vernon. At every city and village he was greeted with the highest tokens of love and veneration. On the 23d of December he met the Continental Congress at Annapolis. Resigning his commission, he said:

> "Having now finished the work assigned me, I retire from the great theater of action, and bidding an affectionate farewell to thy august body, under whose orders I have so long acted, I here offer my commission, and take my leave of all the employments of public life."

Soon a convention was held in Philadelphia to organize the Confederacy of States into a nation. Essentially the present Constitution was formed. By the unanimous voice of the electors, Washington was chosen first President of the United States. He was inaugurated on the 30th of April, 1789. Holding the office two terms of four years each, he retired again in 1796, to the peaceful shades of Mount Vernon. In his farewell address he bequeathed to his countrymen a graceful legacy of patriotic counsel which ever has and ever will excite their profound admiration.

Washington, having inherited a large landed estate in Virginia, was, as a matter of course, a slaveholder. The whole number which he held at the time of his death was one hundred and twenty-four. The system met his strong disapproval. In 1786, he wrote to Robert Morris, saying: "There is no man living who wishes more sincerely than I do to see a plan adopted for the abolition of slavery."

Lafayette, that true friend of popular rights, was extremely anxious to free our country from the reproach which slavery brought upon it. Washington wrote to him in 1788: "The scheme, my dear marquis, which you propose as a precedent to encourage the emancipation of the black people of this country from the state of bondage in which they are held, is a striking evidence of the state of your heart. I shall be happy to join you in so laudable a work."

In his last will and testament, he inscribed these noble words: "Upon the decease of my wife, it is my will and desire that all the slaves which I hold in my own right shall receive their freedom. To emancipate them during her life would, though earnestly wished by me, be attended with such insuperable difficulties, on account of their mixture by marriage with the dower negroes, as to excite the most painful sensation, if not disagreeable consequences, from the latter, while both descriptions are in the occupancy of the same proprietor; it not being in my power, under the tenure by which the dower negroes are held, to manumit them."

Long before this he had recorded his resolve. "I never mean, unless some particular circumstances should compel me to it, to possess another slave by purchase; it being among my first wishes to see some plan adopted by which slavery in this country may be abolished by law."

Mrs. Washington, immediately after her husband's death, learning from his will that the only obstacle to the immediate emancipation of the slaves was her right of dower, immediately relinquished that right, and the slaves were at once emancipated.

The 12th of December, 1799, was chill and damp. Washington, however, took his usual round on horseback to his farms, and returned late in the afternoon, wet with sleet, and shivering with cold. Though the snow was clinging to his hair behind when he came in, he sat down to dinner without changing his dress. The next day, three inches of snow whitened the ground, and the sky was clouded. Washington, feeling that he had taken cold, remained by the fireside during the morning. As it cleared up in the afternoon, he went out to superintend some work upon the lawn. He was then hoarse, and the hoarseness increased as night came on. He, however, took no remedy for it; saying, "I never take anything to carry off a cold. Let it go as it came."

He passed the evening as usual, reading the papers, answering letters, and conversing with his family. About two o'clock the next morning, Saturday, the 14th, he awoke in an acute chill, and was seriously unwell. At sunrise, his physician, Dr. Craig, who resided at Alexandria, was sent for. In the meantime, he was bled by one of his overseers, but with no relief, as he rapidly grew worse. Dr. Craig reached Mount Vernon at eleven o'clock, and immediately bled his patient again, but without effect. Two consulting physicians arrived during the day: and, as the difficulty in breathing and swallowing rapidly increased, venesection was again attempted. It is evident that Washington then considered his case doubtful. He examined his will, and destroyed some papers which he did not wish to have preserved.

His sufferings from inflammation of the throat, and struggling for breath, as the afternoon wore away, became quite severe. Still he retained his mental faculties unimpaired, and spoke briefly of his approaching death and burial. About four o'clock in the afternoon, he said to Dr. Craig: "I die hard; but I am not afraid to go. I believed, from my first attack, that I should not survive it: my breath cannot last long." About six o'clock, his physician asked him if he would sit up in his bed. He held out his hands, and was raised upon his pillow, when he said: "I feel that I am going. I thank you for your attentions. You had better not take any more trouble about me, but let me go off quietly. I cannot last long."

He then sank back upon his pillow, and made several unavailing attempts to speak intelligibly. About ten o'clock, he said: "I am just going. Have me decently buried, and do not let my body be put into the vault until three days after I am dead. Do you understand me?" To the reply, "Yes, sir," he remarked, "It is well." These were the last words he uttered. Soon after this he gently expired, in the sixty-eighth year of his age.

At the moment of his death, Mrs. Washington sat in silent grief at the foot of his bed. "Is he gone?" she asked in a firm and collected voice. The physician, unable to speak, gave a silent signal of assent. "'Tis well," she added, in the same untremulous utterance. "All is now over. I shall soon follow him. I have no more trials to pass through."

On the 18th, his remains were deposited in the tomb at Mount Vernon, where they now repose, enshrined in a nation's love; and his fame will forever, as now, fill the world.[166]

---

[166] *Abbot's Lives of the Presidents.*

INDEX

A

American Flag, vii, 179

B

Ball, Mary, 2
bills of sale, 5
Blue Ridge, 10, 148
British, 6, 12, 16, 18, 24, 37, 39, 43, 44, 45, 48, 49, 50, 55, 57, 62, 65, 66, 67, 68, 69, 70, 71, 72, 74, 75, 77, 83, 84, 86, 87, 88, 89, 91, 92, 93, 94, 95, 103, 107, 110, 111, 113, 114, 115, 116, 117, 118, 122, 123, 124, 125, 126, 127, 128, 129, 130, 131, 132, 134, 135, 136, 137, 138, 139, 140, 141, 143, 145, 146, 147, 148, 150, 151, 152, 154, 155, 156, 157, 158, 161, 162, 163, 164, 165, 166, 167, 168, 169, 170, 171, 172, 173, 174, 175, 176, 177, 178, 179, 181, 183, 184, 185, 186, 187, 188, 189, 190, 191, 192, 193, 194, 195, 196, 197, 202, 203, 204, 205, 206, 207, 208, 209, 211, 212, 213, 214, 215, 216, 217, 218, 219

Butler, Jane, 2, 4

C

Canada, 11, 17, 18, 28, 32, 33, 65, 66, 68, 74, 112, 138, 141, 142, 143, 147, 162, 163, 168, 193, 194
Chesapeake Bay, 1, 197
Christian, 2, 3, 11, 12, 40, 166, 173
Christian virtues, 3
Columbus, ix
courtesy, 3, 23

E

English nobleman, 10
equipage, 4, 68, 78, 91
etiquette, 5, 90, 104

F

Fairfax, Lord, 7, 10, 62, 63
Fairfax, William, 7, 112, 117
Father of his country, x
Fredericksburg, 3, 9

French, v, 11, 13, 14, 16, 17, 18, 20, 21, 23, 24, 25, 28, 30, 31, 32, 33, 34, 35, 36, 37, 38, 39, 43, 44, 45, 46, 47, 50, 51, 52, 53, 54, 55, 56, 57, 59, 64, 65, 67, 72, 75, 83, 94, 99, 138, 142, 147, 193, 211, 215, 217, 218
frontiersmen, 8

H

hunting parties, 7

I

Indian camp-fires, 3
Indian guide, 7, 19, 20
Indian hunters, 3
Indians, 7, 11, 14, 17, 18, 20, 21, 25, 32, 33, 34, 35, 36, 37, 38, 44, 46, 48, 50, 51, 52, 53, 54, 55, 56, 63, 64, 67, 68, 69, 70, 71, 72, 73, 74, 75, 83, 95, 96, 97, 99, 103, 135, 138, 152, 163, 194, 195, 202

L

La Salle, ix, 14, 16
land warrants, 5
Lawrence, Augustine, 3

M

Mexican Gulf, ix
moral courage, 3
Mount Vernon, 4, 6, 7, 27, 45, 55, 65, 76, 78, 82, 84, 85, 86, 88, 101, 106, 107, 109, 110, 112, 117, 128, 130, 133, 137, 148, 157, 204, 216, 219, 221, 222

N

Northern Lakes, ix

O

Oxford University, 1

P

patriarchs, 2, 113
patriots, ix, 84, 91, 111, 126, 132, 133, 136, 148, 152, 153, 158, 187, 192, 194, 198, 211, 215
Pope, Miss, 2
Potomac, 1, 2, 3, 64, 79, 82, 83, 90, 131, 216
promissory notes, 5
public surveyor, 10
Puritan fathers, 11

R

Rappahannock, 3, 4
Republic, x

S

scholar, 5
statesman, v, ix, 61

V

Virginia, 1, 4, 6, 10, 12, 13, 15, 17, 18, 19, 27, 29, 32, 37, 39, 40, 45, 50, 52, 55, 56, 57, 65, 66, 68, 69, 70, 72, 75, 78, 81, 82, 84, 85, 89, 91, 94, 104, 106, 108, 109, 113, 117, 118, 119, 134, 136, 148, 149, 150, 162, 182, 193, 216, 220

Index

W

Washington, ix, 1, 2, 5, 6, 7, 8, 10, 14, 18, 19, 20, 21, 23, 24, 25, 26, 27, 28, 29, 30, 31, 32, 33, 34, 35, 36, 37, 38, 39, 40, 41, 42, 44, 45, 46, 47, 48, 49, 50, 51, 52, 54, 55, 57, 58, 59, 60, 61, 62, 63, 64, 65, 66, 67, 68, 69, 70, 71, 73, 74, 75, 76, 77, 78, 79, 81, 82, 83, 84, 85, 86, 87, 88, 89, 90, 91, 94, 95, 96, 97, 98, 99, 100, 101, 102, 104, 106, 107, 108, 109, 110, 112, 113, 117, 118, 119, 120, 121, 122, 123, 126, 127, 128, 129, 130, 131, 132, 133, 134, 135, 136, 137, 138, 139, 140, 141, 143, 144, 145,146, 147, 148, 149, 150, 151, 152, 153, 154, 155, 156, 157, 158, 161, 162, 163, 164, 165, 166, 167, 168, 169, 170, 171, 172, 173, 174, 175, 176, 177, 178, 179, 181, 182, 183, 184, 185, 186, 187, 188, 189, 190, 191, 192, 193, 194, 195, 197, 198, 199, 201, 202, 204, 205, 206, 207, 209, 211, 212, 213, 214, 216, 217, 219, 220, 221, 222

Washington, George, i, iii, v, ix, x, 1, 2, 3, 6, 7, 10, 13, 19, 29, 30, 60, 90, 109, 119, 131, 145, 166, 167

Washington, John, 1, 2

Washington, Lady, 4, 78, 148, 149, 162

Washington, Mary, 2

West Indies, 7, 134

Westmoreland, 4, 6

wigwams, 1, 11, 20, 97